Three factors prompt this re-examination of the underlying questions that shape mainstream exegesis of Paul's letters. Hermeneutical studies have destabilized assumptions about the nature of meaning in texts; the letters are usually characterized as pastoral but explicated as expressions of Paul's thought; and the impact of E. P. Sanders' work on Paul has sharpened exegetical problems in Romans 1.16–4.25. The outcome is a two-step method of exegesis that considers a letter first in the light of the author's purpose in creating it and second as evidence for the patterns of thought from which it sprang. The passage appears as pastoral preaching, helping the Romans to deal with the implications of the fact that the God of Israel is now accepting believing Gentiles on the same basis as believing Jews. Justification by grace through faith emerges as the theological understanding of God's action in Christ that grounds the pastoral speech.

SOCIETY FOR NEW TESTAMENT STUDIES
MONOGRAPH SERIES
General editor: Richard Bauckham

104

PURPOSE AND CAUSE IN PAULINE EXEGESIS

Purpose and Cause in Pauline Exegesis

Romans 1.16–4.25 and
a New Approach to the Letters

WENDY DABOURNE

CAMBRIDGE
UNIVERSITY PRESS

PUBLISHED BY THE PRESS SYNDICATE OF THE UNIVERSITY OF CAMBRIDGE
The Pitt Building, Trumpington Street, Cambridge CB2 1RP, United Kingdom

CAMBRIDGE UNIVERSITY PRESS
The Edinburgh Building, Cambridge CB2 2RU, United Kingdom
40 West 20th Street, New York, NY 10011–4211, USA
10 Stamford Road, Oakleigh, Melbourne 3166, Australia

First published 1999

Printed in the United Kingdom at the University Press, Cambridge

Typeset in Times Roman 10/12pt [CE]

A catalogue record for this book is available from the British Library

Library of Congress cataloguing in publication data
Dabourne, Wendy.
Purpose and cause in Pauline exegesis: Romans 1.16–4.25 and a new approach to the letters/Wendy Dabourne.
    p.   cm. – (Society for New Testament Studies monograph series: 104)
Includes bibliographical references and indexes.
ISBN 0 521 64003 2 hardback
1. Bible. N.T. Romans I, 16–IV, 25 – Criticism, interpretation, etc.
2. Bible. N.T. Romans I, 16–IV, 25 – Socio-rhetorical criticism.
I. Title. II. Series: Monograph series (Society for New Testament Studies): 104.
BS2665.2.D33   1999
227'.106 – dc21   98–20490   CIP

ISBN 0 521 64003 2 hardback

CONTENTS

PREFACE

This book is one outcome of many years' work, and it is a joy to acknowledge the contributions of a wide circle of teachers, colleagues, students and friends. In particular, Dr John Ziesler, Rev. Toska Williams, Rev. Dr Gordon Watson, Rev. Dr Robin Boyd, Prof. Colin Gunton and the unknown SNTS referee read the entire typescript at various stages of its development and offered encouragement and helpful comments. Special contributions have been made by Mr Seán Jackson, Dr Neil Williams, Ms Wendy Butterworth, the Community at Oxley House and a generous group of friends who checked my typing.

The early stages of the research were undertaken during my Ph.D. studies at Cambridge. Rev. John Sweet, Rev. Dr (now Professor) Christopher Rowland, Dr John Ziesler and, especially, my supervisor Professor Morna Hooker, offered stimulus, challenge and encouragement. Thanks are due to Trinity College for its Research Studentship in Theology and many other benefits and pleasures, to the British Department of Education and Science for an Overseas Research Student's Award, and to Ormond College in the University of Melbourne for a travel grant.

I wish to thank SNTSMS editors Dr Margaret Thrall and Professor Richard Bauckham for their work, and staff of Cambridge University Press for their expertise and helpfulness.

ABBREVIATIONS

AB	Anchor Bible
AnBib	Analecta Biblica
ANRW	*Aufstieg und Niedergang der Römischen Welt*
BAGD	W. Bauer, W. F. Arndt, F. W. Gingrich and F. W. Danker, *Greek–English Lexicon of the New Testament*
BDF	F. Blass, A. Debrunner and R. Funk, *A Greek Grammar of the New Testament*
BFT	Biblical Foundations in Theology
BJRL	*Bulletin of the John Rylands University Library of Manchester*
BNTC	Black's New Testament Commentaries
CBQ	*Catholic Biblical Quarterly*
EBib	Etudes bibliques
EKKNT	Evangelisch-katholischer Kommentar zum Neuen Testament
ExpTim	*Expository Times*
FFNT	Foundations and Facets: New Testament
FRLANT	Forschungen zur Religion und Literatur des Alten und Neuen Testaments
GNS	Good News Studies
GRBS	*Greek, Roman, and Byzantine Studies*
HTKNT	Herders theologischer Kommentar zum Neuen Testament
HTR	*Harvard Theological Review*
IB	*Interpreter's Bible*
IBS	*Irish Biblical Studies*
ICC	International Critical Commentary
IDB	G. A. Buttrick (ed.), *Interpreter's Dictionary of the Bible*
IDBSup	Supplementary volume to *IDB*
Int	*Interpretation*

JBC	R. E. Brown *et al.* (eds.), *The Jerome Biblical Commentary*
JBL	*Journal of Biblical Literature*
JSNT	*Journal for the Study of the New Testament*
JSNTSup	Journal for the Study of the New Testament – Supplement Series
JSOTSup	Journal for the Study of the Old Testament – Supplement Series
LCL	Loeb Classical Library
LEC	Library of Early Christianity
MNTC	Moffat New Testament Commentary
NCB	New Century Bible
Neot	*Neotestamentica*
NIGTC	New International Greek Testament Commentary
NovT	*Novum Testamentum*
NovTSup	Novum Testamentum, Supplements
NTD	Das Neue Testament Deutsch
NTS	*New Testament Studies*
RB	*Revue biblique*
RNT	Regensburger Neues Testament
RSV	Revised Standard Version
SBLDS	SBL Dissertation Series
SBLSBS	SBL Sources for Biblical Study
SBT	Studies in Biblical Theology
SD	Studies and Documents
SJLA	Studies in Judaism in Late Antiquity
SJT	*Scottish Journal of Theology*
SNTSMS	Society for New Testament Studies Monograph Series
SNTW	Studies of the New Testament and its World
SO	*Symbolae Osloenses*
ST	*Studia Theologica*
TDNT	G. Kittel and G. Friedrich (eds.), *Theological Dictionary of the New Testament*
TLZ	*Theologische Literaturzeitung*
TZ	*Theologische Zeitschrift*
WBC	Word Biblical Commentary
WUNT	Wissenschaftliche Untersuchungen zum Neuen Testament
ZNW	*Zeitschrift für die neutestamentliche Wissenschaft*
ZTK	Zeitschrift für Theologie und Kirche

1

ASKING NEW EXEGETICAL QUESTIONS

The work reported in this study of Rom. 1.16–4.25 springs from two main issues. The first is the church's present alienation from the Bible, a widespread concern shared by many Christian NT scholars and affecting NT studies most obviously in hermeneutical questioning and experiment. The second is a concern that mainstream historical-critical study fails to take with full seriousness its own dictum that Paul's letters are *letters* and *pastoral* and must be treated as such. Many colleagues will consider this concern unnecessary, but if it is justified it means that the picture of Paul, his activity and his thought which emerges from mainstream scholarship is suffering significant distortion.

The starting point of the study is a confessional statement about scripture, using the language of our post-Enlightenment culture but in contrast with its secularity:

> The Uniting Church acknowledges that the Church has received the books of the Old and New Testaments as unique prophetic and apostolic testimony, in which she hears the Word of God and by which her faith and obedience are nourished and regulated ... The Word of God on whom man's [*sic*] salvation depends is to be heard and known from Scripture appropriated in the worshipping and witnessing life of the Church.[1]

Engaging as scholar and minister with the problem of alienation from the Bible has led me to conclude that it is not the fault of biblical scholars or of the historical-critical method, although both are often blamed. Nor is it the Bible's fault, although the strangeness of documents that belong to cultures distant from us in time and space is often blamed. Differences of cosmology are a classic

---

[1] Uniting Church in Australia, *Basis of Union*, par. 5.

example, and such problems are not trivial. Beside the real barrier, however, they seem small. In the world of the Bible, God is the Creator and God's purpose is being worked out. God is the measure of truth and justice. In present-day Western culture, God is a private option, an hypothesis that some people accept. The problem of the church's alienation from the Bible lies with the church. The church is too well embedded in the secular culture. This includes biblical scholars who own themselves and their work as part of the church, the body of Christ. Thus, the problem is an aspect of the struggle to be the church in the secular world, and there are no easy answers.

How, under God, can the church tackle the problem of alienation from the Bible? This would require another book. For our study, Newbigin offers a helpful statement:

> [W]e get a picture of the Christian life as one in which we live *in* the biblical story as part of the community whose story it is, find in the story the clues to knowing God as his character becomes manifest in the story, and from within that indwelling try to understand and cope with the events of our time and the world about us and so carry the story forward. At the heart of the story, as the key to the whole, is the incarnation of the Word, the life, ministry, death, and resurrection of Jesus. In the Fourth Gospel Jesus defines for his disciples what is to be their relation to him. They are to 'dwell in' him. He is not to be the object of their observation, but the body of which they are a part. As they 'indwell' him in his body, they will both be led into fuller and fuller apprehension of the truth and also become the means through which God's will is done in the life of the world.[2]

This shows how radical is the action needed. Of course, the church is already indwelling the biblical story by its very existence as a confessing, worshipping, caring people of God. Nevertheless, there is a need to know the story better and to become more at home in it, because Christians are socialized and educated into the conflicting world of our secular culture. What is the role of Christian NT scholars in this undertaking?

The confessional statement offers the affirmation that '[the]

---

[2] *The Gospel in a Pluralist Society*, 99.

Word of God on whom man's salvation depends is to be heard and known from scripture appropriated in the ... life of the Church'. The scripture is described as 'the books of the Old and New Testaments [received] as unique prophetic and apostolic testimony in which [the church] hears the Word of God and by which her faith and obedience are nourished and regulated'. In this relationship, the church can grow towards living more fully '*in* the biblical story'.

If Scripture is to be thus appropriated, Christians must first listen to the 'unique prophetic and apostolic testimony'. It is not a matter of wresting relevance from recalcitrant texts, and approaching Scripture in that spirit is likely to get in the way of hearing the Word of God.[3] The apostolic testimony participates in the historical particularity of the incarnation. The church needs to listen to it, simply to be open to it on its own terms. This is the beginning, not the end, of the process of appropriation. The Christian NT scholar can be an enabler of that listening.

This role definition brings us to the concern of historical-critical scholarship with understanding the text as John's, or Mark's, or Paul's. It demands knowledge of the language of the texts and of their historical, cultural and church contexts. It demands the discipline of being aware of our own presuppositions and circumstances, so that we guard against blurring the distinctive testimony of the writers with personal concerns and emphases. It follows the Enlightenment insistence that the texts are not unmediated revelation or pure theology, but human documents which must be treated accordingly – in Paul's case, as letters, as pastoral, and as Paul's. Further, this role definition can give a purpose and a shape to Christians' practice of historical-critical scholarship. The work is not done simply for the fascination of the chase, but in the service of the church's task of listening. It gives a measure of which questions are most important.

New Testament Studies exists as a discipline in the secular university, and is widely seen to have its integrity as a secular discipline into which the church must not intrude. On the other hand, the documents are scripture – NT – only in the context of the church's life, and the church needs independent-minded biblical scholarship, not at the service of immediate issues or of the church's power structures, but an activity of the body of Christ.

---

[3] With Stendahl, *Final Account*, 21.

This study examines Rom. 1.16–4.25. It is a scholarly study, offering to NT scholarship an alternative way of practising historical-critical exegesis on Paul's letters, and an alternative understanding of this important passage. It is also part of the scholarly work of enabling the church in its task of listening to Paul's apostolic testimony. It is not intended to provide the preacher with sermon material, but so to open up the text that believers may be helped to grapple with Romans and come to know it as part of their own life, part of their participation in the biblical story.

Listening to Paul's apostolic testimony sets us the same task of explicating the text as Paul's that is undertaken in mainstream historical-critical study. Here we encounter the concern that historical-critical scholarship is failing in its endeavour to take Paul's letters seriously as letters and as pastoral. The study opens up these issues, and a new approach to the text is developed. We are not rejecting the historical-critical method, but modifying the way it is usually practised on Paul's letters, especially by developing new or sharpened exegetical questions.

Questions are the most important tool of exegetes. Their skills and knowledge in the areas of the language and culture of the NT and the language and culture of biblical scholarship enable them to use the tools effectively. The basic exegetical tool is the question, What does this text mean? It is shattering to realize that exegetical experiment and hermeneutical study over several decades have broken it. The concept 'the meaning of the text' has been relativized. Is the meaning what the writer intended to say? Does meaning inhere in the structures of the text itself, independently of the writer's intention? Does meaning arise in the encounter between text and reader? A text like Romans yields meaning through readings based on any of these assumptions. When we consider short sections, a greater range is likely to open up. By what criteria can we decide what constitutes '*the* meaning of the text'? If we cannot establish criteria, does the text offer an apparently infinite range of meaning, all of which is at our disposal?

This disabling of the question seems to paralyse us. We advance by recognizing that the blanket question corresponds poorly with actual practice. A text is a series of conventional marks on a sufficiently smooth surface. All our language about its meaning is metaphor. In reading texts in general we conceive the meaning in different ways, depending on the nature of the text and what we want to do with it. A comparison of poetry and instruction manuals makes this obvious. If we find some Sumerian prayers, we feel fairly confident that their meaning for us as historical sources is different from their meaning for the Sumerians who prayed them. Thus, the fact that we are no longer sure how to go about answering the blanket question, What does Romans mean? forces our attention onto ourselves as readers. What kind of a text are we reading? Romans is a letter written as part of Paul's ministry and of the continuing life of the church of the fifties, with no thought that it would come to be scripture. What do we want to do with it? NT scholarship wants to listen to it as Paul's; the church wants to listen to it as part of Paul's apostolic testimony.

In both cases, we must take it very seriously as Paul's. This will move us into the world where God is not a private option, as far as we can be so moved. We must look at Paul's intention. He was writing a letter to the believers in Rome. Our first question, then, is, What was Paul intending to say to the Romans? This will not exhaust the meaning of the text as Paul's. We want to learn from it about Paul's understanding of the gospel, about Paul as a pastor and as a person. The NT scholar's wider task includes using Romans as a source for understanding the church and the world in which Paul wrote, but this limited study offers only an indirect contribution to that work.

We asked what kind of text we are reading and what we want to do with it. Our answers show that the model of meaning applicable here is meaning conceived as contained in the text and in some sense governed by the author's intention. Authorial intention is normally given considerable weight in considering the meaning of a letter. For scripture, this is much more debated. The moves we have made do not, of course, constitute any general answer to the puzzle about the meaning of meaning.

The study of Rom. 1.16–4.25 presented in chapters 2–12 has two aims: to make a substantial contribution to the understanding of the passage as Paul's, and to use it as a test case for developing a new historical-critical approach to Paul's letters. We shall consider carefully their character as letters and as pastoral, and the consequences of the breakdown of the question, What does this text mean? The aims are complementary, and they create interactive elements in the study. Chapter 13 is a review, considering particularly the wider application of the work.

We begin by examining the problems the passage raises.

2

EXEGESIS OF ROMANS 1.16–4.25: THE
BASIC CONCEPTION AND ITS PROBLEMS

Working in mainstream NT scholarship, we approach texts with existing conceptions, conscious and unconscious, of them and of our task as exegetes. Approaching a Pauline letter, we know who Paul was and what this letter is about. The debate provides this basic conception, a framework within which we formulate our questions and wrestle with the problems the text poses.

The basic conception of Rom. 1.16–4.25 is that it is Paul's account of the way God justifies people. Rom. 1.16–17 is the theme statement for this account and/or for Romans. Rom. 1.18–3.20 presents the human predicament, that all are sinners. Rom. 3.21–6 announces God's solution, justification for all who believe through God's gracious action in the Cross. Rom. 3.27–31 spells out some consequences. Romans 4 deals with Abraham's faith. This account may be seen as a presentation of the gospel or of the doctrine of justification, as didactic or polemical. Paul used the language of his time and place, so to understand it we must work to cross the culture gap, study Paul's terms, and recognize the critical importance of the Jew–Gentile distinction. We shall refer to this basic conception as the justification account or justification framework.

Scholars' acquaintance with the problems of the text enriches the basic conception. There are major problems, such as the role of the law, and apparent inconsistencies, such as the appearance of law-keeping Gentiles in an argument that all have sinned. There are problems of detail. Is ὁ κρίνων in Rom. 2.1–5 the Jew or any self-righteous person? Rom. 3.9a; 4.1 present particularly difficult text-critical problems. Some problems arise from lack of information. For instance, we lack sufficient context in contemporary literature to understand fully ἱλαστήριον (Rom. 3.25a).

The basic conception thus enriched constitutes the common ground of the scholarly debate on Rom. 1.16–4.25. It allows for many styles and emphases in interpretation, and vigorous argument about what Paul thought and meant. New exegeses are judged by their scholarly competence, ability to cast new light on some of the problems, and theological substance. Within this framework, the debate proceeds on the assumption that we know what the text is about and are seeking solutions to the problems.

In current exegesis, there are two kinds of challenge to the basic conception. There are suggestions that Rom. 1.16–4.25 is not a justification account. For instance, Minear presents Rom. 1.18–4.15 as part of Paul's theological grounding for his critically important assertion, πᾶν δὲ ὃ οὐκ ἐκ πίστεως ἁμαρτία ἐστίν (Rom. 14.23). It is addressed to one of five groups Minear identifies in Rome, showing the equality of all who are sinners justified by grace.[1] For Elliott, Rom. 1.16–4.25 is concerned primarily with God's sovereignty, integrity and freedom. In particular, the accountability of all people to God is presented to Gentiles, using the Jew as a paradigmatic case.[2] Watson presents a sociological reading, with Romans 1–11 an address to Jewish Christians, mainly to convert them to Paul's view of the law so that the Roman churches may be united as a Pauline Gentile church.[3] Although such interpretations have attracted considerable interest, none has accounted for the text better than readings within the basic conception, so they have not displaced it.

In 1977, Sanders published *Paul and Palestinian Judaism*. This convinced the majority of NT scholars that in the Judaism of Paul's period the law did not function as a means of earning one's own justification. This has led to reconsideration of the role of the law in Rom. 1.16–4.25, since Paul had been seen as arguing against justification by works. It has also given impetus to the recognition of the importance of practical questions about Jew–Gentile relationships in the first-century church. Dunn's *Romans* and Ziesler's *Paul's Letter to the Romans* presented the first attempts to produce whole readings of Romans that take account of Sanders' work. Both accept the basic conception in Rom. 1.16–4.25, and we can see that dealing with the new questions strains it.

Neither commentator takes Rom. 1.16–4.25 as the first major section. Within the traditional pattern of analyses of structure, Dunn sees Rom. 1.18–5.21 as the first major section of the letter body, with Romans 5 setting out first conclusions from the

---

[1] *The Obedience of Faith*, chs. 2 and, esp., 3.
[2] *The Rhetoric of Romans*, ch. 2 and excursus.
[3] *Paul, Judaism and the Gentiles*, chs. 5–7.

presentation of God's saving righteousness to faith, and Rom. 1.16–17 as the climax of the introduction and the theme for what follows.[4] Ziesler breaks with the tradition. Rom. 1.16–17 is the transition to and opening of the letter body, then the human predicament and God's solution are presented in Rom. 1.18–3.31, but Rom. 4.1–8.39 is a complex unit developing four main aspects of this solution. The first is presented in Rom. 4.1–5.21.[5] These differences reflect two problems for exegesis within the basic conception. Does the section end at Rom. 4.25, 5.11 or 5.21? What is the function of Romans 4? In line with tradition, both of these readings stress Abraham's justification by faith as showing the continuity between the gospel and God's action with Israel, but they stress more strongly the issue of Jew and Gentile together within the people of God.

Both scholars explicate Rom. 1.16–17 as presenting the message of justification by faith. Each sows a seed of the element which will strain the framework provided by the basic conception. For Dunn, Ἰουδαίῳ τε πρῶτον καὶ Ἕλληνι is programmatic for the letter, bringing the Jew–Gentile issue into sharp focus, here as a reminder to Gentiles that Jewish prerogative and Gentile outreach are together important to the gospel.[6] Ziesler's special emphasis is on God's faithfulness bringing about a people of God which includes all who are willing to receive. As they move through the text, the impact of the questions raised by Sanders' work is very visible. Ziesler argues that Paul's target is not human self-righteousness, especially Jewish,[7] and he sees his attention directed to questions about the new people of God created by God's new action. This questions contemporary Jewish self-understanding and demands a new interpretation of Israel's election. Ziesler's understanding of righteousness in Paul makes a distinctive contribution, but the Jew–Gentile question strains the basic conception. Dunn sees the important secondary theme of the law raising many of the most difficult problems of understanding Romans. Using a sociological perspective, he expounds Paul's treatment of problems raised by a Jewish misunderstanding of the law as a boundary marker, defining the realm of election and thus of privilege.[8] In his reading, this

---

[4] *Romans*, vii–viii, 38.
[5] *Romans*, 35–6.
[6] *Romans*, 47.
[7] *Romans*, 1–2.
[8] *Romans*, lxvi, lxxi.

strains the basic conception, which nevertheless defines the structure and themes of the passage.

Ziesler concludes that in Rom. 1.18–3.20 Paul is trying to prove not that every individual is grossly and helplessly sinful, but that Jews as much as Gentiles are sinners and answerable to God. This makes the detail of the text more manageable. Finally, however, the argument has provided the basis of justification by grace – 'humanity as a whole, Jew and Greek, is in need of liberation'.[9] Ziesler is too honest to gloss over the inadequacy of Paul's argument, and his exegesis shows the strain this inadequacy creates.[10] The same tension between the basic conception and the interpretation of detail runs in Dunn's exegesis of the passage. He takes for granted the need to demonstrate that all have sinned, speaking of a universal indictment with a major element of attack on Jewish self-assurance. Rom. 3.9–20 is a summing up of the universal indictment.[11] In his *Explanation*, however, it appears far more as the final demonstration that Jews also stand under the condemnation they passed on Gentiles in Rom. 1.18–32.[12] Nevertheless, the basic conception is obviously shaping Dunn's thinking. His *Explanation* of Rom. 3.22c–23 pictures Paul explaining universal sin to Jews who think that they are an exception.[13]

Dunn treats Rom. 3.21–31 as one unit with two sub-sections, the announcement of justification and some consequences for Jewish self-understanding. His exposition shows a continuation of the pattern of his treatment of Rom. 1.18–3.20. Rom. 3.21–6 is an account of justification, but Paul has concentrated on the one controversial element, justification for all on the basis of faith. Dunn treats the passage as exposition, but also as though it were addressed to Jews who thought that they ought to be an exception, thereby achieving a close link with Rom. 3.27–31. Similarly, the pattern of Ziesler's exposition continues. He treats the passage as one unit. In his exegesis of Rom. 3.21–6 as an account of justification, he constantly makes explicit the implication of what Paul is saying, that Jews are no different from Gentiles in this matter. In this context, Rom. 3.27 says that Jews have no boast over against Gentiles – not that they have no boast before God.

9 *Romans*, 100.
10 *Ibid.*, e.g. 100, 109–10 on Rom. 3.23.
11 *Romans*, 51.
12 *Ibid.*, 156.
13 *Ibid.*, 178.

Neither Dunn nor Ziesler has explicitly questioned the basic
conception, but both exegeses show Rom. 1.16–4.25 as a justification account heavily influenced by the Jew–Gentile questions. This
shows more clearly in Ziesler's book because his readership needs
to be introduced to the scholarly conception. Dunn assumes
familiarity with it. One result is that his exposition reads as though
Paul was addressing Jews, although he concludes that Romans is
addressed to Gentiles.[14]

In *The Reasons for Romans*, Wedderburn outlines a reading of
Rom. 1.16–4.25.[15] Rom. 1.16–18 presents three thematic statements. Rom. 1.19–3.20 develops the theme of the revelation of
God's wrath and also is an argument that all, including the Jews
who thought that they were privileged, stand guilty before God.
Rom. 3.21–6 describes how God's righteousness is available to all
through grace. This saving righteousness is exercised through a
judgement of condemnation. God has replaced law with faith, for
Jew and Gentile alike (Rom. 3.27–30). This establishes the law,
which attests the principle of justification by faith in the critical
case of Abraham (Rom. 3.30–4.25). This is the first stage of the
argument of Romans 1–11, in which Paul is defending his gospel
against charges of unrighteousness. This includes a question of
God's own righteousness or unrighteousness.[16] It seems likely that
if this reading were presented on the same scale as Dunn's
commentary, it also would look like a justification account for
Jews, but with a strong reference to the question of God's righteousness.

We may say, then, that current challenges have not displaced the
basic conception of Rom. 1.16–4.25 as a justification account,
although developments in understanding of the law, particularly,
have strained it considerably.

This study starts with the recognition of discrepancies between
the basic conception and Paul's text that are so serious as to
demand that it be directly questioned. They pose problems which
cannot be solved within it. This means not that we have been
unable to solve them with present knowledge or methods, but that
they can be shown to be incapable of solution. Either we are
making a mistake or Paul was. There are three of these discrepancies.

[14] *Romans*, xlv.
[15] *Reasons*, 123–30.
[16] *Ibid.*, 112–14.

The first is between the goal of the argument in Rom. 1.18–3.20 and the content of Paul's text. If Rom. 3.21–6 is Paul's announcement of the revelation of the righteousness of God as the answer to the human predicament, then Rom. 1.18–3.20 must be presenting that predicament. If Paul was trying to do that, he has not made his case. The many recent articles on Rom. 1.18–3.20 and on sections of it show that this argument is a concern in mainstream scholarship.

There are two critical problems. First, there is no proof that all have sinned. It is a commonplace of exegesis that the condemnation of Gentile and Jewish sins is not a conclusion drawn from observation and could not be true of everybody. Rom. 3.9–20 can be taken as proving universal sinfulness by the authority of scripture, cited in the catena, but this involves accepting that Paul places Gentiles with Jews ἐν τῷ νόμῳ (Rom. 3.19). Some exegetes do this,[17] but in the context of an argument proving the sinfulness of Jews and Gentiles, we should expect that τοῖς ἐν τῷ νόμῳ would be taken as referring to Jews unless there were some clear indication to the contrary, and Paul gives none. We could soften the requirement of proof. Bruce, for instance, suggests that Paul does demonstrate the sinfulness of the Jewish and Gentile worlds.[18] Certainly Paul did not think as individualistically as we do, but πάντες ... ἥμαρτον (Rom. 3.23) is part of the basis for justification for πάντας τοὺς πιστεύοντας (Rom. 3.22c). In the fifties, no-one could see whole races as believing. The argument must be taking the individual seriously. Another way of softening the requirement of proof is to suggest that the statements are meant to work in some other way. Käsemann calls them prophetic and apocalyptic denunciations;[19] Wilckens suggests that Paul is working with motifs and themes from Jewish polemic against the Gentile world (Rom. 1.18–32) and from a Jew–Christian conflict (Romans 2).[20] Such proposals imply that Paul was not simply arguing rationally, but aimed to convince his hearers partly by appeals to emotion. Nevertheless, too many Gentiles and Jews could feel with good reason that this very black picture did not apply to them.

[17] e.g. Bornkamm, *Paul*, 121–2; Sanders, *Paul, the Law and the Jewish People*, p. 82 and n. 45. Gaston (*Paul and the Torah*, 29–31) includes this verse in his argument for ὑπὸ νόμον as a technical term referring to Gentiles, but the close parallel with Rom. 2.12 rules this out.
[18] *The Epistle of Paul to the Romans*, 77, 87.
[19] *Commentary on Romans*, 40, 69.
[20] *Der Brief an die Römer*, I, 116, 150–1.

The second major difficulty with the content of the argument is the appearance of law-keeping Gentiles (Rom. 2.14, 26–7). This might help to convince Jews that they are not better than Gentiles, but it is inconsistent with the condemnation of the Gentile world (or the whole world) in Rom. 1.18–32, and introduces the possibility that there are, or might be, some people who did not need grace. The only explanation that saves consistency here is that these are Gentile Christians,[21] but it cannot stand against modern recognition of the importance of the Jew–Gentile issue in Romans. Christian Jews, also, would put other Jews to shame. Further, the Jews' problem with Paul's Gentile churches was that the law was not observed, however much Paul might claim that it was fulfilled.

If Paul's aim was to bring his audience to Rom. 3.20 accepting that the human race as a whole, or every person, has sinned and needs rescue from God's condemnation, then he must be judged to have failed. No new research can make inconsistency consistent or turn such overstated denunciation into convincing rhetoric, let alone proof. This forces us to a challenging conclusion. Either Paul failed with one of the most important arguments in his extant correspondence or he was not trying to prove that all have sinned. If the former is true, the mistake is Paul's; if the latter is true, it is ours.

We come to the second very serious discrepancy between Paul's text and the basic conception. For an introductory justification account, the passage is extraordinarily out of balance. The core teaching gets 6.3 per cent of the text (Rom. 3.21–6) plus an introductory summary, 2.6 per cent of the text (Rom. 1.16–17), a total of 8.9 per cent.[22] This covers six elements: justification for all who believe, the fact that faith is faith in Christ, the way God justifies through the Cross, a statement about God's own righteousness, a summary statement of universal sin, and a claim to scripture support for the thesis. In contrast, the proof that all have sinned takes 62.5 per cent of the account (Rom. 1.18–3.20), while the faith–boasting contrast and the discussion of Abraham together occupy 28.6 per cent. That is, Paul introduces the good news of justification by faith to the Romans he has never seen by giving them a scanty introduction, spending almost two-thirds of his time on sin, presenting a cryptic account of justification, and then

---

[21] e.g. K. Barth, *A Shorter Commentary on Romans*, 35–7.

[22] Percentages in this paragraph were calculated on the basis of a line count of the Nestle–Aland 26th/27th edn text, and rounded to one decimal place.

expounding at length the nature and implications of faith and the history of Israel.

Of course it would be wrong to assume that the proportion of the account spent on any one element should be in direct proportion to its importance. Some things are harder to explain than others. If Jews are harder to convince that they are sinners because of their special gifts from God, then extra time needs to be spent on that. Nevertheless, the content of a message would normally impose some of the proportions of an account of it. In this case, the fact that it has not done so means that the central element, the actual account of justification, is too brief to be clear. It is abundantly clear that the human response required is faith, and that God acts graciously. The explanation of how this comes about through the Cross is cryptic. It cannot pass muster as an introduction for beginners, especially beginners who may be suspicious of the author. This represents a marked tension between Paul's text and the basic conception. Is the mistake Paul's, or ours? Has he created a text that does not say adequately what he intended to say, or have we been working with a wrong idea of his intention?

The third very serious discrepancy between Paul's text and the basic conception is that Rom. 3.21–6 does not work as an introductory announcement of justification. As well as being too compressed, it is also out of balance. Further, the meaning does not match the grammar.

The elements of the account in Rom. 3.21–6 are: justification for all who believe, faith is faith in Christ, all have sinned, they are being justified freely by God's grace, justification is through God's action taken in the Cross, God's own righteousness is shown in that action. There are ninety-nine words in the passage. The announcement of righteousness through faith and the fact that this is faith in Jesus Christ take up the first twenty-five (Rom. 3.21–2c). This element is important and the proportion of the explanation spent on it reflects Paul's particular context, where the relationship with the law is important. It takes 25.3 per cent of the text, and is reinforced by references to faith in Rom. 3.25a, 26. The reminder of the human plight, all have sinned, takes thirteen words (Rom. 3.22d–23), and there is a five-word announcement of gracious justification (Rom. 3.24a). This, the central statement of the justification account, that people are sinners justified by God's grace, occupies altogether 18.2 per cent of the statement, and only just over one-quarter of that is on the positive side. The explanation of the Atonement on which it all depends takes nineteen words, 19.2 per cent of the text, and is extremely cryptic. The nouns ἀπολύτρωσις, ἱλαστήριον, αἷμα are dumped down in rapid succession, with no serious attempt at explanation (Rom. 3.24b–25a). Surely Paul could either have explained clearly or not explained until later. What is clear is that this is action of God's grace, seeking the response of faith. In a justification account the statement about God's own righteousness is a supporting element, not the main point. In some readings it is very important – the gospel is salvation for believers because God's righteousness is revealed in it. Nevertheless, the driving question of a justification account is not, How is God (seen to be) righteous? but, How can sinners be righteous before God? The statement about God's own righteousness is either a guard clause, showing that God takes sin seriously and does not simply call black white,[23] or an explanation of how the revelation of the righteousness of God is also, or includes, a revelation of God's own righteousness.[24] Yet this element occupies 37.4 per cent of Paul's text, including the final reference to faith. A reader unaware of the basic conception would be justified, it seems, in concluding that Paul was intending to speak about faith and God's righteousness, and perhaps the connection between them. Justification by grace through faith would then be part of a discussion of God's righteousness, whereas in the basic conception God's righteousness is part of the discussion of justification.

There is an even greater problem. If the paragraph is an announcement of justification through faith, the grammar does not match the meaning. The problem centres on δικαιούμενοι (Rom. 3.24). Paul's statement is εἰς πάντας τοὺς πιστεύοντας. οὐ γάρ ἐστιν διαστολή, πάντες γὰρ ἥμαρτον καὶ ὑστεροῦνται τῆς δόξης τοῦ θεοῦ δικαιούμενοι δωρεάν (Rom. 3.22d–24a). Δικαιούμενοι is in the nominative case, agreeing with πάντες. That means that according to the grammar Rom. 3.23–4a is a tri-partite statement about 'all': they have sinned, they lack the glory of God, they are being justified freely. According to the justification account, *all human beings* have sinned and lack the glory of God, but only *all believers* are being justified. In the text, the 'all' that refers to believers is the πάντας of verse 22, whereas Paul, with his use of the nominative and his sentence structure, clearly related it to πάντες

---

[23] e.g. Cranfield, *Romans*, I, 211–12.
[24] e.g. Käsemann, *Commentary on Romans*, 101.

(verse 23). If Paul meant to give a justification account, his meaning and his grammar do not match. His grammar works only if the 'all' who have sinned and the 'all' who believe are the same group. Wengst offers this as his response to Bultmann's complaint that the contrast between sin and grace is flattened out by Paul's δικαιούμενοι.[25] In that case, however, we have moved away from a universal account of the justification of sinners to a more limited topic, God's justification of believers. Then Rom. 3.23 ceases to be a summary reference to Rom. 1.18–3.20 and it is no longer clear why Paul had to make that precarious argument. The only alternative is that Paul's account shows him to be a universalist, but if he was, it was clearly not on the basis that everybody had believed.

Further, according to the grammar, οὐ γάρ ἐστιν διαστολή (Rom. 3.22d) gives a ground for the claim that righteousness is for all who believe (Rom. 3.22c), and the whole of the rest of the paragraph spells out the lack of distinction. It is more usual to see Paul explaining that justification is for believers because everybody has sinned and therefore needs grace. Then οὐ γάρ ἐστιν διαστολή underlines this universality. It is not the major basis and pivotal point of the paragraph that the grammar makes it.

In Rom. 3.21–6, the balance of the elements is odd in an introductory justification account and the grammar is wrong. Paul's mistake, or ours?

To summarize, we have three major discrepancies between the basic conception and Paul's text. First, if the passage is a justification account, Rom. 1.18–3.20 must offer a convincing account of the human predicament, that all have sinned and therefore cannot be justified. The text fails to do this. There is no proof and the rhetoric is so overdrawn that many exceptions can be found. The appearance of Gentiles who do the law contradicts the conclusion. Second, if Rom. 1.16–4.25 is a justification account, it is so out of balance that the message of justification is not effectively communicated and most of the account is spent on supporting discussions. These are necessary in the cultural context, but it is surprising that they should crowd out the main point. Third, if Rom. 3.21–6 is the core announcement of justification, the text is out of balance and the grammar does not match the meaning. We cannot hope to solve these problems by further research. Either Paul's justification

[25] *Formeln*, 87.

account has fundamental weaknesses or we are mistaken in assuming that he intended to present such an account. This conclusion faces us with a choice. Do we continue with the basic conception and acknowledge that Paul's argument is inadequate, or do we test the basic conception?

We can make a case for accepting that the basic conception is right and Paul's argument is inadequate. That would be surprising, since the justification theology is profoundly important in his understanding of the gospel as we know it. Nevertheless, it is possible. Sanders holds that Paul's thought moves from solution to problem.[26] The solution is justification by grace through faith in Christ, therefore the problem is that humankind cannot be justified on the basis of its own efforts. This is hard to demonstrate empirically, particularly if it has to be demonstrated for God's chosen people as well as for everyone else. Thus, it is not surprising that Paul's argument in Rom. 1.18–3.20 is flawed.[27] We take it for granted that Paul is difficult and often obscure. He was one of those brilliant thinkers who have enormous difficulty communicating with ordinary mortals. Developing his arguments by dictation, he did sometimes fail to say clearly what he meant. That could account for imbalances and grammatical difficulties. Paul was incompetent as a communicator. Apparently he lost some of his churches. At 2 Pet. 3.16 there is a reference to Paul's letters ἐν αἷς ἐστιν δυσνόητά τινα. Then again, the basic conception has yielded impressive meaning and theology in a long tradition of responsible study. Few scholars have felt impelled to question it, and recent readings on other bases have not persuaded the scholarly community that it should be seriously questioned.

If we want to accept that case and continue using the basic conception to wrestle with an unsatisfactory text, we must recognize what that implies. In Paul's extant writings Rom. 1.18–3.20 is the only attempt to demonstrate the human predicament empirically. For us, that makes it an isolated argument. As historians, we know that it was not so for Paul. Romans is part of a long theological and missionary struggle. If that was the best empirical argument he could produce, surely he would have tried something else long before he wrote this letter. The nearest argument in the extant letters is that of Gal. 3.10–14, that all who rely on the works

---

[26] *Palestinian Judaism*, 443, 499.
[27] Westerholm, *Israel's Law and the Church's Faith*, 158–9.

of the law are under a curse. There Paul argued from scripture, not empirically. We have no evidence that something was forcing him to begin his letter to the Romans with an argument they could hardly be expected to accept.

If we accept that Paul was an incompetent communicator, we must realize that this involves accepting that he was so incompetent that his presentation pulls away from his intention. He was not just using difficult concepts, losing sentences, failing to make points clear, or the like. He gave himself no chance to make his central points clear, being preoccupied with secondary ones. As historians, we must acknowledge that such incompetence is puzzling. There is evidence that Paul was a competent communicator. He founded an impressive number of churches in a hostile world. The churches of Rome, Corinth, Galatia, Philippi, Thessalonica and in Philemon's house kept his letters and shared them around to such good effect that they entered the canon of scripture several centuries later. The clause in 2 Pet. 3.16 looks different in context: ἐν αἷς ἐστιν δυσνόητά τινα, ἃ οἱ ἀμαθεῖς καὶ ἀστήρικτοι στρεβλοῦσιν ὡς καὶ τὰς λοιπὰς γραφὰς πρὸς τὴν ἰδίαν αὐτῶν ἀπώλειαν. Things are hard to understand because of their nature, not because Paul did not explain them clearly. Like other writings, they can be twisted. Similarly, if Paul lost some churches, that could have been because the message he did communicate was not accepted.

It seems that to accept that the mistakes are Paul's, not ours, is to work in the shadow of historical improbability, and to risk assuming that we know better than Paul did what he was trying to do.

What is the case for seeking a better basic conception of the text? First, the present one leaves us with insoluble problems concerned with fundamental issues. Second, the discrepancies we identified are interconnected. Both the account as a whole and Rom. 3.21–6 are out of balance in that they concentrate on important but secondary issues at the expense of justification itself. According to the grammar of Rom. 3.23–4, the 'all' who believe and the 'all' who have sinned are the same group. This implies that πάντες ... ἥμαρτον may not be intended as a statement of universal sinfulness. This links with Paul's failure to demonstrate universal sinfulness in Rom. 1.18–3.20. Perhaps he was not trying to do so. A justification account is a general theological statement, applying to all humanity. The interconnecting problems could question this universal reference. Was Paul's concern more specific? Third, studies taking account of recent work on the law have highlighted in Rom. 1.18–3.20 the argument that Jews are no better off than Gentiles. Could this cast light on the grammar of Rom. 3.23–6, which makes οὐ γάρ ἐστιν διαστολή (Rom. 3.22d) the key statement, not a support for πάντες ... ἥμαρτον (Rom. 3.23a)? This again points to a specific rather than a universal concern. If that had to do with Jew–Gentile relationships, it might lead to an explanation of the imbalance in the whole text, including the space given to Jewish questions in Rom. 3.27–4.25. Dunn suggests that in Rom. 3.21–31 Paul spelt out in detail only the controversial part of his account.[28] This raises the possibility that Romans was part of one of Paul's controversies rather than a justification account. Ziesler's and Wedderburn's accounts encourage us to look in the same direction. If the question of God's righteousness proved to be as important as Wedderburn suggests, Rom. 3.21–6 might not be out of balance at all.

On this view, we must allow and test the hypothesis that Paul was doing something other than giving a justification account, either in general or with emphasis on certain Jewish questions. We need to develop a new basic conception. If Paul was doing something else, and we identified it, we could expect our conception of the passage to change in two major stages. In the first stage, we should see it as a justification account influenced by the 'something else'. In the second, we should be working with a new basic conception because we understood Paul's intention in the new way. It could be that Pauline scholarship is in the process of such a two-stage change, with the changes already brought about by study of the law question representing the first stage.

In taking up this possibility, however, we realize that Paul does say πάντες γὰρ ἥμαρτον καὶ ὑστεροῦνται τῆς δόξης τοῦ θεοῦ δικαιούμενοι δωρεάν (Rom. 3.23–4a), a succinct statement about justification. Our investigation has raised the possibility that the πάντες may refer to a group smaller than all humanity. If that proved to be so, the smaller group would be a living example of Paul's justification theology. Centuries of fruitful scholarly work must not be cast aside lightly. If we simply say that Rom. 1.16–4.25 is not a justification account so it must be about something else, we shall risk throwing a baby out with the bath water. The hypothesis

---

[28] *Romans*, 183.

we need to develop is that Paul was talking about something else, but the justification theology was important for whatever it was.

How do we proceed? We asked whether the mistakes are Paul's or ours. Our hypothesis suggests that at least some of them are ours. Accordingly, we must examine the exegetical methods and procedures we have been using. What are our questions? How do we seek answers to them?

3

ROMANS 1.16–4.25: WHAT DO WE WANT TO KNOW?

To test the hypothesis that Rom. 1.16–4.25 may be something other than a justification account, we must formulate and test an alternative proposal. It should overcome the problems of the present basic conception and not introduce others. We concluded that the difficulties we encountered in exegesis might arise from our failure to understand correctly what Paul was trying to do rather than from Paul's failure to achieve his purpose. Where in our exegetical process could that kind of error arise?

We often describe the process in terms of the hermeneutical circle. In explicating a text, we move between the whole and the parts. Our understanding of the whole guides our understanding of the parts. Study of the parts then modifies our understanding of the whole, and so on. Study of the detail of Rom. 1.16–4.25 in chapter 2 has made us question our understanding of the whole. That is where we are most likely to be making the kind of mistake that would cause the problems we identified. Thus, we are looking for a new understanding of the whole, a new basic conception.

Our understanding of the whole of any text is complex, including, for instance our knowledge of the setting, the writer, the language. Two aspects are most important: *what the text is about* and *what kind of writing we are reading*. The mainstream debate has long been conducted within a consensus understanding of the whole of Rom. 1.16–4.25 so strong that it is rarely discussed. In chapter 2 we made explicit the accepted presupposition that the text is about justification. We did not make explicit the presupposition concerning what kind of writing we are reading. This is because that argument was conducted in the terms of the current debate and the presupposition about the nature of the text does not surface in that debate: the text is theological exposition. This was represented in our argument by the formulation that the passage is seen as a justification *account*.

What do we mean by 'theological exposition'? This will become clearer as we formulate an alternative understanding and expound the text accordingly. For now, we can say that in theological exposition the writer's purpose is to explain theological ideas. If the explanation has a purpose beyond the sharing of ideas, it has little impact on the explanation itself. Implications can come later. This is usually taken to be the case in proposals that Paul's purpose in Romans was to deal with problems in the Roman church, which he does in Romans 14–15, after laying his theological ground very carefully. Thus, Rom. 1.16–4.25 contains statements of what Paul takes to be universal truth. The recurring πᾶς refers to every human being. Theological exposition is addressed to an audience interested in the ideas. It is not concerned with the readers as persons, or with relating the ideas to them in their situation. Accordingly, in mainstream exegesis very little account is taken of Paul's audience.

We can also trace the presupposition that our text is theological exposition in the debates on the purpose of Romans and on Romans as letter. Scholars seek to identify Paul's purpose in sending the Romans a letter comprising a long theological section plus general and specific paraenesis. This approach excludes any possibility that an examination of purpose could bring about reappraisal of the idea that Romans 1–11 is treatise. The approach to the question of what kind of letter we are reading is similar. There is evidence that some scholars are uncomfortable with the idea of a letter consisting largely of theological exposition, yet this is certainly not impossible. The debate proceeds by coming to terms with it. An example is Beker's study of contingency and coherence in Romans. A letter, he says, is a word on target in a particular situation. In this case, he concludes that the circumstances were right for Paul to write a theological tractate for the Romans: 'When a letter assumes the features of a treatise, a problem of major proportions is under discussion. And yet a treatise-type letter does not necessarily negate its particularity.'[1] There is no theoretical reason why Paul should not have written a treatise-type letter, but as long as we try to understand Romans on the basis that it is a letter containing a major treatise, no other view is possible for us. Accordingly, there has been no testing in the debate of the

---

[1] *Paul the Apostle*, 77.

possibility that it might be something that Deissmann would have been happier to call a letter than an epistle.[2]

The justification framework guides mainstream exegesis of Rom. 1.16–4.25. Investigating the problems of the passage has led us to question both elements of that framework. We have strong grounds for suspecting that the passage is not a justification account, and good reason to suggest that it may not be an *account*, i.e. it may not be theological exposition.

The purpose of the following chapters is to develop an alternative exegesis of Rom. 1.16–4.25, arguing that it is valid, it overcomes the problems of reading within the justification framework, and it serves our exegetical purposes better than exegesis in the traditional pattern. This exegesis arose from wrestling with the problems created by the facts that the traditional readings do not match the text, alternatives offered in the debate are no more successful, and some problems are not noticed. The next stages of the argument will be easier to follow if we now present a brief outline of the approach taken and its main results.

The exegesis is in two steps, a teleological and a causal exposition (or reading). The first step, the teleological exposition, is a rediscovery of what Paul was intending to say to the Romans. We call it teleological because the aim is to understand the text in terms of Paul's purpose. It answers the question, Where was this text going *to*? This step depends on careful examination of Paul's purpose in writing and of the nature of the text, and entails a very careful, audience-oriented reading of the text. The second step, the causal exposition, is an examination of the major theological presuppositions underlying what Paul was intending to say, the justification theology and the Creator–creature relationship. We call it causal because the aim is to understand the text as expression of Paul's thought. It answers the question, Where was this text coming *from*? These steps correspond to two interdependent and mutually illuminating elements of meaning in the text.

Exegesis of Rom. 1.16–4.25 by this method offers a radically new view of the nature of the whole. It is not theological exposition but something we describe best as pastoral preaching. It is not a justification account but is about God's righteousness and its implications for the believers receiving the preaching. The driving question is not, How can we be righteous in God's sight since we are sinners? It is, How can God be righteous in our sight if he justifies believing sinners without reference to the Jew–Gentile distinction? The pastoral preaching draws on Paul's theology of justification, and thus gives us access to this aspect of his thought.

The first step is the teleological exposition. In Romans, Paul was making his first contact with the Roman church/es. He did it by beginning to exercise among them his apostolic ministry of preaching the gospel. His letter can best be understood as preaching to believers, rehearsing the gospel as they live under it. The context was the church's agonizing over the question of whether Gentiles who came to faith in Christ had to become Jews. Paul said that this must not be required. He knew that this stand laid his preaching and ordering of church life open to the theological charge of preaching a God who had abandoned Israel and therefore could not be trusted, and to the ethical charge of encouraging antino-mianism and immorality. He also knew that decision-making on this question involved many aspects of community and personal life. These were deep-rooted and affected people's lives in important ways. His purpose in this letter as a whole was to help the Romans to share and act upon his insight into the way believers' lives are shaped by the new action the God of Israel was taking in Christ and the gospel, in this case in the difficult matter of Jew–Gentile relationships within the community of believers.

In Rom. 1.16–4.25, his aim was to help the Romans, especially those with a very conservative understanding of Israel's election, to come to terms with an important corollary of their faith in Christ. God's action in Christ fulfilled the purpose of Israel's election by breaking the bounds of Israel. Realizing this was not simply a step in theological awareness. It involved a new understanding of God and new self-understanding. Such a change affects not just one's actions, but who one perceives oneself to be. The process is painful. Paul did not apologize for the pain, but he was aiming to make it fruitful. God was righteous, and God's righteousness required that God be faithful to the covenant with Israel and be the impartial eschatolo-gical judge. How, then, could God be righteous in justifying on the basis of believing alone? This new action seemed to be God's abandonment of faithful Israel. Paul presented it as the fulfilment of God's faithfulness to unfaithful Israel, and then as the fulfilment of God's purpose in the election of Israel. Thus, Rom. 1.16–17 is not the theme statement for a theological exposition, but a grasping of the nettle of debate: salvation *is* simply on the basis of believing, and this gospel includes the election of Israel. Rom. 1.18–3.20 is not a demonstration that all have sinned, but the stripping away of defences that leaves the conservative believer face to face with the fact that sinful Jew is in exactly the same position as sinful Gentile before God's righteous judgement. Rom. 3.21–6 is not the announcement of justification through faith, but the demonstration that in the Cross God fulfils his righteousness as Israel's saviour and judge, doing it precisely in the action that breaks the bounds of Israel. Rom. 3.27–4.25 is not a discussion of faith and of the continuity of the gospel with God's former action with Israel. Rather, the same conservative believer is shown the history of God's action with Israel in the new light of its fulfilment in Christ. It becomes clear that justification through faith was God's purpose from the beginning. The question here for Paul and the Romans was not how people can be righteous and thus acceptable to a righteous God. It was how God could be seen to be righteous when his new action in the Cross looked unrighteous and had to be viewed, not from the neutral territory of theological argument, but from the midst of the painful life-adjustments it was demanding. This particular question about God's righteousness did not arise from the justification of sinners simply on the basis of their faith, although consideration of that question could have helped to form the theology on which Paul was drawing. It arose from the justification of believing sinners without reference to the Jew–Gentile distinction.

In step 2, the causal exposition, we examine the underlying theology. Traditionally, we have read Rom. 1.16–4.25 as if it were a justification account, either as doctrine – Dodd, for instance – or as a polemical presentation, as in the case of Dunn. *We have been reading a theological presupposition of what Paul was intending to say to the Romans, and reading it as though it were itself what he was intending to say to them.* This has distorted the text, as we saw in chapter 2, and allowed for a misleading element in interpretation of the theology.

We may state the immediate theological presupposition of what Paul was intending to say to the Romans in the form 'every *believer* is a sinner justified by God's grace'. This says nothing about the rest of humanity. We have noted that Paul did not offer any convincing demonstration that all have sinned. When we examine in detail what he was intending to say to the Romans, we shall find that his discussion presupposes that everybody he was talking to was a sinner. When he mentioned God's act of redemption through

Christ, he was referring the Romans to what they already knew. His presupposition was derived from the fact that his hearers had accepted Christ as a means of dealing with their sin. Since Paul clearly believed that the gospel was for everybody, we may state the immediate theological presupposition of this passage in the general form 'human beings are sinners offered justification as God's gift, to be received by faith'. Formulated thus, it is a universal statement, the stuff of philosophical-theological discussion, like the form in which scholarly debate normally handles it. Indeed, its universality is essential to its validity as a statement about how human beings can be acceptable to a righteous God. If this can be achieved by human effort, the prescription is to try harder. This universal form of the presupposition is not the form in which it appears in the text.

Rom. 1.18–3.20 fails to work as a demonstration that all have sinned because it was never intended to do so. That is not its function in what Paul was intending to say to the Romans. Accordingly, it cannot serve that purpose when we study the text seeking insight into Paul's thought. Rather, it shows what sin is, and how sin distorts even the gift of grace, election, into a possession. In Rom. 3.21–6, the justification theology becomes a presupposition of Paul's demonstration of the way Israel's God is righteous in justifying all believing sinners without reference to the Jew–Gentile divide.

A problem with the justification account in traditional readings of the passage is that justification by grace through faith is easily seen as an emergency measure to which God was driven by human inability to overcome sin. This comes through with brutal clarity in the RSV translation of Rom. 3.22d–24a. Οὐ γάρ ἐστιν διαστολή, πάντες γὰρ ἥμαρτον καὶ ὑστεροῦνται τῆς δόξης τοῦ θεοῦ δικαιούμενοι δωρεὰν τῇ αὐτοῦ χάριτι becomes 'For there is no distinction; since all have sinned and fall short of the glory of God, they are justified by his grace as a gift.' *Since* they have sinned and fall short of the glory of God they are justified by his grace. In Paul's text, being justified freely by God's grace is one of three closely related elements providing the ground for the lack of distinction. Yet this translation is widely accepted as expressing his intention. After all, he did not say it very clearly. Most of the official English Bible translations help him out in these verses. In doing so, they obscure what he was intending to say to the Romans. In the context of this logic of emergency, the continuity function of the Abraham argument in Romans 4 is to show that the new measure is not inconsistent with God's previous action with Israel. In searching for what Paul intended to say to the Romans, we found that the discussion of Abraham demonstrates that the divine–human relationship of grace and the response of faith is God's purpose in the election of Israel.

This outline points to something that will be clearer when we have discussed the methodology of this exegesis and the detail of the text. For now, it will suffice to say that the justification theology is a presupposition of what Paul was intending to say to the Romans, but the form in which we find it in the text is shaped by the way Paul was using it. To put it another way, the text is generated partly by the theology, but the form in which we find the theology is generated by Paul's intention in dictating the text.

The passage also reveals a more basic theological presupposition of what Paul was intending to say to the Romans, the relationship between Creator and creature. For Paul, sin is the breakdown of the proper Creator–creature relationship, and salvation is its restoration, with the re-creation of the image of God in the human, the divine glory. The proper Creator–creature relationship is human faith responding to God's grace. The importance of this element of meaning in the text is reflected in mainstream exegeses, notably in the creation faithfulness readings of Käsemann and his school. Barrett's commentary reflects the text more accurately. He recognizes the importance of the theme in Paul's thinking here, but does not impose it on Paul's address to the Romans.[3]

Recognition of this theological presupposition is essential to a proper understanding of the text, but the attempt to treat it as what Paul was intending to say to the Romans distorts the text. Again, the text is generated partly by the theology, but the form in which we find the theology in the text is generated by Paul's intention in creating it.

This outline shows that our reading could overcome the problems we identified in chapter 2.

> Rom. 1.18–3.20 does not demonstrate that all have sinned because it has another purpose.

> The different concerns may well account for what seemed strange imbalances when the passage was read as a justification account.

---

[3] *A Commentary on the Epistle to the Romans*, 81–2.

Rom. 3.21–6 seems to be about God's righteousness as it is expressed in justifying believers. This will probably account for the balance of elements in that pericope.

An argument presupposing that all believers are sinners justified by grace could avoid the problems associated with δικαιούμενοι in Rom. 3.24a.

The justification theology is described as a theological presupposition of what Paul was intending to say to the Romans. This, if credible, explains the role of that theology in the meaning of the passage.

The outline therefore represents an hypothesis worth testing. It also raises major questions.

Why and on what basis does somebody separate theological presuppositions from what Paul was intending to say (not, what he said) to the Romans?

What kind of reading treats the text as having a thread of argument running through it, but also as a painful but necessary pastoral procedure, like surgery?

These questions drive us to some prior ones.

What are we historical-critical exegetes seeking when we study a text?

What do we mean by the questions we ask?

The process of study and interpretation of the NT texts has been continuous from their first readings. In almost two millennia there have been great changes and we can identify periods and styles of exegesis. One cannot rule lines across history, though. Changes come about by changing elements in scholarly understanding. We cannot simply abandon the ambience in which we learnt the Bible or our teachers' influence. This combination of continuity and change can create problems, especially in periods of experiment, such as the present. For instance, what scholars mean by their questions may change, evolving even to a point where an outsider would find a disjunction between what the words of a question said and what the questioner was actually wanting to discover.

One such tension in current exegesis is between the intention of taking Romans seriously as a letter and the fact that we have been reading not Paul's communication but a theological presupposition. If we explore why this has been happening, we shall find some answers about what we are seeking and what we mean by our questions.

There are many reasons, but three interlocking ones seem most important. The real focus of exegesis is on the theology, Paul's thought. As children of the Enlightenment we prefer causal to teleological explanation. We have mistaken the nature of the text. The impact of these factors is strengthened by the fact that the questions of what we are trying to achieve and what we want to know are not normally on a public agenda and discussion of them is not a significant element in the training of new scholars.

Stated so bluntly, the three reasons seem as controversial as the claim that we have been reading a theological presupposition rather than the text as letter. We must explicate them.

We begin with the claim that the focus of exegesis is the theology, Paul's thought. Apparently, the controversial aspect of this is not whether or not it is true, but what the point of saying it is. Of course we are interested in Paul's theology. We see no difference between that and being interested in what he says, taking his letters seriously. Yet one occasionally hears in scholarly conversation an objection that exegesis at the level of what Paul was saying would lead to shallow exegesis. This implies a (submerged!) recognition that there is more to the meaning of the text than what Paul was intending to say and we want an in-depth understanding. If our pursuit of this has led us to miss what Paul was intending to say, we have not fully achieved our goal.

We historical-critical exegetes are heirs of the exegetical tradition. One of the starting points of historical-critical exegesis was the insistence that the biblical texts are not unmediated divine theological truth, but human documents that must be taken seriously for what they are. This includes taking seriously the fact that the Pauline documents are letters, mostly addressed to particular people facing – or creating – particular problems. Yet our inherited understanding of them is as theology first and foremost. More than two centuries of historical-critical study has related these factors by understanding that Paul addressed theological letters to pastoral situations. Beker calls this 'Paul's contextual way of doing theology',[4] and most of us concur.

---

[4] *Paul the Apostle*, e.g. 31, 131.

The second factor contributing to our error of reading a theological presupposition instead of the letter is our preference for causal over teleological explanation. Basically, we understand Paul's letters in terms of his theological thinking. His pastoral, or other, intention is handled as a separate question. For instance, commentators normally treat the purpose of Romans as an introductory question. The commentary will include thorough discussion of the concepts of righteousness and faith, and the question of their meaning will be kept in play, but the questions of purpose will not. A teleological explanation would understand the text in terms of Paul's purpose. As a letter it would be understood as address to his intended audience. Understanding of his theological thinking would contribute to the explanation.

The first step of the two-step exegesis outlined above is a teleological explanation of the text. Expositions within the justification framework are causal explanations. A closer look at Rom. 1.16–17 will clarify this claim. In the commentaries, the usual procedure for expounding these verses is to examine Paul's important concepts and analyse the statement as a theological proposition. The context taken into account is the thought context. For instance, Paul's concept of righteousness is different from ours. The audience is rarely mentioned, and the audience actually being taken into account is The Reader, an ahistorical mind seeking to understand Paul's ideas. In the church of Paul's time, the statement could well have appeared challenging, even inflammatory. Nobody asks whether Paul expected the Romans to respond by analysing it conceptually. The procedure used to arrive at such a reading identifies it as a causal explanation of the text. The debate proceeds on the assumption that this causal explanation is also a teleological explanation. This could be true, *but it would be true only if Paul intended to give an account of his thought.* It could be that because *we* have developed causal explanations of the text, we have concluded that *Paul's* purpose was to express his thought. There is little safeguard against this in the debate.

The teleological explanation of Rom. 1.16–17 in step 1 of our exegesis looks very different. Paul and the Romans were interested in whether Gentile believers had to become Jews. Paul knew that the Romans would have heard about his controversial view, and he could expect that their conceptions of, and responses to, it would vary. With this statement, he was entering the discussion with a clear claim: salvation is indeed for all who believe without any other requirement. This is action of God's righteousness, and it includes the election of Israel and the fulfilment of the word of her prophet. This teleological explanation sees Paul making a particular claim to particular people who might well doubt its validity.

The difference between these two explanations shows in the treatment of terms such as 'faith'. In traditional causal explanation, the exegete observes that faith is needed for salvation. The appropriate response is to give some account of Paul's understanding of faith. In the teleological explanation, Paul was using the word 'faith' to enter into the discussion about whether or not believing in Christ was all that was required for salvation. Thus, the appropriate response is to take 'faith' here to mean 'believing in Christ' without making judgements about Paul's wider understanding.

Our preference for causal explanation is natural to children of the Enlightenment and is encouraged by our inherited understanding of the texts as theological statement. We need a substantial incentive to try another mode of explanation.

The third reason why we have been reading a theological presupposition as if it were the letter is our incorrect identification of the nature of the text as theological exposition. This wrong identification has led us past what Paul was intending to say to the Romans, directing our attention instead to his theological presuppositions. The claims that the current debate presupposes that the text is theological exposition, and that it is best understood as pastoral preaching, will be explicated and fully argued. The contrasting examples already offered should give some indication of what they mean.

In mainstream exegesis of Pauline texts the underlying question is, What does this text mean? It is answered in a single line of exposition, and all the detailed questions contribute to the answering of this unstated question. This presupposes that we can handle the text as letter and as evidence for Paul's thought both at once. We have now identified these as separate concerns. They represent different questions about the texts, the first about what Paul was intending to say to his addressees, the second about Paul's thought. The answers would be the same only if Paul was intending to expound his thought. Accordingly, the unstated question should be acknowledged, rejected and replaced with, We want to explore the meaning of this text. This conclusion is the first-fruits of our examination of the problems of exegesis of Rom. 1.16–4.25, and it coincides with our response in chapter 1 to the breakdown of the tool question, What does this text mean? It is the starting point of the two-step method of exegesis. This method requires that we give more attention to ourselves as exegetes than we see in mainstream exegesis. We do this primarily for the sake of guarding the integrity of the text. We need to consider carefully what questions will enable us to explore the meaning of a particular text. They will include what Paul was intending to say to whomever he was addressing, what kind of discourse this is and what theological presuppositions are in play.

In her article 'In his own Image?', Hooker illustrates from Synoptic studies the way answers to questions are largely determined by the questioners' outlook.[5] Practitioners of source criticism understood the evangelists to be concerned with compiling a careful and complete record of events. The exponents of form criticism saw them as collectors of pericopae that confront hearers with the gospel. For redaction critics, they were theologians uninterested in history. We may add to Hooker's observation that the questioners also determine the questions. To allow our work to be governed by the text is a challenging ideal. She reminds us that we cannot escape from ourselves, and therefore need to be aware of our own presuppositions.[6] This danger of making the NT writer in our own image has been recognized again in the context of reader-response criticism. Beavis comments, '[T]he model of the evangelist *implicit* in most Marcan studies is that of a (modern) scholar writing for other scholars.'[7] Similarly, the model of the apostle implicit in most Pauline studies is of Paul as a scholar writing for other scholars. This Paul is a curious amalgam of first- and twentieth-century models, writing theological arguments for the first numbers of *NTS* or *ZNW*, AD 56.

This charge may seem outrageous. We know that Paul is not like us. We have spent dedicated lifetimes exploring the Classical, Mandaean, Nag Hammadi, Qumran, apocalyptic, Wisdom, rabbinic, mystery religions, magical, Hellenistic popular and every other category of ancient literature, learning languages, examining coins and archaeological sites. We know that Paul's methods of argument differ from ours and we do not reject them just because they are not always convincing to us. Of course we treat Paul as a

---

[5] 'Image', 28–41, 29.
[6] *Ibid.*, 41.
[7] 'Literary and Sociological Aspects of the Function of Mark 4:11–12', 79. Her italics. See also Fowler, *Loaves and Fishes*, 41–2.

scholar. He was. He was trained in the techniques of rabbinic argument and knew his scripture intimately. All this is true – and no defence against the charge. The problem is that we treat Paul's texts as though he were doing what scholars do when they write for each other. He was making the best possible argument. He was speaking mind to mind, not person to person. He was seeking an intellectual response, an assessment that his argument was good enough to establish his conclusion. Any action he hoped for would flow from that.

This approach is so universal that it is hard to illustrate because there are no contrasting examples. It shows most clearly in cases that are extreme, so that it may seem unfair to cite them as examples. The point is that they are not normally noted as surprising. Conzelmann comments that 1 Cor. 3.16 'addresses the reader with surprising directness'.[8] What does this mean? Paul was dictating a letter to the Corinthians. It was to be read aloud by one person while the rest listened. In this setting, Conzelmann's remark can mean only that Paul stopped addressing the Corinthians he had been addressing since 1 Cor. 1.1 and directed a remark to the person reading the letter to them. Conzelmann's words mean that, but we do not suppose that Conzelmann meant it. His words make sense in his own setting. If he wrote, 'Do you not know ...?' in a scholarly article, he would be addressing the reader with surprising directness. Paul's οὐκ οἴδατε; is characteristic of his address to his churches. Conzelmann has slipped into reading Paul's text as if Paul were a scholar writing for scholars.

Barrett argues that in modern book production Rom. 3.28 'could best be placed in a footnote'.[9] This suggestion looks anachronistic if one takes seriously that Paul was dictating something he thought of as a letter, for people to hear. Footnotes are suited to academic discourse, in print. It is not just that Paul lacked the facility to produce a footnote. He was working in a different context, and would not have used such a facility anyway. There must be some other explanation of Rom. 3.28.

Kelber's hypothesis that Paul's choice of the letter form may betray a preference for orality[10] shows how close we often come to assuming that our interest in Paul's thought was matched by his intention to give an account of it. What other literary form would

[8] *1 Corinthians*, 77.
[9] *A Commentary on the Epistle to the Romans*, 82.
[10] *The Oral and the Written Gospel*, 140.

have served Paul's purposes? One can hardly imagine him sending a gospel to the Corinthians.

We make Paul in our own image when we work on the assumption that he was doing the kind of thing we do, and when we unconsciously treat the text as though what we are looking for is what he intended his readers to find, even though we are not his intended readers. This is the phenomenon Hooker noted. It has turned Paul into a scholar and his letters into abstruse scholarly writings, however situational and polemical.

Our tasks are now clear. The first is to show in more detail why and on what ground we have separated what Paul was intending to say to the Romans from the theological presuppositions of what he was intending to say to them. The second is to define the nature of the whole we are reading. Setting aside the presuppositions that Rom. 1.16–4.25 is about Paul's justification theology and a passage of theological exposition, we must try to identify Paul's purpose in writing it, and to understand what kind of discourse it is. The third task is detailed exegesis in the two steps already outlined. This will test our answers to the other questions, and also our claim that separating the question of what Paul was intending to say to the Romans from the study of Paul's thought will serve both our exegetical purposes and the integrity of Paul's text better than the single-strand exegesis we currently practise.

4

THE BASIS FOR SEPARATING PRESUPPOSITIONS FROM INTENDED ADDRESS

The two-step exegesis outlined in chapter 3 deals first with what Paul intended to say to the Romans (teleological exposition) and then with two theological presuppositions of what he was intending to say (causal exposition). We do this because it serves our interests and the integrity of Paul's text better than exegesis answering the single question, What does this text mean?

Our interests are commitment to taking the text seriously as the kind of human document it is, a letter from Paul to the believers in Rome, and concern to understand Paul's thought, his theology. We saw in chapter 3 that they would be completely congruent only if Paul intended to give an account of his thought. Thus, treating the text in a single discussion based on the implied question, What does this text mean? will probably make us blur together the answers to the two questions, leaving both unclear. It will also entail the risk of reading Paul's intended communication through our interest in his theology, thereby making Paul in our own image.

These factors would apply to any contemporary exegesis of any Pauline text. In this study of Rom. 1.16–4.25, there is another. We are seeking a new understanding of the text as a whole, so we have a particular responsibility to define our questions clearly and to deal separately with them, without ignoring the interconnections.

The other reason for trying to separate Paul's intended communication and his theological thought is that this serves the integrity of Paul's text better than single-strand exegesis. It allows us to better identify the nature of the text and Paul's intention in creating it, and without risk of trivializing his apostolic work. Romans is part of that work, not just a reflection on it.

The outlines in chapter 3 give a preview of the new exegesis, indicating that the text will look different.

In chapter 3, we proposed replacing our implicit guiding question, What does this text mean?, with a statement of aim: We want to explore the meaning of this text. That pictures the meaning of the text as complex, something we explore, rather than as unitary, something we follow through. Working as historical-critical exegetes, we are concerned with the meaning of the text as Paul's, and not with the hermeneutical possibilities it might offer if it were cut loose from its first-century, Pauline, letter context.

This explicit statement that meaning in a text is complex corresponds to certain facts recognized in the existing debate. One is that to make sense of what Paul was saying, we must understand the context in which he was speaking. Another is that asking different questions about a text will bring out different aspects of its meaning. No single exegesis exhausts the meaning of a text.

These facts relate to the commonplace observation that a text contains more meaning than the author intended to convey to the audience. The people who take advantage of this include historians and detectives:

> The real history is written in forms not meant as history. In Wardrobe accounts, in Privy Purse expenses, in personal letters, in estate books. If someone, say, insists that Lady Whoosit never had a child, and you find in the account book the entry: 'For the son born to my lady on Michaelmas eve: five yards of blue ribbon, fourpence halfpenny', it's a reasonably fair deduction that my lady had a son on Michaelmas eve.[1]

The deduction is 'reasonably fair' because the account-keeper was not concerned to record the birth. NT scholars, as historians, do the same. Redaction critics use clues the NT writers did not intend to leave.

We may want to say that at least some of the 'extra' we find in texts would be more helpfully classified as information than as meaning. This might apply to the reconstruction of the situation in Galatia that we derive from Galatians, for example. Yet our understanding of Galatians is shaped by that 'information'. Similarly, scholars' conclusions about redaction history affect their understanding of the meaning of the texts. In the case of the quotation above, the information that the child was born helps to account for the fourpence halfpenny expended, but it is indispensable to the meaning of the text of the imaginary account book, and not just to

---

[1] Tey, *The Daughter of Time*, 96.

the meaning of the text of the novel. It would be hard to say that it is *just* information, and not part of the meaning. This is often true. A clear-cut example is allegory, where the point is made by the interrelation of two elements of meaning in the text. On the one hand, we read the adventures of the villain, the knight and the damsel fair and, on the other, we trace the vicissitudes of Virtue under threat from Evil.

Interconnected elements of meaning are clearly visible in Rom. 6.1–11. This passage contains the fullest discussion of baptism in the extant letters, yet it is obvious that Paul's intention was not to discuss baptism as such. He was dealing with the suggestion that believers should sin so that grace may abound. He explained at length that this is nonsense because believers have died to sin through their baptism into Christ. He was drawing on an understanding of baptism to make his point about life in Christ. We know that his intention was to quash the suggestion because that accounts for all of the text, whereas if we concluded that his intention was to instruct the Romans on baptism, we could not account for Rom. 6.1–2.

We note also that this discussion arises from two concepts characteristic of Paul's thought, being in Christ and living to God. They come to explicit expression in Rom. 6.10–11. They are important elements of the meaning of the text, although we could follow what Paul was saying to the Romans without being aware of their importance, even without identifying them as concepts in their own right. For understanding Paul's thought, they are very significant.

It is comparatively easy to identify elements of meaning in Rom. 6.1–11 because the presuppositions are more than usually visible, and because we are familiar with Paul's surviving letters. We now turn to a less familiar text where secondary elements of meaning are not explicit:

> The Parson is very exact in the governing of his house, making it a copy and model for his Parish. He knows the temper, and pulse of every person in his house, and accordingly either meets with their vices, or advanceth their virtues. His wife is either religious, or night and day he is winning her to it. Instead of the qualities of the world, he requires only three of her; first, a training up of her children and maids in the fear of God, with prayers, and

catechizing, and all religious duties. Secondly, a curing, and healing of all wounds and sores with her own hands; which skill either she brought with her, or he takes care she shall learn it of some religious neighbour. Thirdly, a providing for her family in such sort, as that neither they want a competent sustentation, nor her husband be brought in debt. His children he first makes Christians, and then Commonwealth's men; the one he owes to his heavenly Country, the other to his earthly, having no title to either, except he do good to both. Therefore having seasoned them with all Piety, not only of words in praying, and reading; but in actions, in visiting other sick children, and tending their wounds, and sending his charity by them to the poor, and sometimes giving them a little money to do it of themselves, that they get a delight in it, and enter into favour with God, who weighs even children's actions (1 *Kings* 14:12, 13) ... His servants are all religious, and were it not his duty to have them so, it were his profit, for none are so well served, as by religious servants, both because they do best, and because what they do, is blessed, and prospers. After religion, he teacheth them, that three things make a complete servant, Truth, and Diligence, and Neatness, or Cleanliness. Those that can read, are allowed times for it, and those that cannot, are taught; for all in his house are either teachers or learners, or both, so that his family is a School of Religion, and they all account, that to teach the ignorant is the greatest alms ... He keeps his servants between love, and fear, according as he finds them; but generally he distributes it thus, To his Children he shows more love than terror, to his servants more terror than love; but an old good servant boards a child.

This text is an account of the way the Parson rules his household. Clearly, the author's intention was to give this account. We may, however, be more interested in its picture of an hierarchical household. At this point, our interest distracts us from the author's intention. From the text, we could produce a diagram of the household structure, showing the members' functions and relationships. The author did not intend to give this picture; it inevitably appears in the text he created by giving his account of the way the Parson rules the household.

We may call the household structure the sociological presupposition of the intended account of the Parson's ruling of the household. It is integral to the meaning of the text, although not what the text 'says' or what the author was intending to say to the reader. In outlining the two-step exegesis of Rom. 1.16–4.25, we noticed that the text is generated partly by the justification theology, but the form in which we find the theology is controlled by Paul's intention in dictating the text. Similarly, this text is generated partly by the realities the sociological presupposition represents, but the form in which we find the sociological presupposition is generated by the author's intention in creating the text. There is, for instance, no discussion of the roles and relationships of the individual servants.

We have been told nothing about who wrote this text, its context or its origin. We have observed in it both an account of the way the Parson rules his household and a picture of the household structure. We say unhesitatingly that the former is what the author intended to say to the readers and the latter is its sociological presupposition. Why are we sure? The account of the way the Parson rules is what is made explicit, it accounts for all of the text, and it accounts for the presence of the picture of the household structure. If we thought that the picture of the structure was what the author intended to say to the readers, we could not account for all the detail about the Parson's doings.

If we learn that our text comes from George Herbert's *The Country Parson*,[2] we can bring to bear in interpreting it the information that Herbert worked in seventeenth-century England and was gentleman, parson and poet. Further, he says that his purpose in writing was to describe a true pastor in order to give himself a mark to aim at, and perhaps provide the basis for 'a complete Pastoral'.[3] A biographer studying Herbert's personality or an historian interested in the status of women or in attitudes to servants might notice the way the Parson perceives his responsibility and his authority, and compare the relationships with those of other cultures. A reader of the whole book will notice that this account exemplifies the paternalism that characterizes the entire account of the Parson's duties.

What can direct our attention away from what the author intended to say? In examining this passage, we have noticed three

---

[2] *The Country Parson, The Temple*, 68–9.
[3] *Ibid.*, 54.

factors. If another element of the meaning is particularly interesting to us, it will draw our attention. This happens with the picture of the household structure. If we bring to the text questions arising from our concerns rather than from the author's, they will direct our attention away from what the author intended to say. This happens for the biographer and the historian. If we see the passage in the context of the whole work, we may notice elements of meaning that were not significant for the author as he wrote this section. The paternalism is an example. These factors are connected with the fact that we do not belong to the personal and cultural context in which the text was written and intended to be read. We judge it to be a good, not a bad, thing that our attention is drawn to these elements, because they enrich our understanding of a text from which we are alienated to some extent by cultural distance. We shall not, though, let the value of this wider exploration cancel out our awareness of the author's intention. After our exploration, we shall still say that this text *is* Herbert's account of the way the Parson rules his household. We may add that *we find it* an interesting historical source.

We have applied to a non-biblical text the kind of procedure that we have suggested applying to Rom. 1.16–4.25, and that we used in commenting on Rom. 6.1–11. There is nothing startling about our observations. They are simply a conscious observation of processes that are normally either unconscious in our general reading (such as sorting out an author's intention from interesting presuppositions) or part of conscious processes that are not aimed at understanding a text but do enrich our understanding (such as the biographer's and the historian's questions). Why insist that these observations are important? What can we learn from them for our search for a new understanding of the whole of Rom. 1.16–4.25?

They are important for two reasons. They help us to understand how we can have been reading a theological presupposition of Rom. 1.16–4.25 instead of what Paul intended to say to the Romans, and they give the basis in the nature of texts for separating theological presuppositions from what Paul was intending to say to the Romans. It is a matter of fact that texts contain more than their creators were intending to communicate. It is a matter of experience that in reading texts from other cultures we are more likely to give serious attention to this extra than we are in the case of texts from our own cultural context. A good example of this is reading theology from earlier periods, when we can become very attentive to presuppositions, what is considered a valid argument, what questions are worth asking.[4]

That is to say, texts by their nature contain more than their authors were intending to communicate. With familiar texts and texts from our own context, we perform an unconscious sorting process. If we read texts that are unfamiliar because of cultural or chronological distance, or if we use any text to answer questions to which it was not addressed, we become more aware of the extra meaning.

Paul's letters, like the rest of the Bible, fall into a peculiar combination of these categories. They are familiar, yet we read them as strangers. They belong to a cultural milieu different from ours, yet they have been important in forming ours. Further, we read them as heirs of nineteen centuries of intensive study in which they have been considered in various cultural contexts, and used to answer questions other than those that their authors addressed. One result is that an enormous amount of the extra information has come to our attention, and is part of the way we read the familiar texts. We cannot read Paul's letters as ordinary letters because we know too much before we start, yet we are committed to taking them seriously as letters. This constitutes a special case for consciously sorting out what we find when we explore the meaning of a Pauline letter.

What, then, can we learn from our observations to help our search for a new understanding of the whole of Rom. 1.16–4.25? First, the nature of the whole, what it is about and what kind of text it is, is created by the author's intention. Thus, the extract from *The Country Parson* is an account of the way the Parson rules his household, not an analysis of the household structure. Rom. 6.1–11 is an hortatory argument about why believers cannot sin that grace may abound, not teaching about baptism. The extract from *The Daughter of Time* includes an entry from an account book, not a birth announcement. To see what kind of a whole we are reading, we must pay careful attention to Paul's intention, not just his over-all purpose in writing the letter, but also his particular purpose in our passage. This is one reason why we ask not what Paul said to the Romans, but what he was intending to say to them.

Second, what the writer is saying to the reader accounts for all of

---

[4] Athanasius' account of the reasons why the Lord had to die on the Cross ('De Incarnatione' §25) provides a vivid example.

a text and for other meaning that may be found in it. Thus, the description of the way the Parson rules his household accounts for all of the text of our Herbert passage, and for the presence of the other meaning we found, notably the picture of the household structure. Similarly, rejection of the idea of sinning that grace may abound accounts for the whole of Rom. 6.1–11 and for the presence of the discussion of baptism and the concepts of being in Christ and living to God. In the account book, the record of expenditure of the fourpence halfpenny explains why the child's birth is mentioned, whereas we should be greatly surprised at a birth announcement that itemized expenditure on ribbons!

Extra meaning genuinely present in a text is a by-product of the work of writing what the author was intending to communicate. Thus, the two are necessarily related. If we found in a text extra meaning unrelated to what the author was intending to say, we should be reading it in. We should be guilty of eisegesis. Since we are confident that the justification theology is part of the meaning of Rom. 1.16–4.25, we can assume that what Paul was intending to say to the Romans will be related to it, will account for its presence in the text. Thus, if we examine the problems we faced when we read the text as if he had been intending to give a justification account, we should find clues to what he was intending to say to them.

Our observations about the nature of meaning in texts and the way we respond to it as readers also have implications for the way we approach the text after we have identified the nature and subject-matter of the whole.

First, we noticed that a reader who does not belong in the personal and cultural context of a text is likely to be distracted away from what the author intended to say to other elements of meaning. Thus, our practice of trying to reconstruct the situation and understand the cultural milieu will be very important. It will help us to understand the context in which Paul's letter was created and intended to function. We shall need to be aware, too, of our tendency to be distracted away from what Paul was intending to say to the Romans towards other elements of meaning in the text.

The procedure of undertaking first a teleological and then a causal reading will help us to deal with that issue. The teleological reading is our attempt to identify that element of meaning in the text which is what Paul was intending to say to the Romans. In the case of Rom. 6.1–11, for instance, that is his account of why believers do not sin that grace may abound. Questions about his understanding of baptism or his concept of being in Christ belong to the causal exposition, which examines the theology from which his discussion sprang.

Second, we must give attention to what we mean by the statement that what the writer is saying to the reader *accounts for* all of the text. This means that there are no words or phrases unexplained, superfluous to the meaning, apparently inadequate or excessive for the purpose they are serving. The author created a text consisting of these words in this order in the process of carrying out a particular purpose.

Because we are interested in Paul's theology and have a tradition of understanding the text as an expression of his thought, we are likely to take 'accounts for all of the text' to mean 'makes sense of all of the text as springing from a system of thought that we can accept as rational and credible'. Any term that could be devised as a substitute would be open to the same misinterpretation. That is not the meaning of the phrase here, and the difference is crucial. That does not, of course, mean that we should be satisfied with a teleological exegesis that accounted for the text in the sense of leaving no words or phrases unexplained or inadequately explained but appeared to be the product of an irrational mind. That would be acceptable if we had identified the text as nonsense of some sort, or if we had reason to believe that the author was not rational, but we have no reason to believe either that Paul thought to entertain the Romans with something like *The Hunting of the Snark* or that he was not rational. But that is another criterion. If we want to take our text seriously as part of what Paul was intending to say to the Romans, we shall be seeking an exegesis that accounts for all of the text in the sense of leaving nothing unexplained.

We can state the difference another way. Wright demonstrates that Romans is coherent by examining the theology and showing that it represents a rational, intelligible and credible way of under-standing certain issues.[5] In the process, he dismembers the text. He does not read it as a letter. Hays studies the narrative logic of Gal. 3.1–4.11 the same way.[6] The test of the coherence of the text is the coherence of the underlying thought structure. In the two-step exegesis, that coherence is the concern of the causal reading. For

---

[5] 'The Messiah and the People of God'.
[6] *The Faith of Jesus Christ*, chs. 4, 5.

the teleological reading, we seek to understand the text as *coherent communication*. In doing so, we have to produce a reading in which all the words and sentences are functioning in that communication.

This has an important implication for the teleological reading. At that stage of our exegesis, *we must concentrate only on the text in hand*. We do not understand what Paul was intending to say to the Romans in Romans 4 by looking also at Galatians 3 and discussing Abraham in Paul's thought. That, again, belongs to the causal reading and to discussion of Paul's thought using the results of exegesis as data. We may need to use the rest of the Pauline corpus, including Galatians, to reconstruct the situation in which Paul was addressing the Romans, but that is a different matter. This represents an enormous challenge to anybody trained in historical-critical exegesis. We always read one text with part of our attention on the others, and this is so much part of our reading that we are rarely aware of it. It happens because of our interest in Paul's thought. There is nothing wrong with doing this: in fact it is necessary to a full exploration of the meaning of any one text. To read the text as Paul's, we make comparisons only after we have given our full attention to the one text and made sense of it on its own terms as coherent communication.

A small example will help to explain this. In Rom. 2.1–11, there are verses about judgement according to what a person has done. These present no problem for a teleological reading. On the other hand, they raise a vital question about Paul's thought. Is not that inconsistent with justification by faith (*sic*)? In a teleological reading, we trace through Paul's address to the Romans, and Romans 2 accommodates the judgement material without stress. On the other hand, Romans 2 itself presents a major problem to current exegetical effort to understand Paul's thought. If our *whole* teleological reading made nonsense, we should have to try again or else conclude that Paul was inconsistent. If we demand *at each point as it arises* that we can see the underlying consistency, it is very difficult for us to be open to having our ideas challenged by Paul's text. That is one reason why the apparently artificial division between teleological and causal reading is important.

5

HOW TO TRACE WHAT PAUL WAS INTENDING TO SAY TO THE ROMANS

In chapter 3, we proposed that the doctrine of justification is not what Paul was intending to write about in Rom. 1.16–4.25, but a theological presupposition of his intended discussion. Our examination in chapter 4 of what happens when we explore the meaning of texts has shown why and how this proposal is possible. It has also shown us that since we want to understand the text as Paul's, both at the level of what he was intending to say to the Romans and at the level of what it reveals about his thought, our first task is to find out what he was intending to say to the Romans. This task has to come first because Paul's intention created the text and therefore defined what kind of a whole it is – what it is about and what kind of discourse it is. Only when we understand that can we begin to examine the theological presuppositions. They appeared in the text as a by-product of the process of composition. Only when we can see them in relation to Paul's intended discourse can we be reasonably confident that we are reading them correctly. The text itself will provide some tests to assess our reading of what Paul was intending to say. Thus, our whole exegesis will be subject to the text Paul dictated.

Our first task, then, is to develop a teleological reading, an understanding of what Paul was intending to say to the Romans. This will provide essential context for the causal reading, our examination of theological presuppositions. To do this, we must step aside from the mainstream debate on Romans, and ask some different questions. We must first do extensive work in the whole sector of the hermeneutical circle, developing a new hypothesis on what kind of text this is and what it is about. This will replace the old assumption that we are reading theological exposition, a justification account. When we move into the parts sector of the hermeneutical circle we shall be working in the same area as the mainstream debate, but with a different goal and a different basic conception of the text. We shall be trying to understand what Paul was intending to say to the Romans, not asking what the text means. Because it must account for all of the text, this teleological reading will look like a very full exegesis, but it will be awaiting completion by the causal reading. The two stages of work for the teleological reading involve six steps.

Step 1, chapter 6. We work from the problems of the mainstream readings. We are testing an hypothesis that the justification account is a reading of Paul's theological presuppositions and his intended communication was about something else. The intended communication created the text and accounts for all of it. It also generated the other elements of meaning genuinely present in the text. Since we are accepting that the justification account represents meaning genuinely present in the text, the intended communication must be related to it. Study of the problems identified in chapter 2, then, should point us towards a new hypothesis about Paul's intention.

Step 2, chapter 7. We formulate an hypothesis about Paul's purpose. Since his intention created the text, an accurate idea of it should give us a valuable key to the teleological reading. Our passage is part of a longer letter, so we shall look at Paul's purpose in the letter and then in this passage as part of it. We noticed in chapter 4 that reading a text in contexts other than the original is likely to distract readers from what the writer was intending to say to the recipients. Our purpose study will be important in helping us see the text in its original context.

Step 3, chapter 8. We formulate an hypothesis about the nature of the text. This will help to awaken appropriate responses in us as readers, so that we are better able to empathize with Paul's intention and ask appropriate questions.

Step 4, chapter 9. We formulate a substantial hypothesis about the nature of the whole we are reading. This will take the form of a clear summary of what we have learnt so far. It will provide the starting point and framework for the detailed teleological reading, and it will help us to resist the pull of the old (unconscious and therefore very powerful) assumptions about what we are reading.

Step 5, chapter 10. We develop a detailed teleological reading. In this, the aim of our exegesis is to elucidate what Paul was intending to say to the Romans. The questions we ask will arise not from the agenda of the current debate, but from the hypothesis we have so carefully developed. This reading will, of course, test our identification of the nature of the whole.

Step 6, chapter 11. We shall test the teleological reading before we offer it as our best answer to the question of what Paul was intending to say to the Romans and before we use it as the frame of reference for our causal exegesis. We know already that it will have to account for all of the text, although not for all of the meaning that we can find in it. Our study of the nature of the whole will enable us to develop a full set of tests before we embark on the teleological reading.

The process for finding out what Paul was intending to say to the Romans is derived from our understanding of the way we in practice encounter meaning in texts and our careful examination of what it is we want to know.

After we have completed the six steps, we shall be ready to complete our exegesis with the causal reading (chapter 12) and then to review our whole enterprise (chapter 13).

6

WORKING FROM THE PROBLEMS OF INTERPRETATION WITHIN THE JUSTIFICATION FRAMEWORK

We begin our search for what Paul was intending to say to the Romans by examining the points where readings within the justification framework do not account satisfactorily for the text. Exegesis within that framework assumes that Rom. 1.16–17 is the theme statement, Rom. 1.18–3.20 presents the human predicament, Rom. 3.21–6 is the announcement of justification through faith by grace, and Rom. 3.27–4.25 is about faith and the continuity between God's action in Christ and God's earlier action with Israel. In chapter 2, we identified three problems that cannot be solved within this framework. They are so fundamental and so closely interlocked as to question the validity of the framework. (1) Rom. 1.18–3.20 is unlikely to convince an audience that all have sinned. (2) As a justification account, Rom. 1.16–4.25 is out of balance. The main point is not clearly developed, while supporting arguments, essential but secondary, occupy over 90 per cent of the text. (3) As the announcement of justification through faith, Rom. 3.21–6 is out of balance, with grammar and meaning that do not match.

We noted that these problems raise certain issues. These offer starting points for the exploration in this chapter. Was Paul talking to the Romans about something more limited than universal sin and salvation? Are the questions of relationships between Jew and Gentile important to whatever that was? Is Romans part of one of Paul's controversies rather than reflection on the theological bases and outcomes of earlier controversies?[1] These questions raise the further question of what kind of discourse this is.

---

[1] The latter is suggested by Manson ('St. Paul's Letter to the Romans – and Others', esp. 14–15) and Bornkamm ('Testament', 27–8).

Πᾶς in Rom. 1.16–4.25

In Rom. 3.23, πάντες γὰρ ἥμαρτον focusses two problems, the question of universality and the apparent disjunction between Paul's grammar and his meaning. In the justification account readings, 'all have sinned' is both a summary or delayed conclusion of the argument of Rom. 1.18–3.20 and the statement of the need for the grace of Rom. 3.24. We questioned whether this πᾶς refers to all humankind. We might ask, Who, then, is meant by πᾶς? In seeking to discover what Paul was intending to say to the Romans, we ask instead, What was Paul intending to say to the Romans with this πᾶς?

First we must clear the ground. We have always read Rom. 1.16–4.25 on the assumption that it is a particular kind of argument, theological exposition. Reading thus, we find it hard to see how πᾶς could be referring to anything other than all humankind. For this study, we have set aside the presupposition that the passage is theological exposition. Being stitched together with the connectives of logical talk, the text appears as argument of some kind, or at least as discourse with a thread of argument running through it. Having key terms that are theological – salvation, sin, judgement, grace, righteousness – it appears as theological. The most vulnerable element of our old view seems to be 'exposition'. That is interesting, in view of the fact that we have raised the possibility that Romans might be part of one of Paul's controversies.

Some examples show that πᾶς often has a more limited reference than to every human being: 'Everybody (all human beings) needs oxygen to live.' This is a universal use. A speaker with an unreliable microphone will say, 'Can everybody (all of you) hear me?' This reference is universal within a limit. It refers to all the people in the auditorium. Somebody planning a dinner party might say, 'Let's have a roast. Everybody (all people) likes roast beef.' There are millions of vegetarians and probably some others who dislike roast beef, yet a normal listener will not want to correct this speaker. This is a different kind of discourse, and we do not apply the strict standards of logic and consistency that we apply in the first case. With this 'everybody', the speaker is really saying, 'With roast beef, we shall not be taking the risk that a number of guests might not enjoy the meal.' When somebody in trouble insists stoically on being self-sufficient, a friend may say, 'Everybody (all people) needs help sometime.' In logical terms, this is a universal statement. With this 'everybody', however, the friend is saying something like, 'Everybody includes you. It is not good to try to be superhuman in these situations. Please accept some help.' What the friend intends to say to that particular person depends on the fact that the statement is generally true, and the person can be expected to take it as true. The focus of both speaker's and hearer's attention, however, is on the hearer, not on the general statement. Indeed, the intention would not be undermined if there were a few exceptions to the general statement. On the other hand, if we found two human beings who did not need oxygen to live, we should ask serious questions. Different kinds of discourse can make different uses of 'all'.

What was Paul intending to say with the reiterated πᾶς of his address to the Romans? According to the grammatical structure of Rom. 3.21–6, πάντες γὰρ ἥμαρτον (Rom. 3.23a) is part of the grounding for οὐ γάρ ἐστιν διαστολή (Rom. 3.22d). The full grounding is tripartite. Dependent on πάντες are ἥμαρτον, ὑστεροῦνται τῆς δόξης τοῦ θεοῦ and δικαιούμενοι δωρεάν. Among whom is there no distinction in these three respects? Rom. 3.22 is referring to believers in Christ. There is no distinction among believers in Christ, as sinners or as justified.

When we see the πάντες of Rom. 3.23 saying something like 'all believers without distinction' rather than 'every human being', our attention is directed to two features of Rom. 1.18–3.20. There is no reference there to the people under discussion being believers. This would suggest that it is not a grounding for Rom. 3.23, or at least not in the way we have always supposed. On the other hand, there is a distinction running, and it often appears in connection with πᾶς. In Rom. 2.9–10, punishment and reward are ἐπὶ πᾶσαν ψυχὴν ἀνθρώπου τοῦ κατεργαζομένου τὸ κακόν, Ἰουδαίου τε πρῶτον καὶ Ἕλληνος and παντὶ τῷ ἐργαζομένῳ τὸ ἀγαθόν, Ἰουδαίῳ τε πρῶτον καὶ Ἕλληνι. This pattern is immediately picked up in Rom. 2.12–13, with ὅσοι, where the equal treatment of sinners is spelt out in terms of those without the law and those under the law. In Rom. 3.9, everybody, Jew and Greek, is under sin. In Rom. 3.10b–12, 18, there seem to be universal statements with no reference to any distinction, πάντες and οὐκ ἔστιν. These belong to the scripture catena, which is applied in Rom. 3.19–20: ὅσα ὁ νόμος λέγει τοῖς ἐν τῷ νόμῳ λαλεῖ. We argued in chapter 2 that τοῖς ἐν τῷ νόμῳ refers to Jews. The universal statements apply to the whole of the group to whom they refer. The scripture condemnation of them means that *every* mouth may be stopped and the *whole* world arraigned before God. On the basis of definition of terms, this must add Jew to Gentile, with the Gentiles' situation being taken for granted in this verse. Then in Rom. 3.20a, the totally exclusive ἐξ ἔργων νόμου οὐ δικαιωθήσεται πᾶσα σάρξ has the effect of excluding all Israel. The conclusion drawn from the catena includes a stress on 'Jew just like Gentile'.

The pattern we have been tracing identifies the distinction that would be in Paul's and the Romans' minds when distinction is excluded in Rom. 3.22–3. The pattern and that link make excellent sense of the fact that in Rom. 1.16b παντὶ τῷ πιστεύοντι is qualified with Ἰουδαίῳ τε πρῶτον καὶ Ἕλληνι. The distinction would become a key issue in what Paul was intending to say to the Romans. In that case, the elements in Rom. 3.27–4.25 that deal with the distinction would be critical. There are two: the minimizing of the distinction where justification is concerned, for example, Rom. 3.29–30; 4.13–16, and the question of the relationship between God's action with Israel and God's new action in Christ.

In each of these cases, πᾶς is associated with Jew and Gentile. We might almost say that 'all' is made up of Jew and Gentile. There are other uses, though. The uses of πᾶς in Rom. 1.29 and Rom. 3.2 are clearly not evidence for our question, since they do not refer to people, and in Rom. 2.1 the term is part of the address to the interlocutor. Rom. 1.18 and Rom. 3.4, however, look like universal statements and are often taken as parts of Paul's argument for universal sinfulness. In fact, once we give up the presupposition that Paul was trying to establish that all have sinned, we are freed to attend to what he actually said. The πᾶς of Rom. 3.4 is part of a discussion of God's faithfulness to Israel in the face of Israel's unfaithfulness. It extends the τινες of Rom. 3.3, and the terms refer to some of and all of Israel.

Exegesis which treats Rom. 1.18 as referring to Gentiles thereby excludes it from the category of universal statements. Traditional exegesis, however, often treats Rom. 1.18–32 as though Rom. 1.18 is a universal statement, with God's wrath revealed ἐπὶ ἀσέβειαν καὶ ἀδικίαν πάντων ἀνθρώπων. Paul's text reads ἐπὶ πᾶσαν ἀσέβειαν καὶ ἀδικίαν ἀνθρώπων τῶν τὴν ἀλήθειαν ἐν ἀδικίᾳ κατεχόντων. It does not say that God's wrath is revealed against all human beings, or even that it is revealed against the ungodliness and wickedness of all human beings.[2] It says that God's wrath is revealed against all ungodliness and wickedness of a particular category of human beings, those who by or in wickedness suppress the truth. The text does not tell us whether Paul thought that group was co-extensive with humankind. That is a question for the causal reading. Thus, these two uses of πᾶς do not count against the pattern we have observed. That pattern is that when 'all' might refer to the whole human race, the stress is rather on 'all' comprising Jew and Gentile. Both Rom. 3.4 and Rom. 1.18 concern some other 'all', Israel in the one case and ungodliness and wickedness of a specific group in the other.

These observations suggest the hypothesis that what Paul was intending to say to the Romans with the reiterated πᾶς was something like 'all, without distinction between Jew and Gentile'. This points in the same general direction as Dunn's and Ziesler's exegeses, both of which seem to have Paul showing in Rom. 1.18–3.20 that Jews are just as sinful as Gentiles. It coheres with the current recognition that the Jew–Gentile question is more important for Romans than it seems in older exegesis, where it appears as a cultural distinction controlling the way the theology is presented. Universal sinfulness, for instance, had to be demonstrated separately for Jew and Gentile.

Our observations leave us with some questions. While there is reason to believe that Paul's address flows continuously through the whole of Rom. 1.16–4.25, we now have πᾶς in Rom. 3.22–3 referring to all believers, but no reason to believe that πᾶς in Rom. 1.18–3.20 does the same. So far, we have identified it as meaning 'all, Jew and Gentile'. We shall need to find the connection. In each case, πᾶς is connected with sin, judgement or both.

The goal of the discussion in Rom. 1.18–3.20

The study so far encourages us to proceed with our hypothesis that in Rom. 1.18–3.20 Paul may not have been trying to convince his audience that all (meaning all human beings) have sinned. One reason for doubting this is that we find in the text neither proof nor convincing rhetoric to demonstrate that they have. We have now discovered that the emphasis of any πᾶς in the passage that might

---

[2] The universal reference is more often assumed than discussed. Schlier (*Der Römerbrief*, 51) suggests that the lack of the article makes ἀνθρώπων refer to humanity in general.

refer to all human beings is on Jew and Gentile, rather than on the universal reference of πᾶς. We now look at the passages that have traditionally been interpreted as contributing to the demonstration that all have sinned. These are Rom. 1.18–32; 2.1–3; 2.17–24; 3.9b; 3.10–20. We ask whether they add up to an unsatisfactory attempt to do what we thought Paul was doing, or whether there are indications that he may have intended to do something else.

Does Rom. 1.18–32 offer any demonstration that all human beings or all Gentiles have sinned? Once we realize that Rom. 1.18 refers to a specific group of human beings, the answer is that it does not. Paul opened the pericope with the proclamation of the revelation of the wrath of God on all the evil of people who by or in wickedness suppress the truth. How did he develop this? An overview of the passage invites us to seek an answer by studying the expressions that are ways of saying 'because' and 'therefore'. The first of these is διότι in Rom. 1.19. God's wrath is revealed upon the actions of these people because God made himself known to them εἰς τὸ εἶναι αὐτοὺς ἀναπολογήτους (Rom. 1.20b). That is, he made himself known to them either with the result that they are, or in order that they might be, without excuse. In either case, the wrath is revealed because they are without excuse in the face of God's self-revelation.

Διότι in Rom. 1.21 indicates that they are without excuse because knowing God they did not honour him as God or give him thanks. Rom. 1.21b–23 explicates this sin, the passive verbs of Rom. 1.21b indicating already that it carried its punishment from God within itself. This explains the way the refusal of honour and thanksgiving is closely linked with the disabling of minds and hearts.

Based on this situation is διό in Rom. 1.24–5. This is the first of three explicit statements of God's punishment, παρέδωκεν αὐτοὺς ὁ θεός. *Because* of what they had done, *therefore* God gave them up to what they had made of themselves. In content and vocabulary, Rom. 1.25 harks back to Rom. 1.23. It also provides the ground for διὰ τοῦτο in Rom. 1.26–7. Again, the punishment is that God gave them up, and again it is to what they had made of themselves. With the exchange motif and the account of sexual immorality, this links back to the reference to idolatry in Rom. 1.25. The καὶ καθώς that opens Rom. 1.28–31 is the next 'therefore', and the same punishment is pronounced, this time directly on the refusal to acknowledge God. In each of the three cases, an oppressive weight of sin is pictured. Rom. 1.32 offers a climax. The people who by or in wickedness suppress the truth do all these things in defiance of their knowledge that God's judgement is that those who do or approve such things are worthy of death. This outline is nothing more than an attempt to trace through a sequence that is clear in the text. It shows that the first point Paul made in developing the announcement of the wrath of God was that it was revealed upon people who were without excuse. The inexcusable refusal to acknowledge God was itself ungodly and unrighteous. It is also shown as leading to ungodly and wicked actions. These sinful acts arose from the punishment for the original sin, that God gave them up to what they had made of themselves. This again stresses their responsibility for their sins, responsibility reiterated in the statement that they act and think defiance of God's known ordinance (Rom. 1.32). This approach suggests that εἰς τὸ εἶναι αὐτοὺς ἀναπολογήτους at least includes within its meaning the idea that God's judgement of wrath is righteous, and that this idea is important in the discussion. In the passage, there is no attempt to prove that anybody has sinned, simply a statement of their sin. Sin is a datum and the passage is about God's just judgement of wrath. Sinful acts flow from God's punishment of the root sin, and also place responsible sinners under the judgement ἄξιοι θανάτου (Rom. 1.32a).

This line of thought continues in Rom. 2.1, with the charge διὸ ἀναπολόγητος εἶ against the judge who does 'the same things'. Διό in Rom. 2.1 indicates a direct connection. This time, the charge of being without excuse leads to a discussion of God's judgement (Rom. 2.5–11), with the judge who does 'the same things' storing up wrath for himself. There God's wrath is clearly presented as just. In that the diatribe partner is accused of doing 'the same things', Rom. 2.1–3 does talk about sin. As exegetes have long noticed, Paul stated this apparently unreasonable charge without offering either evidence or argument to support it. We notice that he made it the basis of the warning that anybody who does such things is storing up wrath for the day of God's righteous judgement.

Rom. 2.17–24 is about Jews. It mentions Jewish sins, but offers no argument that all Jews were guilty of theft, adultery or temple robbery, or even any argument that all Jews broke the law. The questions about specific sins build towards the conclusion that Jews who boast in the law dishonour God by their law-breaking. This point is given the emphatic final position and the scripture proof. It contrasts sharply with the picture of Jewish identity in Rom. 2.17–20.

In Rom. 3.10–20, the scripture 'proof' that all have sinned is applied to show that the law places the Jews to whom it was given before God's judgement, just like the Gentiles. Rom. 3.20 then becomes a comment about the law, applicable to Jews, not to everybody.

While this review does not lead to firm conclusions, it does show a pattern in the passages. In each, Paul took it for granted that the people had sinned and made some other point on this basis. In Rom. 1.18–32, the sin is the cause and result of being given up by God, and it places sinners without excuse under the judgement ἄξιοι θανάτου (Rom. 1.32a). In Rom. 2.1–11 it is the basis for a warning about not expecting special treatment at the judgement. In Rom. 2.17–24 it is part of the basis for a charge of dishonouring God. In Rom. 3.10–20 it is the basis for saying that the law places Jew with Gentile before God's judgement. Rom. 3.9 is a more isolated text, but it represents the same pattern. However we understand προεχόμεθα and οὐ πάντως, there is a question about a difference between people. The answer is a negative one based on the charge that all, Jew and Greek, are under sin. That is, the statement about being under sin is the ground for whatever the point of this mysterious text is.

Listing the conclusions, we notice that three of the five have to do with God's judgement. Is this significant? Since we have set aside the justification reading, we have insufficient context to investigate Rom. 3.9 any further at present. The treatment of the Jew in Rom. 2.17–24 continues in Rom. 2.25–9. There the true Jew and true circumcision are known only to God. We recall that our examination of the use of πᾶς led to the observation that judgement is important in that context. Further, the whole section concludes with Jew and Gentile before God's judgement. This gives ground for a proposal that judgement may well be significant in what Paul was intending to communicate in Rom. 1.18–3.20.

This pattern of sin as factual basis for some other conclusion strongly reinforces our hypothesis that Paul was not trying to demonstrate that all human beings are sinners. With πᾶς, he seems to have been making a point about 'all' including Jew and Gentile. In the text he was not concerned to define the limits of the 'all', although πᾶν στόμα and πᾶς ὁ κόσμος indicate that in Rom. 3.19 it does cover all human beings. The fact of sin is not even part of the goal of what Paul was saying. It is a presupposition of what he was saying, which apparently had something to do with God's righteous judgement on Jew and Gentile. These conclusions raise to urgency the questions of what kind of discourse this is and to whom it was addressed.

The audience

Concerning the nature of the discourse, we observe that the way Paul was using πᾶς strongly encourages our suspicion that this is not theological exposition. Among our samples of uses of 'all'/ 'everybody', the one most like the pattern we have been discovering is the address to the friend in trouble: the point of the generally true statement is that it is significant for the person addressed. That is the speaker's concern. The general statement as such is not being given attention. That is a possible model for understanding πᾶς here. If it proved to be the appropriate one, it would revolutionize our reading, since it would demand responses very different from those activated by the theological exposition model (in which the use of πᾶς corresponds with the example about all human beings needing oxygen). It would require a reading with constant, careful attention to audience.

We know that Paul's audience was the Romans, but we need to refine that. Our exploration raises one immediate question. Could Paul reasonably have taken it for granted that the Roman believers would accept a presupposition that people, or the people he was talking about, were sinners? In favour of this is his cryptic reference to the Atonement (Rom. 3.24b–25a). Its brevity would be explained if we found that he was directing the Romans to something they knew already and would not need explained. Believers believed in Christ as the one whom God set forth to deal with their sins. Ἱλαστήριον certainly refers to a way of dealing with sin and its effects. This coheres with Paul's starting point for the Resurrection argument in 1 Cor. 15: whoever preached the gospel declared that Christ died *for our sins*, was buried, was raised on the third day, and was seen by witnesses (1 Cor. 15.3–5). 1Thess. 1.9b–10 and Acts 17.31 show the pattern of salvation from the wrath to come. Thus, we have some evidence that Paul could have assumed that the Romans would accept sin as a datum in this way, and stronger evidence that he was making the assumption, reasonably or not. That is good reason to accept into our hypothesis the idea that what Paul was intending to say to the Romans presupposed that the people he was talking about were sinners. Hypotheses are for testing.

The balance and grammar of Rom. 3.21–6

Our investigation of Rom. 3.23 led to exploration of Rom. 1.18–3.20. We now return to δικαιούμενοι (Rom. 3.24a). Cranfield summarizes the problems of the relation of verse 24 to its context:

> The difficulty of the explanation which lies nearest to hand, namely, that δικαιούμενοι is dependent on the πάντες of v. 23, is that, on this view, what seems to be a substantial contribution to the thought of the paragraph as a whole (if ὅν in v. 25 is understood as introducing an ordinary relative clause, it actually includes the whole of vv. 24–26) is formally part of the explanation of οὐ γάρ ἐστιν διαστολή, which itself supports the πάντας of v. 22a.[3]

We examined this in chapter 2. The grammar works only if πάντες (Rom. 3.23) refers to the same group as πάντας (Rom. 3.22). This problem disappeared when we examined πάντες (Rom. 3.23) without assuming that Paul was giving a justification account. It is believers, and only believers, among whom there is no distinction in the three respects listed.

The other problem is the role of οὐ γάρ ἐστιν διαστολή in the paragraph. According to the grammar, all of Rom. 3.23–6 is an explanation of οὐ γάρ ἐστιν διαστολή (Rom. 3.22d). If we accept that Paul meant what he said, the paragraph looks different. Since οὐ γάρ ἐστιν διαστολή has this key role, the stress in Rom. 3.22 is different. In traditional readings, the key phrase is διὰ πίστεως Ἰησοῦ Χριστοῦ. Εἰς πάντας τοὺς πιστεύοντας simply underlines that. When οὐ γάρ ἐστιν διαστολή has its major role in the paragraph, the key phrase in Rom. 3.22 is εἰς πάντας τοὺς πιστεύοντας. The point at issue is not believing in Christ, but all believers in Christ. This is consistent with observations we have made already. If it is correct, we shall need to reread Rom. 3.21–2.

How does the rest of the paragraph look as an explanation of οὐ γάρ ἐστιν διαστολή? First, Paul listed the three respects in which there was no distinction. Next, he rehearsed briefly how 'all' were

[3] *Romans*, I, 205.

being justified freely. It was by God's grace, through the redemption which is in Christ Jesus, whom God set forth (purposed?) as ἱλαστήριον (expiation? propitiation? Mercy Seat?) through faith, by (in?) his blood. Then he explained why God did it in this way. It was for the demonstration of God's righteousness in two respects, and so that he might be righteous. We have noticed already that the second step is too brief to be a clear Atonement account, and have suggested that Paul was referring the Romans to something they already knew. The structure of the paragraph suggests that Paul was referring them to what they knew for the sake of what he wanted to say about it, namely, *why* God was justifying people in this way – in order to be seen to be righteous and to be righteous. This would account for the fact that 37.4 per cent of Rom. 3.21–6 deals directly with the question of God's righteousness.

A question about God's righteousness

This evidence suggests that we are looking at theodicy. Paul was facing a question about whether God was indeed righteous. The key role in the passage of οὐ γάρ ἐστιν διαστολή suggests that the question was about God justifying believers without distinction, that is, without distinguishing between Jewish and Gentile believers. Although we are not used to the question in this form, we recognize a major issue of Paul's ministry, a question that research suggests the Romans were facing, the relationship between Jew and Gentile in the church.

This way of looking at the text casts light on two other problems. The καί of εἰς τὸ εἶναι αὐτὸν δίκαιον καὶ δικαιοῦντα τὸν ἐκ πίστεως Ἰησοῦ (Rom. 3.26b) is usually translated 'and'. This is so awkward that Käsemann goes to the length of suggesting liturgical parallels.[4] 'Even' is more natural to the construction, yet few participants in the mainstream debate believe that a good argument can be made for this. In the context we are now hypothesizing, it is natural to the meaning as well as to the construction – God acts in order to be righteous even in justifying on the basis of faith. 'Even' has a note of surprise about it.[5] The expectation is that that would be unrighteous, but God has acted so that it is righteous. Τὸν ἐκ πίστεως Ἰησοῦ describes the person with reference to faith. There

---

[4] *Commentary on Romans*, 100.
[5] BAGD, καί, I.2.g.

is no other criterion of judgement. The second problem is the role
of Rom. 3.1–8, which often appears to be an aside. It also is
concerned largely with the question of God's righteousness, and the
question arises because at that point there seems to be no place left
for Israel (Rom. 3.1; cf. Rom. 2.25–9). Rom. 3.1–8 and Rom.
3.21–6 both deal with God's righteousness as faithfulness to
election and as justice in judgement. We recall the other points
about God's righteous wrath and judgement in Rom. 1.18–3.20.
This may be a key concern of the whole passage. If we find it to be
so, Rom. 3.1–8 will probably not appear as a digression. These
observations do not account for the charge of encouraging sin in
Rom. 3.7–8. Our hypothesis will need to open up a reading of the
passage which includes that.

We have been examining Rom. 3.23–6 on the basis that according
to the grammar the whole depends on οὐ γάρ ἐστιν διαστολή.
Cranfield qualified this, saying that it is true if the ὅν of Rom. 3.25 is
introducing an ordinary relative clause. Presumably, he was alluding
to the proposal that Paul used a pre-Pauline formula. This proposal
arises primarily from the difficulties of reading the text within the
justification framework, and the variety of reconstructions of the
original formula does not encourage confidence in it. While it is
possible that Paul was alluding to a traditional formulation he
expected the Romans to recognize, the proposal is not necessary to
our hypothesis so far, and the arguments for it are not strong enough
to impose it at this stage of our investigation.

Summary: clues and questions towards a new hypothesis

Here we review our investigation so far. Setting aside the presupposition that Paul was giving a justification account, we are using the
difficulties of reading Rom. 1.16–4.25 on that presupposition to
help direct our attention to what he was actually saying. We have
found the following:

> In Rom. 3.22d–24a, πᾶς refers to all believers, with the
> emphasis on all without distinction. Examination of πᾶς in
> Rom. 1.18–3.20 showed a persistent reference to Jew and
> Gentile, with Rom. 3.19 adding Jew to Gentile as sinners
> before God. This distinction would therefore be in the
> minds of Paul and his audience when distinction was
> excluded in Rom. 3.22.

Whereas it is clear that in Rom. 3.22d–24a the reference of πᾶς is to all believers, in Rom. 1.18–3.20 the focus is on Jew and Gentile, with no concern to define the limits of the 'all' except in Rom. 3.19, where the reference is to all humanity.

In Rom. 1.18–3.20, none of the passages traditionally taken as contributing to the demonstration that all have sinned has that function. Sins are data, the basis for making some other point. This suggests that Paul was presupposing that all the people concerned had sinned, and was arguing from this. There is evidence to suggest that he was intending to talk about God's judgement.

The unsatisfactory Atonement account in Rom. 3.24b–25a is explained if Paul was not offering an explanation of the Atonement, but referring the Romans to something they already knew. They believed in Christ as one who died for their sins. With other NT evidence, this suggests that Paul could reasonably have spoken to the Romans on the presupposition that all the people he was talking about were sinners.

If we follow the grammar and the balance of elements in the pericope, Rom. 3.21–6 seems to move towards the conclusion that God acted in the Cross in order to be seen to be righteous and to be righteous even in justifying believers in Jesus. Given the role of οὐ γάρ ἐστιν διαστολή, this implies that there was a question about God's righteousness if God justified all believers without reference to the Jew–Gentile distinction. This reading gives καί in Rom. 3.26 its proper weight. It allows the possibility that Paul was referring the Romans to what they knew about how God justified for the sake of what he wanted to say about why God did it that way.

This reading of the thrust of Rom. 3.21–6 offers the possibility of accounting for Rom. 3.1–8, a problem in many traditional readings.

Following the grammar moves the emphasis in Rom. 3.22 from διὰ πίστεως Ἰησοῦ Χριστοῦ onto εἰς πάντας τοὺς πιστεύοντας. This would involve a rereading of Rom. 3.21–2.

Our examination raised some major questions for consideration in formulating a new hypothesis about what Paul was intending to talk about and in what kind of discourse.

The fact of sin was a presupposition, not the goal, of what Paul was saying in Rom. 1.18–3.20. What was the goal? We have two clues. There is a clear concern with Jew and Gentile in Paul's πᾶς. The conclusions drawn from the fact of sin include a strong element of judgement. The Jew–Gentile concern connects with our observations about Rom. 3.21–6, and we know it was a major concern for Paul and the church of his day.

The question of the nature of the discourse is looming large. We found one clue. Paul's use of πᾶς in Rom. 1.18–3.20 looks like the usage where the truth of a general statement is being taken for granted and the statement is intended to say something in particular to the addressee. Such discourse would be very demanding for us to read.

We need to develop a clearer view of the audience Paul was intending to address than simply that they were the believers in Rome.

We need a new understanding of Rom. 3.21–2.

In this investigation, we are using the problems of reading Rom. 1.16–4.25 within the justification framework to help us find the starting point of a new hypothesis about the whole. We started from three problems that we have argued are insoluble within the old framework. We now have evidence that Paul's intention in Rom. 1.18–3.20 was not to convince his audience that all have sinned. Reading Rom. 3.21–6 on the assumption that the grammar and meaning do match went some way towards making sense of the balance of elements in that pericope. We have not drawn even a tentative conclusion about the balance of elements in the whole passage. We have not drawn any conclusions about law-fulfilling Gentiles (Rom. 2.14, 26, 27). Since we have concluded that the context is not an argument that all have sinned, there is no question of how they can be seen to be consistent with such a conclusion. On the other hand, we have not found a way of seeing them as consistent with the references to 'every mouth' and 'the whole world' in Rom. 3.19. This points us again to the questions of Paul's purpose in this section, and of the nature of the discourse.

A major outstanding problem is the role of the law. In older exegesis, it was understood to have been misused as a means of trying to earn justification. In the light of recent research, stress has been put instead on its role as a boundary marker between Jews and Gentiles. Law references in the passage are in four groups. In Rom. 2.12–29 it is a criterion of judgement. It is an ambiguous criterion, in that it seems that all people are to be judged according to whether or not they did what the law requires, but the law itself is the criterion only for Jews. In Rom. 3.19–20, the law condemns as sinners those who come under it, the Jews, and brings knowledge of sin. Rom. 3.21 refers to a revelation of the δικαιοσύνη θεοῦ apart from the law and to which the law bears witness. This is paralleled in Rom. 3.27–31, where justification is by faith and not works of the law, and the law is established by this. In Rom. 4.13–16, promise and faith are set over against law, with an emphasis on the promise to the seed of Abraham, ἐκ τοῦ νόμου and ἐκ πίστεως (Rom. 4.16b). These observations do not lead to a conclusion about the role of the law, but it is involved with the Jew–Gentile distinction, and with the continuity between God's action in Christ and his former action with Israel. Here we have another question about Rom. 1.18–3.20 that has led us to the theme of judgement.

Hypothesis about Rom. 1.16–4.25

We can now formulate an hypothesis that Paul was intending to talk to the Romans about a particular problem. It seemed that God's righteousness was put in question if justification of sinners was simply on the basis of faith in Christ without distinction between Jew and Gentile. On that hypothesis, the Jew–Gentile distinction will be a major issue. This is consistent with its appearance in Rom. 1.16, with the fact that 'all' in Rom. 1.18–3.20 seems to be made up of Jew and Gentile, and with the theme in Rom. 3.27–4.25 of the continuity between God's action in Christ and God's former action with Israel. It seems to provide the field of reference for understanding the role of the law in the passage. It also opens up the possibility of a reading that would correct a significant problem of the traditional readings, namely that both the passage as a whole and Rom. 3.21–6 are out of balance. This hypothesis should help us with the question of Paul's audience. He was dealing with the problem that God's righteousness seemed to be put in question when the Jew–Gentile distinction was over-ridden. How would that problem arise? For whom was it a problem? For whom in Rome? What kind of a problem was it for them? It seems obvious that it would have been a theological problem, but did it have other dimensions as well?

We can also formulate some questions to consider in developing the hypothesis.

> The role of Rom. 1.18–3.20 is a major question. We have several strands of evidence suggesting that it is concerned with God's judgement. This reminds us that a major use of the δικαι-vocabulary, and therefore a significant element of its meaning, is juridical. That may point us to the connection with Rom. 3.21–6.
>
> We should formulate Paul's purpose more precisely. Since his purpose created the text, this question is likely to interact with the questions of the audience he intended to address and of the nature of his discourse.
>
> The hypothesis demands a new reading of Rom. 3.21–2. If the Jew–Gentile distinction and God's righteousness are interlocking central questions, Rom. 1.16–17 is also going to look different. In particular, the hypothesis that Paul's main concern was with God's righteousness raises the possibility that δικαιοσύνη θεοῦ may have more to do with God's own righteousness than is usually supposed.

In one fundamental respect this hypothesis reverses the traditional readings. When the passage is read as a justification account, the concern is with how sinful human beings can be righteous in God's sight, and justification by grace through faith is the solution. On our hypothesis, the concern is with how God can be righteous in the sight of whatever human beings Paul was considering, and justification by grace through faith is the problem, or part of it. The traditional readings are anthropocentric. Our hypothesis suggests that to understand what Paul intended to say to the Romans we need to read theocentrically. We are reminded of Bultmann's dictum that in Paul's writing '[e]very assertion about God is simultaneously an assertion about man and vice versa'.[6]

---

[6] *Theology of the New Testament*, I, 191.

7

PAUL'S PURPOSE IN CREATING THE TEXT

The second step in our search for what Paul was intending to say to the Romans in Rom. 1.16–4.25 is to identify as precisely as possible his purpose in writing. This will help us to see the text in its original context, so that our attention is directed to those elements of its meaning that are what he intended to say. It will help us to develop empathy with the nature of the text, so that we respond appropriately. It is important for developing a reading that will account for all of the text.

Our question is, What response was Paul trying to elicit from the audience he was addressing in Rom. 1.16–4.25? We shall try to discover what response he was seeking with the letter as a whole, and then consider how his purpose in our passage contributes to it. Did he want his hearers to understand and approve his theology? To give him help? To be guided in handling a problem of their own? Something else altogether? Our work in this chapter is limited by the fact that we have not yet identified the audience or the nature of the text, but by the time we are ready for the detailed teleological reading, we shall have a working hypothesis about Paul's purpose.

We are asking what response Paul was trying to elicit from the people he was addressing. At its best, the normal purpose question in the mainstream debate is, Why did Paul write this letter to these people at this time? The difference between these two purpose questions is important. Our What response ...? question arises from the demands of the teleological reading, the attempt to identify what Paul hoped the Romans would hear when the letter was read to them. The Why ...? question lends itself to turning purpose into a sub-set of cause. This shows in titles like 'A Convergence of Motivations'[1] and *The Reasons for Romans*. The

---

[1] Beker, *Paul the Apostle*, 71.

purpose question is then drawn into the preference for causal explanation, and contributes to a reading of the text as expression of Paul's thought.

As evidence for an answer to our question, we have the letter itself and information about Paul, the Romans, and the situation and problems of the tiny churches not yet labelled 'Christianity'. One of our major problems in trying to enter into the situation is that Romans belongs to the period when Christianity was not yet established as separate from Judaism.

We begin with the letter, accepting that it is one letter. Gamble's argument that chapter 16 is part of the letter is persuasive,[2] and none of the redaction theories explains why someone would put pieces together less than coherently.

The letter is not the same evidence for us as it is for the rest of the debate. It is clearly a letter, with the frame well enough marked: greeting Rom. 1.1–7, thanksgiving section beginning at Rom. 1.8 and merging into the letter body by Rom. 1.17, concluding requests and courtesies Rom. 15.14–16.27. For the mainstream debate, the problem arises from the letter body, 10.5 chapters of theological exposition and a paraenetic section: the long theological exposition is not a comprehensive account of the gospel or of Paul's theology, but neither does it appear to be treating a specific issue. For us, the problem is different. In questioning the assumption that Rom. 1.16–4.25 is theological exposition, we have placed the same question over Romans 5–11, and the answer need not be the same for all the material. We are not sure what kind of a letter we are reading. Further, we have developed an hypothesis that Rom. 1.16–4.25 is not about how believers are justified but about how God can be righteous in justifying believers without distinguishing between Jew and Gentile. Mainstream readings of Romans 5–11 could be equally astray. Accordingly, we can make only limited observations about the content of the letter. Within these constraints, what evidence can we derive from the letter?

Paul made one direct statement about his purpose: τολμηρό-τερον δὲ ἔγραψα ὑμῖν ἀπὸ μέρους ὡς ἐπαναμιμνήσκων ὑμᾶς διὰ τὴν χάριν τὴν δοθεῖσάν μοι ὑπὸ τοῦ θεοῦ εἰς τὸ εἶναί με λειτουργὸν Χριστοῦ Ἰησοῦ εἰς τὰ ἔθνη, ἱερουργοῦντα τὸ εὐαγ-γέλιον τοῦ θεοῦ, ἵνα γένηται ἡ προσφορὰ τῶν ἐθνῶν εὐπρόσ-δεκτος, ἡγιασμένη ἐν πνεύματι ἁγίῳ (Rom. 15.15–16). One

---

[2] *The Textual History of the Letter to the Romans*, 65–95.

purpose was to remind the Romans. Of what? To what end? We are accustomed to thinking of the letter in terms of problems needing solutions, and we have identified a substantial problem in Rom. 1.16–4.25. Nevertheless, the letter can be seen to be full of reminders of familiar things such as the Cross, the church's experience of the Spirit, God's faithfulness, teaching about the way believers should live. Whether simply as reminders or helping to solve problems, these would serve the end he mentions, carrying out the ministry God gave him so that the offering of the Gentiles would be acceptable. It seems that Paul wanted to remind his hearers of the gospel and of proper responses to God's grace so that their life in Christ would be enriched, to be part of an acceptable offering to God.

We can gather some information from the letter frame. The occasion of the letter was Paul's expectation that at last he would be able to visit Rome (Rom. 15.22–4). The letter would therefore serve to some extent as a self-introduction, since he knew few of the Romans. Paul included some requests: a hope for an hospitable reception and support for the Spanish mission (Rom. 15.24), and requests for hospitality for Phoebe (Rom. 16.1–2) and for intercession for the Jerusalem visit (Rom. 15.30–2). One of the responses he was seeking must have been action on these requests, but it is hard to see that as his whole or main purpose in writing. If it were, we should expect the requests to be linked much more explicitly to the body of the letter.

Two linked concerns dominate the letter frame, the gospel and Paul's calling as apostle to the Gentiles. In this connection, we note his tone of authority, which is reflected in the body of the letter (for example Rom. 6.12–23; 11.17–24; 12.1–15.6). He was talking *about* being apostle to the Gentiles and therefore to the Romans (Rom. 1.5–6, 14–15; 15.14–21), and he was speaking *as* apostle to the Gentiles, though careful to avoid any suggestion of interference or lording it over their faith (Rom. 1.11–13; 15.14–15). Scholars of epistolography note that the thanksgiving often gives an indication of the purpose of a letter,[3] so the interlocking themes of visit, gospel and apostleship to the Gentiles may be significant for identifying Paul's purpose.

We move now to the letter body, the part where we move farthest

---

[3] e.g. White, 'Saint Paul and the Apostolic Letter Tradition', 438; Fitzmyer, 'New Testament Epistles', 224.

from the mainstream debate. We can agree with the identification of Rom. 12.1–15.6 as a paraenetic section, on the basis of the imperatives and the content. Chapters 12 and 13 appear to be mainly general instruction, appropriate to most Christian congregations, although we may suspect that some elements would be particularly relevant here. Rom. 14.1–15.6 is often seen as treating a Roman problem, but scholars cannot agree on the problem. Close examination of the text suggests that this is because Paul was more concerned with the principles for dealing with such problems than with the particular problem. His main concern is with not usurping God's judgement, with considering one another, with following Christ's example. Their attitudes to food and holy days allow people to consider themselves strong or weak, but what follows from being strong or weak is the way to treat other believers, not the solution to problems about food and holy days. I suggest, therefore, that Paul was showing with this example how believers should deal with such problems. That raises the question of why these problems warranted more detailed attention than other issues in this section.

Rom. 15.7–13 is a conclusion. The injunction to welcome one another is directed to Jews and Gentiles. Its importance is marked by the grounding in Christ and in four different scripture quotations. Is it a conclusion to the discussion of ritual observance, which has the injunction to welcome but no explicit mention of Jew and Gentile, or is it a conclusion to something more, perhaps the whole letter body, which does raise Jew–Gentile issues?

In the chapters usually seen as theological exposition, we can say with some confidence that Romans 9–11 is a clearly demarcated discussion of Israel's unbelief, focussed on the problem of whether God has abandoned Israel and concluding that God has not. Rom. 1.16–8.39 has no clear structural markers, and no such single clear theme. We have an hypothesis that Rom. 1.16–4.25 is about how God can be righteous in justifying believers without distinguishing between Jew and Gentile. In Romans 5–8 we can observe that sin and the law are major issues, apparently connected (Rom. 5.12–21; 6.15; 7), and there seems to be a solution in Rom. 8.1–17. Rom. 5.1–11 and Rom. 8.18–39 have strong eschatological elements, and references to the justification and salvation of believers.

Having taken an overview of the text in descending order of clarity of evidence, we now ask where Paul expected the Romans to begin. The opening (Rom. 1.1–17) is dominated by the gospel. For a greeting, Rom. 1.1 and 1.7 would be expansive; Rom. 1.1–7 is overwhelming. It defines Paul's apostleship by the gospel. The thanksgiving merges into the body of the letter. Rom. 1.8–15 mentions Paul's hopes and obligations as a preacher of the gospel, especially to the Gentiles and therefore to the Romans. In Rom. 1.16–17, the preaching seems to have begun. If the gospel was not at the centre of Paul's attention when he began the letter, he certainly went out of his way to give the Romans the impression that it was. If he wanted to move away from the gospel after that, he would have needed to do something to alert his Roman listeners.

Thus, the opening suggests that Paul's intention, or part of it, may have been to preach the gospel by letter. What would this mean? Scholars who suggest that in Romans Paul was preaching the gospel do not usually take this up in undertaking exegesis of the text. This gives the impression that for them preaching means giving a general account of the gospel. The suggestion seems to be a way of accounting for the fact that Paul does not appear to be dealing with a particular problem. Yet our review of the contents suggests that one problem was receiving considerable attention – the relationship between Jew and Gentile in life under the gospel. This was clearly part of the question about God's righteousness in Rom. 1.16–4.25, and the issue of God's faithfulness in Romans 9–11 is closely related. The food and holy days issue could have been wholly or in part a Jew–Gentile problem, and the linking together of questions about sin and the Torah is at least potentially part of the same constellation. The issue looms large in the closing stages of the letter, with the heavy weighting of authority given to the injunction to Jew and Gentile to welcome one another, the concern about the offering of the Gentiles to God, the references to the Gentile mission and the Jerusalem visit, and the final doxology.

If Paul was preaching, he was preaching to believers, so that the presence of a particular issue is readily intelligible. He was aiming not at conversion but at growth in the life of faith. The presence of the Jew–Gentile issue is readily intelligible, since at that time it was an important factor in life under the gospel, and we know that Paul had strong views about it. The suggestion that he was preaching within the framework of a particular issue might enable us to account for the fact that the body of the letter is not a systematic account of the gospel.

Can we relate the features we observed in the letter to Paul's and the Romans' situations and their participation in the church's life in the fifties?

Clearly, Paul understood his mission to the Gentiles as part of God's purpose (for example Gal. 1.1–7; Rom. 15.15–16). In Christ, God had acted within Israel in a way that could be understood only through Israel's experience of God's action, but had acted for all people. Were the bounds of Israel, then, to be extended or broken? Was Israel to expand through the incoming of the Gentiles, with all Jewish institutions part of the working out of God's action, or was the gospel to go out from Israel? Facing this question, Paul was involved in a struggle in which the gospel and the church's identity were at stake.

Of course, the issue did not appear first in that theoretical theological form, but in the form of practical questions. In the records we have, the clearest example is the question of table fellowship (Gal. 2.11–14). There would be pastoral questions about believers whose Gentile families would resist their becoming Jews. If they had decided to become Jews, presumably they would be prepared to inflict and to bear the consequent suffering. If they had believed in Jesus, received the Spirit, even been baptized, and were then confronted with this demand, the case would have been different. Missionaries encountering people who would like to join them but did not want to become Jews must also have questioned whether they were excluding people by imposing a barrier that should not have been there. The question was whether Gentiles who believed in Christ had to become Jews.

Paul's view and practice was that this was not appropriate and must not be required. For us, knowing Christianity and Judaism as separate religions, it is hard to realize how radical a decision this was when there was no concept of 'Christianity' and the churches were not clearly differentiated from Judaism, with its variety. The letters show this as a theological decision. Characteristically, Paul went to the gospel to decide a question about life under the gospel. In Christ, God was creating the relationship of human faith responding to and depending on God's grace. This relationship will be destroyed if another requirement is added. Paul was insisting that the proper response to God's grace was no longer faith plus Torah observance, but faith alone. Torah obedience had a place only if it was already part of the believer's faith response. Even then, it must be subordinated to the needs of the fellowship of believers. To some other believers, this looked like proclaiming a

God who had abandoned Israel and therefore could not be trusted. If that was his gospel, it was not good news. It was dangerous and should be stopped. In practice, the problem centred on keeping or not keeping the law. This meant that in the Hellenistic world Paul's position could be, and apparently sometimes was, understood in terms of freedom from restraint, so that he was charged with antinomianism and encouraging sin (for example Rom. 3.7–8).

Thus, the Jew–Gentile questions that we identified in the letter were part of Paul's life, central to his calling as apostle to the Gentiles. They were also part of his immediate situation. When he was composing the letter he had just been through many months of struggle and conflict over them. Romans deals with themes that appear in earlier letters, and several scholars have made lists of parallels with Galatians and the Corinthian letters.[4] Looking forward, Paul was preparing to deliver the Gentile churches' offering to the church in Jerusalem. His determination to risk presenting it himself shows that for him it was not merely poor relief. His fears, that he would be in danger from unbelieving Jews and that the gift might not be acceptable to the Jerusalem church (Rom. 15.30–1), suggest that he saw it as a symbol of the unity of the church. Rejection of the gift would amount to rejection of the Gentile churches, and of the gospel he preached. This would split the church and probably make the Spanish mission more difficult. For Paul, the truth of the gospel was at stake.

This problem provides the context for the Jew–Gentile concerns. It also leads us to the solution of another problem in Romans. Paul addressed the Romans as ἔθνη, suggesting that he saw them as one of 'his' Gentile churches, but much of the letter sounds very Jewish. The problem arose from the Jewish matrix of the gospel. There was no other language available to discuss it. Gentile believers would have had no choice but to learn the language in the process of trying to come to grips with the issues. In Rome, there were Jews among them, as there were in the 'Gentile' Corinthian church (Acts 18.8; 1 Cor. 1.14).

We have considered Paul who wrote the letter, and his interest in the issues we identified in it. These issues were central to the life of the whole church in this formative period. Now we consider the Romans to whom Paul wrote. What would we like to know about them? The clue is in the phrase 'to whom Paul wrote'. Our present

---

[4] e.g. Bornkamm, 'Testament', 23–5; Wilckens, *Der Brief an die Römer*, I, 47–8.

purpose is to understand what Paul was wanting to say to the Romans. Accordingly, we need to picture the community he had in mind as he dictated the letter. Our sources are the letter and some independent historical data.

We noted that the question at the centre of Paul's mission was also at the centre of the church's life, and that it appeared in practical as well as intellectual theological forms. Thus, we expect that because the Roman believers were believers, they were actively interested in it. Wherever Jew and Gentile came together in Christ, these issues had to be faced and answers lived out. Under what conditions, for instance, could or would Jewish and Gentile believers eat together? Such questions do not go away. Only an all-Jew or all-Gentile church could avoid them. Far from being like that, the Roman church/es, according to our evidence, were likely to be feeling the issues particularly acutely.

The scanty evidence suggests that the church in Rome grew up first in relation to the synagogues. Claudius made a decree, probably in AD 49,[5] expelling the Jews from the city. Suetonius' statement that this was because of disturbances caused by a Jew called Chrestos[6] suggests that it was because the gospel itself was causing trouble in the Jewish community. We cannot be sure that this was the reason for the edict,[7] and we cannot know how thoroughly it was enforced, but it must have removed from the church at least the leaders among those believers who were Jews or Gentiles who had been conspicuously engaged with synagogues. Thus, the churches would have developed for several years of their short history under more strongly Gentile influence. This would not have cut them off entirely from Jewish influences, since it seems unlikely that all believers with synagogue associations would have been expelled. We can expect that there would have been a difficult period after AD 54, when Claudius' death opened the way for the return of the exiles. They would find the Roman church changed. They would also bring expectations and practices from the churches in which they had been involved elsewhere. Thus, the Romans would have had an active interest in the questions discussed in the letter.

---

[5] Achtemeier argues that there is no incontrovertible evidence for the date ('Unsearchable Judgements and Inscrutable Ways', 523–4).

[6] *De Vita Caesarum* 25.4.

[7] Benko, 'Pagan Criticism of Christianity during the First Two Centuries A.D.', 1056–61.

Given their history and Rome's position as a centre of travel and trade, they may well have had more than normal interest in the experiences and problems of other churches.

This external evidence converges with what we have found in the letter to suggest that Paul was writing to the Roman believers about questions that he expected would be of practical interest to them. The questions demanded action, and the action would both reflect and help to form people's understanding of the gospel and their response to it. The nature of the questions and our sketch of the Romans' own situation suggest that they would probably have created tensions and stresses for the Romans. The nature of the letter, however, speaks against the hypothesis that Paul was writing to deal with problems so that he could have a good visit when he came. It is perfectly possible for a community to handle problems in a constructive way that reflects its health, and the letter appears to be addressed to a church that Paul was glad to see as healthy and flourishing (for example Rom. 1.8–13; 6.17; 15.14). There is no reason not to take these positive statements seriously. Comparison with the thanksgivings in other letters suggests that Paul gave thanks for what he believed was there. He gave thanks for qualities or activities of the Thessalonians (1 Thess. 1.2–10), Philippians (Phil. 1.3–7) and Philemon (Philem. 4–7), but in the Corinthian letters the thanksgiving focusses on God's action, gifts and faithfulness (1 Cor. 1.4–9; 2 Cor. 1.3–7), and in Galatians it is replaced by the long doxological expansion of the greeting (Gal. 1.4–5). Further, the only possible problem would be one of Jew–Gentile conflict, so it would have been tactless to address them as a Gentile church and then start talking to them as if they were Jews. His language suggests that he was dealing with a problem that they shared, not one that was splitting them into hostile factions. Again, why would Paul overcome his reluctance to intervene in the affairs of a church whose father he was not? Intervening from a distance, he would risk worsening the situation or alienating the Romans. It is hard, too, to see how he could think that intervention would be effective when he handled the problem with such delicacy that we cannot reconstruct it. He did not approach the Galatians or Corinthians like that.

To form a picture of the Romans Paul was addressing, we must also consider the relationship between him and them. Traditionally, Romans was read on the basis that Paul, not having been to Rome, did not know the Romans and was giving his views to people who knew nothing of them. This *tabula rasa* view suits the perception of the text as theological exposition, so it has lasted longer as an effective (although unnoticed) presupposition of exegesis than it has lasted in the debates about Romans. When we noted the tone of authority in the letter, we noted also Paul's tact in exercising it. Perhaps he knew that he was a controversial figure and exercised his authority accordingly! We know that some of his friends and former co-workers were in Rome at the time of the letter (Rom. 16.3–15). We also know that Rome was a centre of trade and travel. As Malherbe has pointed out, this must have meant that Christian communities heard about each other, and not all the news was bad or produced problems.[8] Paul was talking to the Romans about problems that were important to his and their lives in Christ because they were part of what it meant to be believers in Christ at that time. He must have expected that they would be interested to hear such a discussion *from* a person *of whom* they had heard various, probably conflicting, reports. Almost certainly, they would have had a variety of attitudes towards him. This was his first direct contact with them, and he hoped that it would be the beginning of a fruitful association. This view accounts better for the evidence than the more simplistic suggestion that Paul was writing to combat opposition and misunderstanding that had reached Rome ahead of him.

We conclude that Romans represents the first direct contact between the apostle to the Gentiles and the church at Rome, and that Paul chose to make that contact by beginning to exercise his apostolic ministry among them. The bulk of the letter is a preaching of the gospel as it bears on the intractable issue at the centre of Paul's calling and of their life. On this view, the almost lyrical appeal in Rom. 15.7–13 to welcome one another, Jew and Gentile, is the climax of the letter. It can bear the weight of this significance because it is based in Christ's action, in Jewish tradition, and in scripture. It represents Paul's goal in his preaching: to help the Roman believers to share and live out his view of the obedience the gospel demanded in this matter. Whether or not he knew that there was friction in Rome, it is clear that at that stage of the church's life the coming together of Jew and Gentile posed problems. This passage shows it not as a problem to be handled but as a gift of God to be received with joy. That would cast a new light on the

---

[8] *Social Aspects of Early Christianity*, 63–5.

problem aspects. This was the response he was seeking. The practical requests in the letter frame would then be expressions of this commitment, or even the normal support the tiny churches offered one another.

This identification of the response Paul was trying to elicit matches well with his own statement about writing reminders with a view to the Romans forming part of an acceptable offering, the Gentiles (Rom. 15.15–16). If the offering of the Gentiles as part of the church was an offering made by Jew and Gentile together in Christ, it would represent the fulfilment of God's purpose.

This is our first hypothesis about Paul's purpose in writing Romans. If it is to stand, we shall need to show how Rom. 5.1–11; 8.18–39; 12.1–13.14 have their places in this preaching, and give a fuller account of the rest of the letter body. This is an example of work in the hermeneutical circle. It depends on a full teleological reading of Rom. 1.16–4.25, and will be taken up in chapter 11.

We turn now to Paul's purpose in writing Rom. 1.16–4.25, its function in the letter. Our hypothesis is that Paul was dealing with a problem that God's righteousness was put in question if God justified believing sinners on the basis of faith without distinguishing between Jew and Gentile. In terms of the goal of the whole preaching, this discussion has two significant features. It focusses on the heart of the gospel, God's saving action in the Cross, and it does this in such a way as to remove a barrier to mutual acceptance. This barrier corresponds to the objection to Paul's insistence that Gentile believers must not be required to become Jews, the objection that Paul was preaching a God who had abandoned Israel and therefore was untrustworthy and no God.

Looking at the passage in this context, we notice that Paul was not on the defensive. He was saying that through the Cross God is righteous in graciously justifying believing sinners simply on the basis of their faith. This appears as the fulfilment of God's faithfulness to Israel. Rom. 1.17 shows it as the fulfilment of the Habakkuk prophecy; chapter 4 shows believers as the heirs of the promise to Abraham. This argument relates to the Ἰουδαίῳ τε πρῶτον καὶ Ἕλληνι of Rom. 1.16b, which at least implies that there is a place in the universal gospel for Israel's election. In Rom. 3.29–30, Paul was saying that those who know that their God is the only God should know that he is God of all peoples, and will treat others as he treats them. Thus, we have reason to believe that Paul was not defending salvation through faith alone as not inconsistent with

God's faithfulness to Israel. Rather, he was presenting it as the fulfilment of God's faithfulness to Israel. This is consistent with the tone of authority we noted in the letter, and with the suggestion that Paul was preaching by letter. Although the problem facing the churches set the agenda, Paul was preaching to the Romans, not answering objectors on their terms. We shall need to take up this point in dealing with the nature of the text. It affects the way we perceive and respond to what Paul was saying.

We may now make the hypothesis that in Rom. 1.16–4.25 Paul was grounding his preaching in God's saving action, showing that God fulfilled the election of Israel in a way that removed the distinction between Israel and the Gentiles in the matter of salvation. His purpose in this presentation was to give the Romans greater freedom for each other and greater openness to the other things he had to say by removing a barrier to the mutual acceptance of Jew and Gentile in the church. The boldness of his claim is far more than is immediately obvious. It would have massive implications for the understanding of Israel's election and therefore for the self-understanding of the Jewish believers involved. It would demand the response of the whole person, not just intellectual assent.

This hypothesis raises a question. If Paul was dealing with God's faithfulness, why did he discuss God's righteousness? One of the basic forms of gospel proclamation in the NT is the promise of salvation at God's final judgement. The language of Rom. 1.16–17 – σωτηρία, ἀποκαλύπτεται, δικαιοσύνη, the promise contained in ζήσεται – was orienting the Romans to a preaching in that framework, and this orientation was maintained through the passage. In that schema, God has the role of eschatological judge. When God is acting as eschatological judge, the criterion of God's covenant faithfulness is God's judicial righteousness.

We conclude our first investigation of Paul's purpose in creating our text by saying that he was taking the first step in a preaching of the gospel to the Roman believers. This preaching presented the gospel through the lens of the church's problem of whether Gentiles who believed in Christ had to become Jews. Paul's aim was to help the Romans to share and act on his understanding that mutual acceptance of Jew and Gentile as believers was a necessary response to God's action in Christ. In this first step, he was presenting that action in such a way as to show it as both the fulfilment of God's purpose in the election of Israel, and God's overcoming of the Jew–

Gentile distinction. The response he was seeking from the Romans was greater freedom for each other in the gospel, and greater openness to the conclusions he drew from this view of God's action.

To deepen our understanding of Paul's purpose, we need to examine further the nature of text and audience. We shall take up that investigation in chapter 8.

8

THE NATURE OF THE TEXT

In this chapter we take the third of the six steps involved in our teleological reading of Rom. 1.16–4.25, formulating an hypothesis about the nature of the text. This explicit hypothesis replaces the implicit presupposition of the mainstream debate that the text is theological exposition. We describe the nature of the text *in order to awaken the appropriate responses in ourselves.* Since the identification of the text as exposition has been implicit, the responses it has generated have all the power of tools unconsciously applied to the text. We therefore need to formulate our new hypothesis as fully and explicitly as possible, and be very conscious of what we are doing when we are working with it on the teleological exposition.

Because the question is an unaccustomed one, at least in the form in which we are asking it, we shall present the hypothesis in four major statements about the way we perceive and respond to the text. For each of these, we shall supply as much evidence as is possible without entering into detailed exegesis, and discuss the changes it requires in our responses to the text.

1. *In our teleological reading, we are seeking what Paul was intending the Romans to hear when the letter was first read to them.*

In this case, our first and fundamental observation about the nature of the text helps to form our response by defining more closely our goal in reading. We have already argued that we exegetes need to separate out our questions about the meaning of a text. We need to ask first what Paul was intending to say to the Romans and then what we can learn about his theology from what he said. Our first statement gives a closer definition of 'what Paul was intending to say to the Romans'.

Romans is a first-century letter. How is it different from our letters? Why is the fact a ground for asserting that our concern in the teleological reading is with what Paul intended the Romans to hear when it was first read to them? Does it have other implications for our reading? Paul dictated the letter to Tertius (Rom. 16.22). Questioning has not overset this consensus view. The objections arise mainly from the difficulty of composing such a long and intricately developed piece of work by dictation with first-century materials and facilities. This reminds us that composing the letter would be a long process, with interruptions. Accordingly, the coherence we find suggests that the content was planned. If the question should arise in exegesis, we can reasonably assume that Paul knew in general what was still to come when he was dictating it.

When it was complete, the bulky papyrus would be given to a messenger to take to Rome. In the first-century Mediterranean world, non-official mail had to be sent by a private messenger, often a traveller to the same destination, and its delivery was subject to all the hazards of travel. Since it could fall into the wrong hands, a letter was often intended to be supplemented by a spoken report from the messenger.[1] It seems that Paul was unusually fortunate, in that he could rely on colleagues and friends as messengers. Romans seems so full a statement that we gain the impression that he was not relying on his own words being supplemented,[2] although the messenger might be helpful in the church's discussion.[3]

When the letter arrived it would be read to the gathered congregation (Col. 4.16; 1 Thess. 5.27; Philem. 1–2), in Rome probably to several congregations at different times. We need some slight acquaintance with palaeography and ancient education to realize what 'read to' means. Most documents were written without accents, punctuation or breaks between words, so a reader would work over the letter before attempting to read it to the group. Anybody sufficiently educated to do this would take it for granted that the letter must be read with attention to bringing out its meaning, so that the reading might seem to us to be something of a

---

[1] On letter-carriers, see White, *Light from Ancient Letters*, 214–16; letter 10, p. 34; McGuire, 'Letters and Letter Carriers in Christian Antiquity', 150, 185, 199–200.

[2] McGuire cites statistics from Wikenhauser showing that Paul's letters were exceptionally long by the standards of even literary letters ('Letters and Letter Carriers in Christian Antiquity', 148).

[3] This seems more likely than Doty's suggestion that the letters were to be supplemented (*Letters in Primitive Christianity*, p. 46 and n. 60).

performance.[4] The greeting in Rev. 1.3 is to ὁ ἀναγινώσκων καὶ οἱ ἀκούοντες. Since Romans survived to be copied, shared around and finally included in the canon, we may assume that the Romans went back to it after the first reading, but they would probably do this by rereading it or sections of it when the church gathered, and talking about it. Thus, nobody would have read it the way we read a letter. Even ὁ ἀναγινώσκων would be working on the mechanics of reading and the needs of the audience, not simply reading for the argument or the ideas.

We infer that Paul composed Romans by speaking and he intended to speak to a gathered congregation. Thus, the analogies in our world would be addresses to groups that are not in a position to interact with us as we proceed, such as sermons or lectures. A preacher or teacher characteristically draws on a wider knowledge and understanding to say something particular to a congregation or class. She is usually conscious of more meaning in the discourse than the listeners are expected to hear. Clearly, the Romans kept the letter and reread it, thus exploring its meaning further, and it would seem wrong-headed to suppose that Paul did not hope that they would do so. Romans represents an enormous amount of time and effort on the part of Paul, Tertius, the messenger, ὁ ἀναγινώσκων and the Romans. Nevertheless, since it was for a listening audience it had, to that extent, to function like a speech. It would be created to make an impact at first hearing.

This conclusion already represents a response different from the responses usual in the debate to the fact that Romans is a letter. Because of the radicality of our questioning in this study, we are faced with an unknown – a text whose nature we have to identify – and we have asked how we can be helped by the known fact that it is a letter. In the debate, on the other hand, we move from a 'known' fact – that Romans includes a long treatise section – and we are faced with the problem of what kind of a letter it can be. In the first case, we begin with the independent fact about the nature of the text; in the second we begin with the starting position the academic debate has reached.

Studies of epistolography have deepened our knowledge of ancient letters, especially of epistolary conventions. We see again Paul's freedom and authority as apostle, as he adapted the Hellen-

---

[4] Marrou, *A History of Education in Antiquity*, 165–6; Bonner, *Education in Ancient Rome*, 220–5. Quintilian explains the role of the comic actor in the teaching of boys, including the reading of speeches (*Institutes of Oratory* I.11).

istic formulae to the service of the gospel.[5] The massive scholarly effort, however, has had only a little impact on exegesis and debates on Paul's theology. This is not surprising, since the body of a letter can serve so many different kinds of purpose and subject. In our reading, we may find help with some points of detail from those studies.

At this point we should consider a probable objection to our procedure. In asking what Paul was intending the Romans to hear when the text was first read to them, we may seem to be asking a question which it is neither possible nor desirable to answer. As regards the possibility of answering it, we share a problem that faces all historical-critical exegesis because all of it takes account of a writer's intention: even if we did arrive at the right answer, we should have no means of knowing it. Further, it may be argued that we should be reading the text, not dealing with some psychological entity in Paul to which we do not have access – unless his text fulfilled his intention perfectly and we can hear it exactly as he intended it to be heard, two unlikely contingencies. Nevertheless, Young and Ford are right in saying of 2 Corinthians, 'No general theory can be allowed to rule out what seems to be appropriate to this particular text. 2 Corinthians is a functional link in a specific chain of communication between Paul and the Corinthians, and the intention of Paul is a key element in this.'[6] Romans is not one of a series of letters, but otherwise the same applies to it. NT scholars are not normally persuaded to desist from investigations because the evidence is insufficient. In this case, it is better than it is for sociological studies, for instance. We have defined our task of reading according to Paul's intention by saying that we are seeking that element of meaning in the text that represents what he was intending to say. Paul's intention created the text, that element of meaning exists in it, and we have developed some criteria for identifying it. Only after we have tested it shall we offer our teleological reading as our best answer to the question of what Paul was intending the Romans to hear.

Concerning the desirability of asking this question, we note Barton's comment about the understanding of authorial intention in historical-critical exegesis: '[It is] a caricature of historical

---

[5] White, *Light from Ancient Letters*, 19–20.
[6] *Meaning and Truth*, 147. Their understanding of intention, however, is multi-faceted, while ours is specific.

criticism to speak as if it were wedded to the author's intention in this very narrow sense of "what the author was explicitly wanting to say at the moment of composition"; neither literary nor biblical critics have at all often been as indifferent as this to "the text itself." [7] But Romans is a letter, so for our teleological reading we are necessarily interested in what Paul was 'explicitly wanting to say at the moment of composition'. It does not follow, however, that in our exegesis we are 'wedded' to that, since it comprises teleological plus causal exposition. Barton's comment presupposes the historical-critical approach that deals with the texts as expressions of Paul's thought, however polemical or pastoral.

In taking the text seriously as a letter, we encounter the question of the role of authorial intention in meaning. Debates on this issue are usually in the context of hermeneutics, and for NT scholarship tend to draw on literary theory. In neither of these contexts is a high priority given to letter as letter. We observed in chapter 1 that the model of meaning actually appropriate in reading a text varies with the nature of the text and our purpose in reading it. While authorial intention can be placed low in considering the meaning of literary texts, it is much more important for letters, like Romans, which are direct communication from one person to particular others. This factor tends to fall from consideration for two reasons. Historical-critical exegesis has characteristically considered the letters as expressions of Paul's thought rather than as communication, thus making them more amenable to literary criteria of meaning. As Young and Ford observe, inclusion in the canon brought about an effective change of genre from occasional letter to scripture.[8] Ricoeur's comment that Paul's letters are addressed as much to the modern as to the original readers[9] is possible only because they have become part of the canon, and it clearly involves treating them differently from ordinary letters. We recognize, however, that scripture is made up of a variety of genres, including letters. Our task at this stage is to treat Romans as whatever kind of letter we can find it to be. In doing so, we are not ignoring the fact that it is scripture, but recognizing for our generation that this scripture has the form of an occasional letter.

---

[7] *Reading the Old Testament*, 170.
[8] *Meaning and Truth*, 228.
[9] *Interpretation Theory*, 93.

2. *Romans as letter was created and received by speaking and listening. Thus, for teleological reading it calls for responses appropriate to speech.*

We must make sense of all of the text in sequence, assuming that Paul intended a single, sequential communication. We must assume that it will be simple in the sense of being uncomplicated, suitable for hearers. This does not mean that it will be easy. It need not have been for the Romans, and as listeners-in across nearly two millennia we may well find it difficult. We may expect, however, that points may be made at length, and words may be spent on providing such aural markers as emphasis, or indicators that new matters are being taken up. The introductory questions in Rom. 4.3 and Gal. 3.2 are examples of the former. Rom. 3.31; 6.1 take up issues arising from what has been said, and turn the audience's attention to discussion of them. Since listeners lack time to puzzle over difficult constructions, we must take what would have been the most obvious interpretation of any obscure construction.

Already in the 1950s, Dahl noted that Greek prose is generally closer to speech than are modern literary works. Since texts were for hearing rather than seeing, he urged that in order to follow the flow of thought in the Pauline letters we should prefer aural signals to the visual ones provided by modern typography, chapter and verse divisions, headings and systematized outlines.[10] This insight is being confirmed and extended in more recent studies of orality.[11] In reading Romans as a letter, we need to go further, too. Dahl wrote, in the tradition of mainstream exegesis, of following the flow of *thought*. We have to follow the flow of Paul's *address to the Romans*.

Again, Romans as a first-century letter demands from us responses different from our accustomed ones. We shall not be able to move back and forth in the text in the way we do as readers. We shall not be able to do what Wilckens does at Rom. 3.27, and read something in the light of what comes after it.[12] The linearity of speech also carries the implication that it is unlikely that Paul was expecting the Romans to hold over a point until it became clear several of our chapters later. Wright presupposes this with his

---

[10] 'The Missionary Theology in the Epistle to the Romans', 79. (Originally published 1956.)
[11] A helpful example is Achtemeier's 'Omne Verbum Sonat', esp. 18–23.
[12] *Der Brief an die Römer*, I, 247.

argument that Paul's references to justification by works in Rom.
2.1–16 represent a system that will not come into action until
appropriate recipients have been created by the process described in
Romans 3–8.[13] The fact that listening audiences do not have time
to formulate and discard hypotheses about difficult passages puts a
question mark over readings of Rom. 1.17, such as Lagrange's[14]
and Minear's,[15] taking ἐκ πίστεως εἰς πίστιν with δικαιοσύνη
θεοῦ rather than with ἀποκαλύπτεται.

Romans comes to us as a text like the other texts on our desks,
and so invites the kinds of responses we give to them. The fact that
it belongs to a realm of speaking and hearing challenges our
patterns of response. We need to explore the difference between it
and the other texts on our desks, keeping in mind the significance
of the fact that as text it belongs to a realm of speaking and
hearing. We can be helped by studies of orality and literacy.

The basic distinction we must recognize is that between oral and
literate cultures. We twentieth-century Western scholars belong to
and are deeply formed by a highly textual sub-culture of a print-
literate culture that is already moving into new media worlds. We
cannot observe oral and literate cultures from neutral ground, but
must ask how oral cultures differ from literate ones.

In our culture, writing and print shape not only communication
but modes of thought, and in Synoptic studies we had to learn that
there are no such things as oral texts, verbal 'texts' waiting to be
written down. Patterns of thought and the functioning of individual
and communal memory are different in oral cultures. For us the
most important aspect of this is that in a truly oral culture thought
has to be much more concrete and presentation has to be shaped by
devices like contrast, repetition and rhythm, because words once
spoken are past. One cannot refer back, as we do with written notes
and printed books. Elaborate chains of argument with each step
stated concisely and only once are impractical.[16]

Our immediate reaction to this contrast is that Paul belongs with
us on the literate side of the divide. His letters were written; they
come from a culture that valued greatly the written words of
scripture; there is a constant stitching together with the argumentative connectives of thought or speech that has some roots in

[13] 'The Messiah and the People of God', 116–17.
[14] *Romains*, 20.
[15] *The Obedience of Faith*, 41–2.
[16] Ong provides a useful account. *Orality and Literacy*, ch. 3, esp. 31–57.

writing. Ultimately it was not impossible for either Paul or the Romans to refer back, although it would have been difficult (and probably inconceivable) for Paul, as requiring a major interruption while Tertius found the place in the featureless landscape of a papyrus text,[17] and impossible for the Romans in the course of a reading of the letter, although not afterwards. Does not this suggest that we can look on the orality of Romans as comparatively incidental, and not the major challenge it has seemed?

To answer that, we need to realize that in real life the basic oral–literate distinction is blurred. The skills of writing and reading enter a culture and develop within it. In use, the attitudes and skills of orality and literacy interact with each other and with the culture in a process of mutual enrichment.[18] Experts trace stages by which literacy spreads and establishes its influence. Havelock's schema is a good example. He lists craft literacy, semi-literacy, recitation literacy, scriptorial literacy, typographical literacy.[19] Of course, 'a culture' here cannot be understood monolithically, either. Geographical location and social class, for instance, will contribute to a very varied tapestry. By Paul's time, reading and writing had had several centuries to make their mark on the culture of his world.

In seeking to understand where Paul and we fit on an orality–literacy spectrum, it is illuminating to examine the relationships between writing and speech. In our scholarly sub-culture, writing is dominant. It is important in forming thinking, and is the primary means of communication. Speech is secondary. A characteristic form is the lecture, which normally takes its reference points from printed texts. We may be annoyed if somebody lectures by reading the typescript of a book in preparation. Our annoyance shows that there are proper differences between writing and speech; the fact that such lectures do occur indicates that the distinction can be over-ridden. Even proper lectures usually ask audiences to do with their ears what they are trained to do with their eyes, follow and assess complex arguments. The other characteristic form of scholarly speech is debate, in seminars or the like. Some people are adept at developing and communicating ideas in this medium;

---

[17] Deissmann, *Light from the Ancient East*, figures 18, 26, 41; Reynolds and Wilson, *Scribes and Scholars*, 2–5.

[18] Thomas gives a good account of the complexities in *Literacy and Orality in Ancient Greece*, Introduction and ch. 2.

[19] *Origins of Western Literacy*, 20–1.

others find it difficult. To present a substantial argument, we prepare a paper, again subjecting speech to writing.

None of us would advise a speaker learning the craft to speak as she writes. We are more likely to be encouraging such a person to overcome this disability. Yet two of the greatest Roman rhetoricians, Cicero and Quintilian, advised orators that one should speak as one writes.[20] We noted Dahl's observation that Greek prose is more like speech than is ours. These observations encapsulate the subjection of writing to speech in Paul's world. The primary mode of communication was speech. Public oratory was important in forming policy and administering justice. It was in the administration of sprawling empires that writing came into its own.[21] In education, the dominance of speech may be observed in the fact that reading meant reading aloud, and in the movement down the school system of the teaching of oratory or declamation.[22] Most literature was suited for reading aloud. It is a commonplace of Pauline scholarship that anybody in the cities of Paul's world could listen to many public speakers.

The secondary nature of written tradition in the church illustrates the dominance of speech. We find Paul using letters as a substitute for being with his churches;[23] the gospels were not written until decades after the events they interpret and thus record. Eusebius quotes Papias as preferring oral testimony, even though indirect, to mere books.[24] Similarly, there stood alongside the written Torah an oral tradition that would be recorded in writing over a number of later centuries.

There was often something second-hand about an encounter with a document. Most people were illiterate, dependent on somebody who could read to them. Harris argues that the conditions for producing more than a low level of craftsman's literacy in a community did not exist in the ancient world, and estimates an over-all level of literacy below 15 per cent for relatively highly

[20] Cicero, *De Oratore* I.33.150–2; I.60.257; II.22.96. Quintilian, *Institutes* XII.10.49–55.

[21] Bowen, *History of Western Education*, 1, 194–7; Easterling, 'Books and Readers in the Greek World: 2. Hellenistic and Imperial Periods', 17; Harris, *Ancient Literacy*, 206–18.

[22] Bonner, *Education in Ancient Rome*, 251–3, 331.

[23] e.g. White, 'Saint Paul and the Apostolic Letter Tradition', 439; Stirewalt, 'Paul's Evaluation of Letter-Writing', 192.

[24] *Ecclesiastical History* III.39.3–4. Alexander demonstrates a similar view in the wider society ('The Living Voice').

literate Rome and Italy in the late Republic and high Empire.[25] Dewey presents an alternative scholarly view that this estimate is much too high.[26] For those with the skill, reading was not the automatic process it is for us. At the most mechanical level, the person who creates a text does so by inscribing a series of conventional marks on a sufficiently smooth surface. At the same mechanical level, we may describe the reader's activity as unlocking the meaning locked up in the cipher. Modern printed books with clear, even type, chapters, paragraphs, sub-headings, even illustrations, allow for an eye–brain process. Not only is there no need of speech; it would slow the process. A manuscript, written with attention to the economical use of relatively expensive materials,[27] without our aids to the eye, was much more in need of being unlocked by a voice, and that was what normally happened.[28] Our reading material and processes free us to concentrate directly on ideas; theirs reflected, and contributed to, the dominance of speech. Ong writes,

> The reestablishment of the written or printed word in the oral world means that the word must somehow be restored to the mouth, the oral cavities and apparatus where the word originated. [In print cultures, this is minimized.] The case was different in the highly oral cultures in which the biblical texts came into being, where reading was less deeply interiorized, that is to say, where reading called for a more conscious effort, was considered a greater achievement, and was less a determinant of psychic structures and personality, still basically oral in organization.[29]

This dominance of speech created skills different from ours in Paul as author and the Romans as listeners. The difficulty one of us would face in composing a letter as long and complex as Romans under the conditions then prevailing is no measure of the degree or kind of difficulty Paul faced. Similarly, the Romans' listening skills would be better than ours, but also shaped by different experience.

[25] *Ancient Literacy*, 11–24, 266–7.
[26] 'Textuality in an Oral Culture', 39.
[27] Harris, *Ancient Literacy*, 194–6.
[28] B. M. W. Knox gathers evidence showing that there was nothing surprising about silent reading, but does not dispute that reading aloud was the norm. 'Silent Reading in Antiquity'.
[29] 'Maranatha', 258–9.

Reading Romans as speech, we must do our best to read with our ears and pay attention to aural indicators in Paul's text.

Thus, although it is a text from a literate culture, its oral character makes it decisively different from our texts. How, then, do we see the relationship between orality and textuality in Romans?

Ong offers an illuminating distinction. Writing (or print), he says, is not to be conceived as a means of preserving what somebody wants to say so that it can be transmitted to recipients separated from the speaker by time and/or space. A text is written for readers who are individuals, and can be collectively conceived as a readership; oral communication on the scale of Romans is spoken for listeners who collectively constitute an audience. The writer communicates with the readership virtually entirely by words.[30] The readership of an Hermeneia commentary differs greatly from the readership of a devotional study of the same text. The readership is not present to the author, although it affects the way the text is written. It consists of individuals who as readers are independent of one another. Speeches are spoken for audiences. The speaker is present to the audience and therefore communicates not only by the words, but also through use of the voice and through the complex we call body language.[31] The audience is present to the speaker, and can affect the speech not only in the planning but also by its reactions. The members of an audience are present to each other, and the audience as an entity reacts to the speech as it proceeds. (An interesting sidelight on both the reality of this distinction and the dominance of writing in our culture is the woodenness we often notice in speeches read by public figures facing our media.)

This contrast illuminates a number of elements in our own situation as readers and in the text of Romans. Recognizing their occasional nature, we have held that Paul's letters were substitutes for his presence with the churches. Comparing that with our situation in our highly literate culture, we realize that we, too, sometimes use letters as a substitute for being there, as when we write to friends, or send a greeting to a celebration at which we should like to be present. Our books and articles, however, are not

---

[30] 'The Writer's Audience is always a Fiction', 56–8. In modern books, this can be modified by such factors as page lay-out and illustrations. Page lay-out in early printed books shows how slowly this advantage was taken up.

[31] Cicero, *De Oratore* III.56–60; Quintilian, *Institutes* II.12.10.

substitutes for personal presence. We take advantage of the writing/ print medium to develop long, complex arguments, and to make demands on our readers that are alien to oral settings.

In contrast, we find in Romans extensive evidence that Paul was doing everything he could to reach across the time-space gap which separated him from the Romans and which is represented by the fact that it is a text. He calls them ἀδελφοί; he draws on their existing knowledge or understanding with οἴδαμεν and ἀγνοεῖτε; he draws on their memory of being baptized (Rom. 6.1–11); he draws on scripture; he uses the teacher's techniques of the diatribe to help them to keep pace with what he is saying; he leads them carefully through complex points (for example Rom. 4.10); he waxes passionate and lyrical (Rom. 8.31–9; 15.8–13).

Even in our world a personal letter can be the nearest thing to snap frozen speech that the written medium allows. Ong's distinction is important for the contrast between speech and writing, between orality and literacy, but it does not rule out the practical fact that writing does also preserve words and facilitate long-distance communication.[32] We may say that the textuality of Romans represents the fact that Paul and his audience were not present to one another, so that the interactive elements of the speaker–audience situation were missing; its orality is represented by the facts that he was speaking, and that he was speaking for what he knew would be an audience, not a readership. He worked within the linearity of speech and hearing, which presents different opportunities and constraints from those the written media offer us.

In a sense, the textuality of Romans was the alien thing about it for Paul, and we find him struggling against it. From our scholars' standpoint in a highly textual sub-culture of a highly literate culture, its orality is the alien thing, and we have to come to terms with that.

Corresponding to the dominance of speech was the pervasive influence of rhetoric in the Graeco-Roman world. Letter-writing was taught as a branch of rhetoric. Looking to the study of rhetoric for help with our teleological reading of Romans, we find that the yield is disappointingly small, but the little we do gain is very significant.

---

[32] Lentz, *Orality and Literacy in Hellenic Greece*, 3–4; Thomas, *Literacy and Orality in Ancient Greece*, 28.

The work of Betz on Galatians[33] and of Young and Ford on 2 Corinthians[34] might give us hope that studies of rhetoric would help with the question of the literary genre of Romans. 'Letter' is too vague. Here we are largely disappointed. Scholars applying rhetorical theory to Romans do not necessarily find themselves forced to question seriously the traditional framework of exegesis.[35] Reading within that framework, many have identified it as demonstrative or epideictic. This is hard to define,[36] but its application to Romans means that Paul's aim was to strengthen the Romans in commitment to an agreed value and encourage them to act on their conviction. This could include trying to improve their understanding or to make clear the urgency of the need for action. This happens to converge with our identification of Romans as preaching, and it agrees with what Paul said in Rom. 15.14–16. It does not offer a formal structure to guide our reading. It does suggest that the element of apology some scholars find in Romans was not sufficient to form the character of the discourse. If it had done so, we should expect that Romans could be seen to have the form of an apologetic letter, or at least some marked characteristics. Rhetoric formalizes patterns of ordinary speech, and the ancient rhetoricians knew that untrained people will offer defences that follow the shape of a formal forensic speech.[37]

Sharpening earlier references to Romans as protreptic,[38] Aune[39] and Guerra[40] argue that Romans can be identified as a λόγος προτρεπτικός. Although this genre does not appear in the extant rhetorical handbooks, perhaps because of the conflict between philosophy and rhetoric,[41] the identification serves the same purpose in our enquiry as rhetorical ones. It is clear that προτρεπτικὸς λόγος was a type of speech and writing recognized in the

---

[33] *Galatians.*

[34] *Meaning and Truth*, esp. 36–44.

[35] e.g. Wuellner, 'Paul's Rhetoric of Argumentation in Romans'; Jewett, 'Following the Argument of Romans'; Kennedy, *New Testament Interpretation*, 152–6.

[36] Good introductory outlines are offered by Kennedy (*New Testament Interpretation*, 73–7) and Perelman and Olbrechts-Tyteca (*The New Rhetoric*, 47–53).

[37] Quintilian, *Institutes* II.17.5–6.

[38] Berger, *Formgeschichte des Neuen Testaments*, 217; Stuhlmacher, *Der Brief an die Römer*, 17.

[39] 'Romans as a Logos Protreptikos'; cf. *The New Testament in its Literary Environment*, 219.

[40] *Romans and the Apologetic Tradition.*

[41] Aune, 'Romans as a Logos Protreptikos', 96.

ancient world,[42] and there is a good, not definitive, case for assigning Romans to it. The value of this identification to us is limited by the fluidity of the genre. The clearest identifying factor is purpose. The writer or speaker is urging the audience to a way of life or, in derived forms of the genre, radical action. Jordan gives the critical identification point as the situation of radical choice.[43] Jordan and Guerra accept that protreptic could also be used to encourage continuing or renewed commitment in those who had already made the choice.[44] The second identifying factor is method or content. The protreptic encourages commitment negatively by showing the inferiority of all alternatives and positively by presenting the supreme desirability of the cause espoused. It may also include direct urging to accept the invitation.[45] While protreptics take a wide variety of literary forms,[46] these three elements at least reasonably often formed a structural feature, so that a ground-clearing negative section was followed by the positive presentation and then by an invitation. This looks like another case of a literary or rhetorical form following the patterns of everyday speech. Guerra tries to firm this structure into an identifying feature of the genre, but this would exclude Romans, since the A, B, C structure is there broken down by Romans 9–11, which he identifies as a return to the negative,[47] giving an A, B, A, C structure – supposing one agrees that Romans 1–8 comprises one ground-clearing and one positive block. The characterization of Romans as προτρεπτικὸς λόγος converges with the rhetoricians' characterization of it as epideictic and with our characterization of it as preaching.

Another way of drawing on rhetorical theory is to see how Paul was using rhetorical techniques. Elliott asks how Paul was defining and modifying a rhetorical situation, and thereby reads Romans 1–4, with its Jewish content, as addressed to Gentiles.[48] Although he refers to the letter as hortatory, and this is reflected in his exegesis, he does not identify clearly the relationship between exhortation and theological exposition. This approach offers us no

---

[42] *Ibid.*, 91–109; Jordan, 'Ancient Philosophical Protreptic', 309–10; Guerra, *Romans and the Apologetic Tradition*, 1–22.

[43] 'Ancient Philosophical Protreptic', 333.

[44] *Ibid.*, 330; Guerra, *Romans and the Apologetic Tradition*, 170.

[45] Guerra, *Romans and the Apologetic Tradition*, 170.

[46] Jordan, 'Ancient Philosophical Protreptic', 328; Aune, 'Romans as a Logos Protreptikos', 97.

[47] *Romans and the Apologetic Tradition*, 144.

[48] *Rhetoric*, ch. 2 and excursus.

help with the genre question and, since in practice it involves the application of an esoteric discipline to a known text, does not offer us real hope of help with our radical question about the nature of the text. Again, rhetorical rules are a formalization of processes of ordinary speech.

Our study leads us to concur with S. E. Porter's carefully argued conclusion that there is little ground for treating the letters as if they were formal speeches and applying the categories of formal Graeco-Roman rhetoric.[49] Accordingly, the most important rhetoricians' contributions to our teleological reading are summed up in Kennedy's statement that '[a] speech is linear and cumulative, and any context in it can only be perceived in contrast to what has gone before, especially what has gone immediately before, though a very able speaker lays the ground for what he intends to say later and has a total unity in mind when he first begins to speak'.[50] However much the Romans might have learnt from rereading the letter later, it is designed, like a speech, to communicate a message as it was being heard.

Historical-critical exegetes are likely to experience as limiting the constraints of reading the letter as speech. We need to be clear what these constraints are. In identifying what Paul intended to say to the Romans, we are dealing with linear speech. On the other hand, we may sometimes need to examine other contexts in which a word or concept is found in order to understand it as nearly as possible in Paul's way. This process is analogous to using a lexicon in reading a foreign language. For this purpose, the context literature includes parts of the letter that from a listener's point of view are still to come, as well as other contemporary documents. In the causal exposition, the second part of our total exegesis, we shall be seeking patterns of thought in a known text and therefore approach it in a more familiar way.

3. *In Romans, Paul was preaching the gospel to a believing community.*

We formed this hypothesis in studying Paul's purpose. It provides our best answer to the question of literary genre, a limited but useful answer. We now define and describe what we mean by 'preaching', show how that identification will shape our response to

---

[49] 'The Theoretical Justification for the Application of Rhetorical Categories to Pauline Epistolary Literature'.

[50] *New Testament Interpretation*, 5.

the text, and take note of the way these responses differ from our accustomed ones.

A number of earlier expositors have suggested that in Romans Paul was preaching,[51] although they still treat it as theological exposition. This seems to be a way of accounting for the perception of Romans as systematic but not a full account of the gospel. Paul can be seen as preaching and as engaged in very abstract discussion, hard for listeners to follow.[52] Certainly such preaching occurs, but given Paul's missionary record, we should hesitate to accept that he would have preached in such a way. Our examination of the use of πᾶς in Rom. 1.16–3.26 suggests that he was not doing so in Romans.

It may be objected that the mainstream debate does not simply treat Romans as theological exposition, but recognizes in it a variety of literary forms such as exhortation, doxology, liturgical forms, even liturgical and credal quotations. This recognition is important in the debate as the basis of form-critical studies of pre-Pauline tradition. These are important for understanding the history of the church and those aspects of Paul's thought that are revealed in his adaptations of traditional material. A classic example is the identification of a pre-Pauline formula in Rom. 3.24–6. We find, though, that these observations are sometimes in tension with the way the text is treated as theological exposition. Commentators generally approach Romans just as they would anybody else's theological exposition, except that they are expounding it, not debating with it. The literary forms generally lose their own character and become elements of the exposition. For example a quoted prayer is being cited, not prayed.

What do we mean by calling Romans preaching? Paul was addressing believers, so it is not missionary preaching, although traces of his missionary preaching have been found in it.[53] Readers who find strange the concept of preaching the gospel to believers

---

[51] e.g. Gaugler, *Der Römerbrief*, 5; Kertelge, *The Epistle to the Romans*, 20–1; Wire, 'Pauline Theology as an Understanding of God', 162; Black, *Romans*, 20; Scroggs, 'Paul as Rhetorician', 271–98.

[52] In 'Following the Argument of Romans', Jewett described the letter as 'situational' (382) and as 'highly abstract' (383). Although this language disappears from the amplified version in Donfried's second edition of *The Romans Debate*, the impression remains. See also Dahl, 'The Missionary Theology in the Epistle to the Romans', 74.

[53] Some commentaries; Bultmann, *Der Stil der paulinischen Predigt*, 3, 107–9; Bussmann, *Themen der paulinischen Missionspredigt auf dem Hintergrund der spätjüdisch-hellenistischen Missionsliteratur*, ch. 5, esp. 108–9.

may find Beker's concept of contextual theology helpful: '[Paul] was able to bring the gospel to speech in each new situation without compromising either the wholeness of the gospel or the specificity of the occasion to which it was addressed.'[54] Preaching to believers is characteristically concerned with the way the gospel addresses particular believers in their particular situation, with articulating its claim on their obedience. This coheres with our hypothesis about Paul's purpose. It is what we mean by 'preaching' in this study. It is different from the concept of Romans as teaching, which is more a matter of improving their understanding of the gospel, although hard and fast distinctions cannot be made.

'Paul's contextual way of doing theology' is not, though, another way of saying 'preaching to believers'. Beker discusses 'contingency' and 'the specificity of the occasion to which it was addressed'. He stresses the importance of actual situations and real people, but in highly abstract language. This seems to shape his own thinking into a far from concrete form. 'Paul's contextual way of doing theology' is Paul's way of doing something we do. He is doing theology, but instead of discussing theological problems on an academic agenda, he is discussing theological problems arising in particular situations. While it is true that Paul was doing theology, and to such good effect that the church has been indebted to him ever since, some such phrase as 'pastoring theologically' would better characterize the processes Beker describes. This formulation equally respects the central idea that Paul was concerned with the truth of the gospel in particular situations. It brings out the action aspect, and also the fact that Paul was addressing people, not situations or occasions. 'Paul's contextual way of doing theology' leads us to read Romans as theological exposition. Beker captures this when he writes, 'This particular problem gives Paul the opportunity to address the church about the fundamental role of Israel in salvation-history in the framework of the universality of God's grace in Christ for all people.'[55] Fitzmyer conflates lecturing and preaching in his examination of the language and style of Romans.[56] Against this perception, we are stressing the difference.

Beker's approach is typical of present-day exegesis of Paul's letters. In the modern West, people usually understand themselves in psychological and sociological terms, and pastoral care tends to

---

[54] *Paul the Apostle*, 33–5, quotation, 34.
[55] *Ibid.*, 92.
[56] *Romans*, 92.

operate accordingly. Further, it is usually conceived as work with individuals. The care of a congregation, as distinct from the individuals in it, does not come readily to mind. Paul was writing to congregations. His language of sin, grace and righteousness is for us the specialized language of a specialist discipline, theology. The pastoral concerns for which 'theological language' is used become a separate specialist discipline, with a title like Spiritual Direction. To be or not to be religious is in our world a matter of private preference. With our unconscious assumption that our culture is normative for humanity, we forget how unusual in human terms is this privatization of religion, and we take Paul with us into the world of 'theology'. Then we abstract from his language, making the Paul of scholarly writing even more like us. We write about 'justification'. Paul talked about justifying and being justified, but the noun δικαίωσις appears only twice in the NT: εἰς δικαίωσιν ζωῆς (Rom. 5.18b) and ἠγέρθη διὰ τὴν δικαίωσιν ἡμῶν (Rom. 4.25b). We need to remind ourselves that Paul's purpose as we identified it in chapter 7 can properly be called pastoral. Mainstream exegesis calls the letters pastoral and therefore seeks the problems to which they were addressed. That approach suggests that Paul's pastoral method was to identify the theological problem involved in a situation and write a theological argument to deal with it. That is not what we mean by 'preaching', or even by 'pastoring theologically'.

'Preaching' is the answer we can give to the question of Romans' literary genre. What is the use and what are the limits of this identification? It is very important to realize that this label is anachronistic. We do not know what preaching to believers was like in Paul's time, and our picture of Jewish preaching is inadequate. This creates two important limitations. First, we cannot expect any help with questions of form or structure. Second, we must not be tempted to go on and claim that we now have, in Romans, an example of first-century preaching in the church. We lack the historical evidence for that.[57] What we have found is that

---

[57] Bultmann notes that we have no sermons from Paul (*Der Stil der paulinischen Predigt*, 3). Preaching in Diaspora synagogues seems a likely model, but Sanders points out that we have no samples (*Paul, the Law, and the Jewish People*, 130–1). Thyen's effort to trace the preaching style uses indirect evidence (*Der Stil der jüdisch-hellenistischen Homilie*, 67), and details of style are not what we need. Examples offered by Wills ('The Form of the Sermon in Hellenistic Judaism and Earliest Christianity') and Siegert (*Drei hellenistisch-jüdische Predigten*) are unhelpful for Romans.

in Romans Paul was doing something that is best described according to our experience as very good pastoral preaching. He was addressing the gospel *to* these people, not talking *about* it. This identification is thus a tool to guide our responses.

What is the difference between preaching, to which we shall be responding in this study, and theological exposition, to which we have been responding in the mainstream debate? We can see this most clearly by looking first at purpose. The expositor is concerned primarily with ideas, and the aim of theological exposition is the assessment that a convincing case has been made. There may be a desire for action on the basis of a positive assessment, but that is a subsequent issue. The preacher is concerned primarily with hearers, and the aim of preaching is conviction leading to action. The hearers should be led to new or deeper understanding of and obedience to the gospel as it addresses them in their situation, not simply to assent to a doctrinal account. A preacher therefore seeks to engage people's feelings and wills, as well as their minds. We can see evidence of this in Rom. 1.16–4.25 in the drama of the presentation, the lively dialogue sections, the appeals to personal experience, and the deference to sacred authority. We have looked already at the things Paul did to try to engage directly with his hearers. As readers of this preaching, we miss tones and emphases provided by the voice, and the body language. Of course, the Romans heard the letter with somebody else's voice and presence, although we do have reason to believe that there would have been a reader available whom Paul could trust for a sympathetic presentation. He had friends in Rome (Rom. 16.3–15) or may have been able to brief a literate letter-carrier, probably a colleague.

If we respond to theological exposition, we deal with the ideas. Our question about δικαιοσύνη θεοῦ, for instance, is, What did Paul mean by this term? If we are responding to preaching, we visualize Paul concentrating on his hearers as he dictates, and drawing on a fuller understanding to say something in particular to them. Then we need the best possible understanding of Paul's concept, but our attention will be focussed on the way the phrase is functioning here. It appears in Rom. 1.16–17. Seeing the text as theological exposition, participants in the mainstream debate put δικαιοσύνη θεοῦ into its thought context very carefully. The ideas Paul was using are studied in depth. Reading the text as preaching, we need to take that work with us as we consider it in this preaching. So far, we have identified the relevant issue as the relationship of Jews and Gentiles in Christ, with the question of how God could be righteous if he justified believing sinners on the basis of faith, without reference to the Jew–Gentile distinction. Having examined the concept and the situation, we find Paul making a claim which would have seemed to many of his hearers to impugn God's righteousness as the faithful covenant God of Israel. In the same statement, he was claiming this as the effective expression of God's righteousness. A little reflection on the problems of Jew–Gentile relationships in the church will show us that it would have been improbable to the point of impossibility that the Romans would have reacted to Rom. 1.16–17 in the dispassionately analytical spirit of the modern scholar, or that Paul intended that they should. It amounts to a bold claim in a painful debate: 'Yes, my brothers, salvation is indeed for all who believe without any other condition, and in so saving us God is revealing his righteousness as the God who elected Israel, and fulfilling the word of the prophet.' We can only conclude that Paul meant to make the Romans feel a dilemma and want to know what was coming next.

If it will stand the test of exegesis, our identification of the text as preaching to believers resolves what has been seen in the debate as the problem that Romans is a letter. Whereas the debate has moved in the direction of accommodating our understanding of what letters are like to the perception that Romans contains a long treatise section, we have set aside that perception. Our re-examination of the text has led to a view of Romans that lies well within the bounds of what we understand by an occasional letter, even though it is not dealing with a situation peculiar to Rome. We have not tried to fit it into some preconceived idea of what an occasional letter should be. Paul *could* have written letters that were official documents in the church;[58] he could have written a letter-essay to the Romans.[59] Such proposals accommodate the 'treatise section'. Starting from the text and from knowledge of Hellenistic letters, we have concluded that he did not do so.

We have now identified the text as preaching that was meant to be read to a listening audience, as text belonging to an oral-aural milieu outside our experience. We can sum up the guidance this gives for the teleological reading by saying that it imposes a criterion of intelligibility. Our reading must be something that we

---

[58] Berger, 'Apostelbrief und apostolische Rede'.
[59] Stirewalt, 'The Form and Function of the Greek Letter-Essay'.

can reasonably suppose that Paul would expect to be accessible to his hearers.

Preaching involves a relationship between preacher and congregation. Theological exposition presupposes a relationship between expositor and readership or lecture audience. These relationships are different. Because we have identified Romans as encapsulating the preacher–congregation relationship and not the expositor–readership relationship, the text will look different. We take up this issue as we turn to the question of Paul's audience.

4.   *In preaching, Paul was speaking with authority to a committed audience, not with some diffidence to an adversarial one. In Rom. 1.16–4.25 he was addressing the Roman believers via a narratee, a believer responding to the gospel from within a conservative Jewish frame of reference. This character we call The Conservative.*

Preaching to believers presupposes a committed congregation, and this is the first step we take in defining Paul's audience. The question of audience has already arisen in chapter 6. When the truth of a universal statement is being taken for granted and attention is on what it means for speaker and addressee, then the question of who is being addressed is urgent.

In the mainstream debate on Romans, the question of audience does not have this specificity and urgency. It is a preliminary question, often asked in the form, Was Paul addressing Jews or Gentiles? The answer identifies the frame of reference within which Paul was thinking and with which we must work if we are to understand his thinking. Particularly in the case of Romans 1–4, however, it is comparatively easy to read the text as a universal theological statement whose context is of quite minor importance. Then the question of audience is reduced to a question of the context within which Paul was developing his thought. The audience is a readership.

Detailed exegesis normally proceeds with virtually no attention to Paul's audience. The tacitly presumed audience is The Reader, a mind interested in the apostle's ideas. This is matched by the tacit assumption that Paul's aim was to bring to expression or communicate his ideas. Heil's reader-response exposition illustrates this.[60] Heil carefully places Paul in his historical setting and discusses

---

[60] *Paul's Letter to the Romans.*

issues shaping his thought. In contrast, he describes the readers, the Romans, in less historical detail, placing more emphasis on categories from rhetoric in his discussion of reader response. In his detailed discussion of the text, the audience appears as Universal Man, responding to the ideas with feelings as well as with intellect. In more traditional exegesis, the assumption concerning Romans 1–4 tends to be that Paul is addressing theological exposition to the Romans whom he has not met, and periodically turning aside to deal with problems or objections by addressing an Interlocutor, in the style of the diatribe as it was understood on the basis of Bultmann's work. Guerra's is an example of a more focussed treatment,[61] interrelating questions of content, purpose and audience. He does not, however, break out of a static model in which certain elements in Paul's letter can be related to certain elements in the Romans' situation, such as Jewish-Christian suspicion of Paul's gospel, or relationships with the civil authorities.

This treatment of audience corresponds to the way scholars write for a readership rather than an audience. We decide on our readership and write accordingly. For instance, we explain background more fully in a book for the interested lay person, or quote in the original languages for scholars. We may also, sometimes almost unconsciously, vary our prose style or mode of argument to accommodate different readerships. Once the readership is decided, the path is set. It does not require detailed attention as we proceed.

This pattern reveals its weakness even within mainstream exegesis by producing some extraordinary results. There are readings that have Paul demonstrating its need for the gospel to an audience which exists by virtue of the fact that all its members are among those few in their world who have accepted it. This is a major element of the difficulty that led Morris to accept the suggestion that Paul was writing to the Romans as Romans, not as Christians[62] – a piece of scholarly sleight of hand that would surely have startled Paul considerably.

Dunn's commentary represents a pioneering venture into exegesis with real reference to Paul's audience. He refers to the audience frequently, but in a manner which suggests that it has not occurred to him to think through the question. He begins with a blunt statement that Paul is writing to Gentiles, but by the end of the

---

[61] *Romans*, e.g. x, 1, 126, 136, 143.
[62] *The Epistle of Paul to the Romans*, 65; Godet, *Commentary on St. Paul's Epistle to the Romans*, I, 148–9, referring to Hofman.

next paragraph has Paul aware of the ethnic composition of the churches in Rome and feeling a need to provide counsel about how Jew and Gentile in the church should perceive their relationship (p. xlv). His comprehensive study of the information available about the church in Rome brings him to a picture of a church originally rooted in synagogue communities and still not clearly distinguished from the Jewish community, but with a large Gentile majority and a Jewish minority with good reason to feel themselves vulnerable, so that Paul felt a need 'to warn his gentile readers against any feelings of superiority over their Jewish fellows' (p. liii). This context makes something of a puzzle of the vigour with which Paul deals with the Jews' false presumption of ethnic privilege in Romans 2–4, certainly not taking care of their vulnerability!

He calls Romans 'a letter to be read out as live exposition, and to be heard (and understood) at one or two sittings' (p. xiii). This makes explicit the presupposition of the debate that the letter is exposition. It also states the generally accepted fact that it would have been read out to the Romans. Unusually, Dunn carries this awareness into his commentary, and often refers to the audience as listeners or hearers (for example pp. 104, 140). He even has an aside on Rom. 3.9: '... though, of course, the way the text was read out would help inform the sense' (p. 158). On the other hand, sometimes they become readers (for example p. 105), even a readership (p. 158). At Rom. 3.2, they are to respond to λόγια as 'a gentile readership' (p. 138). Facing up to Rom. 1.23 they become 'readers and listeners' (p. 72). Does this mean that those who read out the letter to the house churches warrant special mention here?

Dunn generally shows Paul's audience as being instructed. This matches his perception of the text as exposition. On the other hand, phrases such as 'a pricking of the balloon of Jewish presumption' (p. 108) presuppose a desire to change attitudes, and by head-on attack. At Rom. 3.1 'the slightly agonized cry of Jewish self-identity responds in bewildered protest' (p. 138). The diatribe is more interactive. Paul is doing more than talk to his audience. This raises the question of the way he was hoping they would respond.

Dunn's attempt to take account of the audience is a laudable advance in exegetical practice. His infelicities and most readers' failure to notice his treatment of audience are indicators of the state of the debate.[63] They show us how great an effort will be required

---

[63] Even Stowers, with a specialist interest, examines Dunn's introductory state-

to read Paul's letters as consistent address to their audiences rather than as exposition which needed only to be accessible to The Reader of his time and place.

At this stage, we need to identify more closely our question about the audience. The historical-critical ideal is sometimes expressed by saying that we try to understand the text as the Romans, Paul's first-century audience, would have understood it. This places the exegete with the historical audience as actual recipients over against Paul as sender. We are placing ourselves with Paul. Since we are interested in Paul's intention and in the letter as Paul's, we are not at present concerned with the question of how accurately his perception of the audience matched the actual Roman congregation/s.[64] Accordingly, the text will be a more important source than other historical information.

Ong has said that the writer's audience is always a fiction.[65] Since the writer has readers or a readership, not an audience, he holds that the writer has to fictionalize an audience in order to write. This is true, in its degree, of even the most personal letter, since the writer does not know, for example, how the person will be feeling when the letter is read. This fictionalizing of the audience, then, is part of the textuality of Romans. Our concern with the fictionalized rather than with the actual audience focusses our teleological exposition on Paul and the response he was hoping to elicit from that audience.

To develop our picture of Paul's fictionalized audience we have two main kinds of information. One is our view of the Eastern church as Paul knew it and of the Roman church. A letter-writer's fictionalized audience is not a fantasy, but a more or less unconsciously held view of the actual addressees. The other is the content of the letter, which offers some direct information on the way Paul saw the Romans and also provides the agenda. The concerns he was talking about would contribute to the way he fictionalized his audience.

Apart from the unique church in Jerusalem, Paul's experience was mainly of the house churches of his own mission field. Our sources give us no reason to suppose that his experience of the church at Antioch or what he had heard about the church in Rome

ments about audience, but not his treatment in the exegesis (*A Rereading of Romans*, 22–3).
[64] See Sumney, *Identifying Paul's Opponents*, 116.
[65] 'The Writer's Audience is Always a Fiction', 59–78.

would cause him to correct his expectation of something similar in Rome. Concretely, the fictionalized audience would probably consist of three or four dozen people, perhaps a household or two, or a household and some friends, gathered in somebody's house.[66] (The geography of Rome, the history of the synagogues, and the references to households in Romans 16 all suggest that there would probably be several such gatherings, but we need not suppose that Paul was particularly conscious of this as he addressed them. In the letter, he was always treating the Roman church as enough of a unity to be addressed as one.) There would be some known faces, but in the letter Paul seems more concerned to reach out to the unknown ones. He would have addressed many such gatherings in the course of his mission. Acts 20.7–12 suggests that he was capable of talking at length, and had listeners who were willing and able to attend to him. This constitutes a private rather than a public setting for what Paul was saying. He was not addressing a large assembly, but speaking to a small group such as he knew.[67]

The letter makes it clear that he was thinking of them as Jews and Gentiles together (for example Rom. 15.7–13). We need to consider this. Paul was addressing believers in Christ, but his letters suggest that he thought of the churches as consisting of Jews and Gentiles (for example Gal. 2.14–15; Rom. 11.13). This is different from our categories of Jew, Jewish Christian, Gentile, Gentile Christian. The churches of the fifties were moving towards being 'Christianity'. The concepts 'Christianity' and 'Christian' are so formative in our thinking that it is hard to empathize with Paul's conception of the churches as made up of Jews and Gentiles, not Jewish Christians and Gentile Christians. This is a critically important element of the culture gap between us and Paul, existing as it does at the point where we feel that we are on common ground with Paul, standing in a Christian context, however different from his. Accordingly, we shall avoid using the term 'Christian' except in modern contexts, and we shall not use the terms 'Jewish Christian' and 'Gentile Christian' at all. In using the terms 'Jew' and 'Gentile' to refer to the Roman believers, we shall also recognize that they do not represent clear-cut attitudes or consistent collections of characteristics. We know that Jews and Gentiles of the time were variously related to one another's cultures, and we could expect

---

[66] Murphy-O'Connor, *St. Paul's Corinth*, 153–8.

[67] See Stowers, 'Social Status, Public Speaking and Private Teaching: The Circumstances of Paul's Preaching Activity'.

that on the issues Paul was discussing in Romans, attitudes would differ. For instance, the Jews Prisca and Aquila might be less bound by the requirements of the ritual law than some of the Gentiles who had been associated with the synagogue before they received the gospel, and see the questions about the role of the law in a different light.[68] Taking Paul seriously in this way will create some difficulties and require some effort, but it will help us to enter into his perception of his audience.

Our study in chapter 6 raised the questions of whose was the problem about God's righteousness in justifying believers apart from the covenant, and what kind of problem it was. It is part of the problem of the church's relationship to Judaism, which emerged as a practical problem but was identified as a theological problem – literally, a problem about God. Theoretically, there would be three possible lines of solution. First, the gospel, being God's fulfilment of Israel's election, could be the ingathering of the Gentiles. Then believers would remain within Judaism. Against that solution was the church's experience that the Holy Spirit was given apart from the covenant, and many Diaspora churches were predominantly Gentile. Second, the church could be a new people of God replacing Israel, so that the old covenant was superseded. Against it was the undoubted rooting of gospel and church in Israel, and the fact that a God who abandoned the chosen people could not be trusted, so that such a gospel would not be good news. Paul's view that the gospel was threatened where Gentile believers accepted law and circumcision was apparently seen as denying God's faithfulness, as well as encouraging antinomianism and immorality.

For Paul, the saving power of the gospel was action of Israel's God whom he knew. He would not ask whether God was faithful in this new action, but how. This brought about a radical reappraisal of his understanding of God's action with Israel, creating radical alteration in his self-understanding, his identity as a Jew. Thus, the pastoral dimension of the problem was not simply at the level of who might eat with whom and under what conditions. The vindication of God's righteousness entailed a new self-understanding for Jewish believers, and demanded care for them from the Gentiles. This is a deeper and more disturbing issue than

[68] Wilckens, *Der Brief an die Römer*, I, 39–41; Dunn, 'The Incident at Antioch'; Barclay, 'Paul among Diaspora Jews', 92–8.

the comparatively – only comparatively! – external questions about the law. In whatever terms this could be recognized in Paul's culture, it was a pastoral challenge.

Part of the way the roles of preacher and congregation appear in the text is that Paul's approach differs from the one we tend to assume. With the presupposition of theological exposition goes the idea that he was giving the Romans an account of his gospel, with some element of apologetic. He was hoping to persuade them of the validity or acceptability of his view, and they would judge whether or not his case was convincing. Some expositors find in the letter traces of Paul's diffidence in writing to the Romans. This view is subject to Campbell's objection that Paul would hardly have submitted his gospel to the Romans for assessment.[69] It also fails to sit comfortably with the identifications of the text as epideictic or protreptic. It is clearly not how Paul understood what he was doing. He was not presenting a proposal or arguing a case, but preaching the gospel. His 'solution' to the 'problem' was integral to the gospel he was called to preach. Far from trying to persuade judges of the validity of his view, he was leading fellow-believers into this dimension of the gospel and their obedience to it, and doing so with the authority of the apostle of God to the Gentiles. This included showing them where they were wrong in attitudes or views they might have been holding, consciously or unconsciously (for example Rom. 2.17–24; 11.13–22).

Reading on the presupposition that Paul was preaching with authority to a committed and co-operative audience is difficult in the context of a debate in which conflict has the status of an hermeneutical key. In the debate on Romans, this hermeneutical key is sometimes used with full awareness, as when Paul is seen to be dealing with opposition to himself or his views that had already reached Rome. Perhaps more often, it is not recognized, but the habits of mind of modern Western adversarial academic debate are unconsciously laid on Paul and his work. It is of the essence of our academic debate that each writer is trying to convince a critical audience which includes peers who will want to argue against this case and put up alternative views. We can see such a process operating, for instance, in Michel's proposal that Romans is a Lehrbrief in which Paul defends himself against charges of denying

---

[69] 'Why did Paul Write Romans?', 264–5.

the advantages of Israel and opening the way to antinomianism.[70] The question of whether some of the Romans saw themselves as Paul's peers and wanted to judge his effort is outside our present concern. To understand the letter as Paul's preaching, we need to see how *he* perceived the relationship. He addressed the Romans as an apostle commissioned by God (Rom. 1.1), whose responsibility included them (Rom. 1.5–6, 11–15; 15.14–16). He saw himself as having authority to commend them (Rom. 6.17), and guide them (Rom. 14.1–15.7). He was realistic and tactful in not handling that authority inappropriately (Rom. 1.12; 15.14–15, 22–3), but he did not let it slip away. Thus, resisting habits of mind formed in the mainstream debate is part of the challenge the text offers us.

The last item in our examination of the way Paul fictionalized his audience is his expectation of the ways the letter might be received. We have suggested that the Romans would have heard conflicting reports about Paul, doubtless ranging from the very favourable view of Prisca and Aquila, who had been willing to risk their necks for him (Rom. 16.3–4), to energetic condemnation. Further, the Roman believers would have had varying backgrounds in Judaism, the Gentile world and Jew–Gentile contacts. Thus, while he preached with his proper authority he would be expecting a variety of attitudes towards himself and his preaching. He was talking to people, and we shall narrow our responses if we think of him addressing a 'problem' or a 'situation'.

We can examine Paul's intention in relation to his Roman audience by using the concepts of implied author and implied reader developed in reception theories of reading. These are applied to NT studies in reader-response and narrative criticism. Fowler presents a useful set of figures.[71] A text is written by a real author and read by real readers – Paul and the Romans. It generates an implied author and an implied reader (in the case of Romans, an implied audience), who are figures within the text. They are necessarily flat characters, since only those aspects of a person that are activated by the text appear. A text may include a narratee, who is distanced from the implied reader, and therefore subject to her observation. An example is the Objector in the Bultmannian view of diatribe in Paul, observed by the implied audience, the Roman church as Paul fictionalized it. There may be, correspond-

---

[70] *Der Brief an die Römer*, 30–1.
[71] 'Who is "the Reader" in Reader Response Criticism?', 10–11; *Let the Reader Understand*, 31–6.

ingly, a narrator apart from the implied author. In the diatribal exchanges in Romans, the implied author would also be the narrator in relation to the Objector as narratee. We can apply these roles to Romans. Paul is the real author. The implied author we call The Apostle. This is the way we find Paul presenting himself to the Romans. He is called by God as apostle (Rom. 1.1). His task is to preach the gospel in order to bring about the obedience of faith among the Gentiles (Rom. 1.5–6), and that is what he is doing in this letter (Rom. 15.15–16). As apostle, he speaks with authority, and is confident about his message. We notice the style of his authority. His first description of himself is as δοῦλος Χριστοῦ ᾽Ιησοῦ, a characterization that each of the Romans could have claimed.[72] His authority is exercised within the common allegiance to Christ as Lord, so it is not of the kind that lords it over others. He treats the Romans with respect and asks for their support, especially as intercessors. We have noted explicit signs of his authority in the text. We note also the tone of one commissioned to say something that has a serious claim on the listeners' attention and obedience. He speaks as a Jew who has learnt something profoundly and disturbingly new about Israel's God, and wants the Romans to enter into that new truth in the ways appropriate to them.

Kingsbury's definition of the implied reader is helpful: '[t]he implied reader is that imaginary person in whom the intention of the text is to be thought of as always reaching its fulfilment'.[73] The implied audience of Romans is a community of Jewish and Gentile believers who are learning to live together in Christ. The Apostle respects it and rejoices in it. It is an open and attentive audience, with serious questions about the issues under discussion, and willing to make an effort to understand the preaching. It has that proper humility which is willing to learn and open to change. By the end of the letter it will have increased freedom and harmony in Jew–Gentile relationships. We call the implied audience The Congregation.

We have examined the evidence that Paul was doing all he could to reach across the time-space gap between himself and the

---

[72] While some scholars, such as Stuhlmacher (*Der Brief an die Römer*, 21), see this as a claim to authority, Dunn (*Romans*, 7) points out its application to many believers in the NT.
[73] *Matthew as Story*, 38.

Romans. In the process, he was doing all he could to create that implied audience out of each group of real listeners in Rome.

We have been considering the audience Paul was intending to address in Romans as a whole. What of Rom. 1.16–4.25? Here, especially, a number of scholars have found the argument so Jewish as to see it in dialogue with the synagogue. In the terms in which we have been discussing audience, The Congregation is invited in this passage to observe and learn from The Apostle's engagement with a narratee whom we call The Conservative.

What brought us to this hypothesis? Reading the passage attentively to discover what audience is being addressed, we find features that mark it out from its context in this letter and the Pauline corpus. There the speaker is constantly engaging and including the audience. Verbs are often first or second person plural, the Romans are addressed as ἀδελφοί (Rom. 7.1, 4; 8.12; 10.1; 12.1; 15.14, 30; 16.17), there are questions, there are phrases such as οἴδαμεν δέ and ἀγνοεῖτε. In Rom. 1.16–4.25, in contrast, most of the terms of address are in the diatribe passages, and there is lavish use of the second person singular while there is none of the second person plural as address. Until very recently, exegetes have usually treated these diatribe passages as a rhetorical or debating device in which Paul turns from the Romans to address an imaginary interlocutor. Once we envisage Paul having in his mind's eye a small group of believers in a private house, this becomes difficult to accept. This view of diatribe belongs rather to the market place. Far from turning aside from the audience, the diatribal elements in Romans tend to sharpen the address to the audience. Diatribal mini-dialogues or addresses were used as a teaching device,[74] as is clearly illustrated in Seneca and Epictetus. There they are often parts of a much longer address to an individual.[75] They are used like that in Rom. 1.16–4.25 – to handle matters that are particularly difficult for the listener, who has been understanding God's election in terms of privilege. Thus, Rom. 2.1–5 brings home the judgement of Rom. 1.18–32 to such a judging person and Rom. 2.17–24 challenges his view of Israel's boast over against the Gentiles by showing how Jewish sin dishonours God in Gentile eyes. Rom.

---

[74] Stowers, *The Diatribe and Paul's Letter to the Romans*, e.g. 76–7, 182–4.

[75] e.g. Seneca, *Ep*. 66.40 includes an example of a response to an objector, while 14, 18, 38 are among numerous examples of Seneca raising Lucilius' expected objection himself and answering it. In Epictetus an objector is invoked in II.23.16, for instance.

3.27–4.2 opens Paul's demonstration that the gospel of grace, which seemed to overturn God's election of Israel, is the fulfilment of God's electing purpose. Rom. 3.1–8 is often seen as an example of Paul hard-pressed by an objector, but it is more intelligible when one recognizes that the speaker, not the debating partner, has the initiative. These diatribal passages are unusually long for Paul, and form a major part of the passage. Further, the διό of Rom. 2.1 follows from Rom. 1.18–32, the description of God's righteous judgement in Rom. 2.6–11 continues the sentence that begins in Rom. 2.5, the second person singular address of Rom. 2.17–24 continues in the question and answer discussion of circumcision in Rom. 2.25–7, and Rom. 3.1 arises from Rom. 2.17–29. When we read with our ears and recognize the sound of a speaking voice in the text, these diatribal passages fit naturally into the flow of speech as highlights of an address to an individual at the high points of his questioning of what is being said.

The last explicit address to the Romans, the implied audience, is in Rom. 1.15. Then the preacher begins turning to the conservative believer, framing his address in terms of Jewish questions and Jewish presuppositions. This is particularly noticeable in Romans 2. The root of the exegetical problems in this chapter is that the whole discussion proceeds on Jewish presuppositions that seem, from where we stand, to be pre-Christian. Whatever the details of their interpretations, exegetes are agreed that in Romans 4 Abraham is claimed as a witness for Paul's view. The preacher begins turning back to the implied audience in Rom. 4.23–5, where 'we' is 'we believers' whose lives are determined by God's fulfilment of the promise. In Rom. 5.1, there is again direct address to the implied audience.

These features of the text are best explained by hypothesizing address to a narratee. This figure becomes the recipient of a whole, coherent discussion, not of a series of asides from a discussion which becomes fragmented when they are taken seriously as asides. We call him The Conservative. Viewed in this way, the passage is an example of what Graeco-Roman rhetoricians called προσωπο-ποιία/prosopopoeia, speech in character.[76] Stowers, reading within a different framework, sees two successive examples, address to an imaginary Gentile in Rom. 2.1–16 and a discussion with a Jew who

[76] Often, but less helpfully, translated 'impersonation'. Quintilian, *Institutes* IX.2.29–32; Kennedy, *Greek Rhetoric under Christian Emperors*, 64; Stowers, *A Rereading of Romans*, 16–21.

has taken it upon himself to teach Gentiles in Rom. 2.17–4.22/23. He notes the return to address to Paul's epistolary audience towards the end of Romans 4.[77]

How did Paul expect this to work? We have noted that he would have expected the Romans to have varied views on the issues, and varied attitudes towards himself. At the level of the text, we observe that the implied author, The Apostle, is preaching the message entrusted to him by God to a called and strong community of the saints, The Congregation. He has indicated his eagerness to preach to them. With the confessional formula οὐ ... ἐπαισχύνομαι (Rom. 1.16a), he has conjured up the common experience of confessing the faith in the face of opposition, or at least lack of sympathy. He has stood with them, and encouraged them to see themselves as standing with him. In Rom. 1.16–17 there follows a clear statement of the gospel as the power of God for salvation παντὶ τῷ πιστεύοντι, Ἰουδαίῳ τε πρῶτον καὶ Ἕλληνι. That is controversial. It confirms what they have heard about The Apostle. In the rest of Rom. 1.16–4.25, he works through what it means for the person who will have most difficulty in coming to terms with it, the conservative believer who believes, either as a Jew or as a Gentile with a strong commitment to Jewish ways, that the proper Gentile response to the gospel is to believe it and to act on the conviction that doing so effectively makes one into a Jew, a member of the people to whom the promise was given. By speaking in this way, The Apostle gives the individual members of The Congregation the opportunity to receive and relate to what he is saying according to the way it encounters them in their particular situations. This procedure also takes seriously the very real difficulties that many of his contemporaries obviously had with Paul's gospel. Nobody is being ridden over rough-shod. This picture is quite sufficiently credible to be taken into our hypothesis about the nature of the whole we are reading in Rom. 1.16–4.25.

The four statements we have explicated in this chapter give us our hypothesis about the nature of the text. Romans is a letter which was dictated and intended to be read aloud to the gathered church. In teleological reading, therefore, *we are seeking what Paul was intending the Romans to hear when the text was first read to them.* As a letter for reading aloud, *it participates in the nature of speech, and therefore we must make sense of it as speech.* We must

---

[77] *A Rereading of Romans*, 36–8; ch. 4.

make sense of all of the text in sequence, assuming that there is a single strand of address that is simple enough for listeners to follow. 'Simple' here means 'uncomplicated', not 'easy'. It need not have been easy for the Romans, and as listeners-in we may well find it difficult. The oral-aural context requires us to allow ourselves to be guided by aural markers in the text, and when we encounter a difficult or obscure construction, to take the meaning that would be most immediately obvious to a listener. *We identify the text as preaching, not theological exposition, and believe that Paul understood himself to be speaking with authority to a co-operative audience, not with some diffidence to an adversarial one. Rom. 1.16–4.25 is addressed to the Roman believers mainly via a narratee who is a believer responding to the gospel from within a conservative Jewish frame of reference.* Using the personae we have established, we shall take the teleological exposition as reading The Apostle's preaching to The Congregation, mostly via The Conservative. The fact that we still have the causal reading to come will free us from trying to deal with all the problems of the text, or attempting to grasp all the meaning it contains, so that we can concentrate on that element of meaning in the text that represents Paul's intention.

9

HYPOTHESIS DESCRIBING ROMANS 1.16–4.25

Developing a teleological reading of Rom. 1.16–4.25, we complete our work in the whole sector of the hermeneutical circle by formulating an hypothesis describing the whole we are reading. Following our work in chapter 3, we need to describe what it is about and what kind of text it is. This hypothesis, consciously developed and used, will provide a new basic conception to guide our detailed reading. The studies in chapters 6–8, of the issue at stake, Paul's purpose and the nature of the text, provide the material.

Our hypothesis will be tested by the teleological reading it yields. By definition this does not deal with all of the meaning in the text, so it will not be comparable with readings in the mainstream debate, and therefore cannot be effectively tested against them. Before we offer it as our best answer to the question of what Paul was intending the Romans to hear when the text was read to them, we shall subject it to three tests. It must account for all of the text,[1] making sense of it in sequence and without demanding impossible feats of comprehension from first-century listeners in the Roman church. This involves overcoming the problems identified in chapter 2. We must be able to see it as an intelligible part of the whole meaning of Romans. This requires that we can see it as the first stage of Paul's preaching and also as compatible with the justification account as a related element of meaning. It must *either* be something we can accept that Paul could have said in the situation *or* force us to ask reasonable questions about our understanding of the situation and/or of Paul.

In describing the basic conception with which the mainstream debate operates, we can distinguish between what kind of text this is and what it is about. It is theological exposition; it is about

---

[1] See above, pp. 42–3.

justification. We shall formulate our hypothesis by considering first the nature of the text and then what it is about, but recognize that the identification of the text as preaching precludes a clear separation.

Rom. 1.16–4.25 is the first stage in a preaching of the gospel by Paul, apostle of God to the Gentiles, to the believers in Rome, establishing contact by beginning his ministry with them. We called the text preaching because we saw that Paul was addressing the gospel *to* these believers, not talking to them *about* it. Preaching to believers is expressing the way the gospel addresses them in their situation. The preacher seeks to engage feelings and wills as well as minds. Paul's particular purpose was to help the Roman believers to own and act on his insight that the gospel calls Jew and Gentile in Christ to welcome one another. He preached with the authority of God's apostle, treating the Romans as a committed and co-operative audience, open to receive help with some of the difficulties of this gospel demand. He dealt with problems and objections, but he did not respond to objectors on their terms. They might have raised the issues, but he formulated the questions and set them in their proper contexts.

The context of this preaching was the church's struggle to work out its relationship with Judaism as believing Jews and Gentiles came together in Christ. The touch-stone issue was the role of the Torah, mark of Israel's identity as God's covenant people. Our study of the Roman churches suggests that they would be experiencing the tensions themselves and have an interest in the problem for the whole church. The letter indicates that Paul saw the Roman church as healthy, working with the stressful issues but not beyond valuing the guidance he was called to offer. Clearly, he held that Gentile believers should not become Jews. The letters show this as a decision based on God's action in Christ. It attracted two major criticisms: it implied that God had abandoned the election of Israel and thus was no God; it encouraged lawlessness and immorality. Paul was preaching to Roman believers who had heard about his view, but not from him, and whose own experience would give rise to a variety of views on the subject. For Paul, his view was not one among a number of approaches to a problem, but an integral part of the gospel God had called him to preach to the Gentiles.

In chapter 7 we saw that in Rom. 1.16–4.25 Paul was grounding his preaching in God's saving action, showing that God had fulfilled the election of Israel in a way that removed the distinction between Jew and Gentile in the matter of salvation. Negatively, this would remove a barrier to mutual acceptance. Positively, it would show God's action as carrying with it the demand for mutual acceptance.

Knowing that his audience would have varying ideas about the gospel, Jewish tradition and himself, Paul preached this part of his message as address to the kind of listener most likely to find it unacceptable, a believer responding to the gospel from a conservative Jewish position. This narratee we call The Conservative. Thus Paul gave the Romans the position of onlookers, and onlookers whom he had done all he could to gather to his side in the discussion. The Conservative's position is one that Paul and others of his flocks had experienced themselves. He knew what it was like to realize and respond to the newness of God's action in Christ. As preacher, he was not theologizing about God's action from a neutral standpoint, but was with other believers, living through the unclarity and day-to-day problems inseparable from the obedience of faith. His pastoral aim was to give The Conservative the freedom to receive and live out a new vision of Israel's God – and, inevitably, of Israel, including himself. The Romans could respond to the discussion in ways appropriate to them, moving towards the freedom Paul was seeking for them.

This passage is about God's righteousness. In its preaching context, Rom. 1.16–17 is a claim that the salvation offered in the gospel is indeed for all who believe with no other requirement, and this is revelation of God's righteousness. It includes the election of Israel. The language establishes the framework of the preaching as the familiar one of salvation at God's eschatological judgement. This claim raised major questions. How could God be righteous as Israel's covenant God if he justified believers without distinguishing between Jew and Gentile? How could he then be righteous as eschatological judge, which involved saving Israel and condemning the wicked?

Rom. 1.18–3.20 deals with sinners, Jewish and Gentile. The first point made is that they are without excuse. In this discussion, sin is a datum and the conclusions, as far as we could trace them, are about God's judgement. Πᾶς is used in ways which stress that 'all' is made up of Jew and Gentile. These elements of our exploration converge at Rom. 3.19–20. The Torah places Jew with Gentile so that the whole world is arraigned before God's judgement (Rom. 3.19). Rom. 3.20 excludes the possibility that the Torah may make

Israel different. It brings knowledge of sin. Within this discussion, Rom. 3.1–8 examines the apparent abandonment of the covenant if Jewish sinner is no different from Gentile sinner. Rather than demonstrating that everybody is a sinner in need of grace, Rom. 1.18–3.20 is leading The Conservative to recognize that Jewish sinner is in the same position as Gentile sinner before God's judgement. This questions his understanding of Israel's election and of God's righteousness.

Following out the grammar of Rom. 3.21–6, we found Paul showing that God is indeed righteous in justifying believers without distinction between Jew and Gentile. This reverses the question usually identified in the debate. Paul was not talking about how sinners could be righteous in God's eyes, which involves the question of how God could be righteous in justifying them simply because they believed. Rather, he was talking about how God could be righteous in the eyes of these particular sinners (Paul and the Romans) if he justified all of them on the basis of their faith in Christ without reference to the Jew–Gentile distinction. This involves the question of how God can be righteous as faithful to the covenant if he over-rides the distinction.

The relationship between Rom. 1.18–3.20 and Rom. 3.21–6, plus the placing of the discussion about God's covenant and righteousness in Rom. 3.1–8, suggests that the question of God's faithfulness was being raised at the point where God justified believers without distinguishing between Jew and Gentile. Paul moved the question back to the point where their sinful actions have already over-ridden the distinction. Then the question of God's faithfulness does not concern elect Israel so much as elect but unfaithful Israel – no unfamiliar question for The Conservative.

Our studies of Paul's purpose and of the nature of the text enable us to draw a conclusion from our observations in chapter 6 about πᾶς in Rom. 1.16–3.26. It is operating to focus universal statements whose truth is taken for granted on the 'we' of the text, The Apostle, The Conservative and The Congregation in the context of the believing community of Jews and Gentiles. There is no explicit concern with whether the πᾶς includes all humanity. This confirms our suspicion that Paul may have been talking about something more limited than universal sin and salvation. He was talking about the way God's saving action affected these particular people. This coheres with our identification of the text as preaching. It also solves the problem of the connection between πᾶς (Jew and

Gentile) in Rom. 1.18–3.20 and πᾶς (all believers) in Rom. 3.22–3. They are linked by the address to The Conservative. In exegesis, we may define the link further. The church context also explains how sin can be a datum in Rom. 1.18–3.20. The Conservative thinks in terms of Jews and 'Gentile sinners', but he has accepted Christ as a ἱλαστήριον because he is a sinner. The issue was not one of Gentile believers being sinners over against Jewish believers who were not. It was about the impact of the gospel on his assumption that Jews were different before God from Gentiles.

It appears that by Rom. 3.26 Paul had posed and resolved the question of God's righteousness not by defending God's action, but by showing it as righteous and as questioning the questions posed against it. This turns the criticism onto the questioner. If God acts inconsistently with existing ideas of righteousness, the human being can either accept the criteria and conclude that God is not righteous, or take it as axiomatic that God is righteous and re-examine the criteria. The latter, Paul's procedure here, puts the person under the microscope instead of putting God there. For The Conservative, it means an overhaul of beliefs about God so deeply held that he had probably scarcely been aware of them, and with that an overhaul of his understanding of Israel, and of himself as a person in relationships, especially with Gentile believers.

In Rom. 3.27–4.25, three characteristic features of Judaism are discussed. Paul shows God's action in Christ as establishing or fulfilling or reinterpreting monotheism, Torah and God's election of Abraham. In chapter 6 we noticed elements in this passage that minimized the Jew–Gentile distinction. We can hypothesize that The Apostle examines God's past action with Israel in the light of the new action in Christ and the gospel, and shows the continuity.

In sum, our hypothesis is that Paul was preaching to a committed and co-operative church about God's righteousness active in Christ and the gospel as saving power. His presentation had the inseparable aims of showing this as righteous action of Israel's covenant God, and as making a claim on believers, that they accept the overriding of the Jew–Gentile distinction that had been part of their world-view and identity. He did this largely by inviting the members of the congregations to stand with him as he helped a narratee to respond to the way it challenged his position as a conservative Jewish believer. This hypothesis identifies the text as part of Paul's apostolic work, not a reflection on it.

How shall we use this hypothesis for the teleological reading?

Our concern is to identify that element of meaning in the text which is what Paul intended the listening Romans to hear. We shall therefore make use of the personae in the text which we identified in chapter 8. We shall consider what we find The Apostle saying to The Congregation, especially as they observe his encounter with The Conservative. The text is present for us to make these observations, and we shall write in the present tense. Only if the teleological reading can pass our tests shall we present it in the past tense as our best answer to the question of what Paul was intending to say to the Romans in the first century.

The text requires from us responses appropriate to speech and to preaching. Applying the criterion of intelligibility, we must accept the linearity of speech and the speaker's need to provide aural guides for the hearers. The teleological reading should be sufficiently uncomplicated for attentive and involved listeners to follow. We must set aside the adversarial style of our own work and attend to Paul as to one preaching with authority to a committed and responsive congregation.

10

THE TELEOLOGICAL EXPOSITION OF
ROMANS 1.16–4.25

We now move from the whole sector of the hermeneutical circle to the parts. We begin to test our hypothesis by undertaking the detailed teleological reading of Rom. 1.16–4.25, trying to trace the element of meaning in the text which is what Paul was intending the Romans to hear when it was being read to them.

This chapter is written in the present tense about what we find that The Apostle, the implied author, is preaching to The Congregation, the implied audience, mostly via address to The Conservative, the narratee. Only after we have tested our reading shall we be able to refer to it in the past tense as what Paul was intending to say to the Romans. It will be our best answer to that historical question.

We shall take the text in sections, presenting for each a teleological exposition and a methodological commentary. The teleological exposition is an account of what The Apostle is saying to The Congregation or The Conservative, showing how the text works. The methodological commentary is concerned primarily with the way we have arrived at this reading. Interaction with the rest of the scholarly debate will be kept to a minimum. Our goal and questions are different from a commentator's.

The challenge of writing and reading this chapter is to concentrate on the task in hand. In seeking what Paul was intending the Romans to hear, we must focus our attention on this one text, and attend to it as address *to* the Romans. We are seeking out one element, the controlling element, of the meaning. There is more to explore in the causal reading.

In Rom. 1.1–16a, Paul established the personae of the text, the implied author and the implied audience. The implied author is The Apostle, called by God to preach the gospel to the Gentiles, including the Romans. The implied audience is The Congregation, the called and faithful community of the saints in Rome, to whom he is obligated and with whom he is hoping for a fruitful visit. The negative confessional formula οὐ ... ἐπαισχύνομαι (Rom. 1.16a) implies not that he might be ashamed, but that he confesses and preaches Christ even in the face of opposition. We know from the letters and Acts that persisting in this had often got him into trouble. To be 'not ashamed of the gospel' was a demand placed on the Romans as well.

Rom. 1.16–17 – teleological exposition

When we approach this statement asking what The Apostle, the implied author, is saying to The Congregation, the implied audience in the historical situation we have been describing, we are struck by its clarity and boldness. It will make The Congregation sit up and ask questions.

There is nothing controversial about saying that the gospel is God's power for salvation, but the rest amounts to a claim that salvation is for all who believe without any other condition, and this is because (γάρ, Rom. 1.17a) of the nature of the gospel, which is God's revelation of his righteousness in a sphere of faith. This revelation includes the election of Israel (Ἰουδαίῳ τε πρῶτον καὶ Ἕλληνι, Rom. 1.16b) and fulfils the word of her prophet (Rom. 1.17c). The Congregation will not ask what The Apostle means by πίστις or δικαιοσύνη θεοῦ. They will hear a statement that believing the gospel, believing in Christ, is all that is required for salvation, and that this gospel is the revelation of God's righteousness. It is not merely a demonstration of the fact that God is righteous. It is δύναμις, powerful action that reveals God's righteousness – they might even say, is God's righteousness. The questions they will ask arise from their understanding of δικαιοσύνη θεοῦ. How can the God of *this* gospel be righteous, since the action said to reveal this righteousness seems to be an abandonment of the election of Israel? How does *this* eschatological judge reveal the righteousness of Israel's eschatological judge, whose righteousness consists in judging justly and saving his people Israel? In the context of the church's problem, The Apostle seems to be claiming to have his cake and eat it too. He is preaching salvation for everyone who believes, and in the church's experience that category overlaps only a little with Israel. At the same time, he is saying that this gospel is the righteous action of the God who elected Israel from among the nations, and whose righteousness therefore consists at least partly in faithfulness to Israel. How will he make good this claim?

We need to look more closely at the way he has built up this picture. The language – δύναμις, σωτηρία, ἀποκαλύπτεται, ζήσεται, δικαιοσύνη – orients The Congregation towards a preaching in the familiar framework of the eschatological judgement. The gospel was preached as offering salvation at that judgement. This meant that those who accepted it would be given the verdict Δίκαιος and enter upon the blessings of salvation. In this preaching, God appears in the role of eschatological judge.

When The Apostle says παντὶ τῷ πιστεύοντι, The Congregation will not hear a statement of the universality of the gospel. Rather, within their own context, they will hear this preacher saying, as he is known to claim, that all you have to do in receiving the gospel is to believe. Concretely, Gentile believers do not have to become Jews. Hardly have The Congregation taken in this point than it is followed by another which sounds inconsistent with it: Ἰουδαίῳ τε πρῶτον καὶ Ἕλληνι. To put the Jew first is to claim that the gospel includes the election of Israel. Surely you can have one or the other, but not both!

The Apostle says that the gospel is this saving power because God's righteousness is revealed in it. The Congregation's understanding of the righteousness of the God of Israel, their saviour, includes as a major element the idea that it is a saving force. At the same time it resists the idea of action that would over-ride the election of Israel, as this insistence on faith seems to do. The righteousness of the God of the covenant by definition includes faithfulness to the covenant. The Apostle, however, goes on to underline again the centrality of faith. In this gospel, God's righteousness is revealed ἐκ πίστεως εἰς πίστιν. This revelation is in a sphere of faith, and that is where one must be to encounter it. Furthermore, the word of the prophet testifies to it: 'The one who is righteous by faith shall live.' Thus, The Apostle describes God's righteousness in terms of action that seems to question God's righteousness as elect Israel understands it. In the same breath, he is claiming that it is the fulfilment of a word of one of Israel's prophets.

At this stage, according to our hypothesis, The Apostle is still addressing the implied audience, The Congregation, but already has an eye to the narratee, The Conservative. The language of the preaching here, the language of eschatological judgement, is very

Jewish. So, necessarily, was the language of the debate about whether Gentiles who believed had to become Jews. We have framed the two major questions The Congregation will ask within that framework. They would not mean quite the same to all the members. Gentiles who were tempted to see the church as replacing Israel (Rom. 11.13–24) might feel that this statement was pulling them back into a past they had thought they had left behind, whereas to Prisca and Aquila and others who thought like Paul, it could seem a helpful and challenging way of saying it. To The Conservative it would seem suspiciously like a contradiction in terms. How could God be righteous in action that seemed to abandon Israel's election? The question was there for all of them, in various forms. It is perhaps The Conservative who will most want to ask how this could be the righteous action of Israel's eschatological judge.

Rom. 1.16–17 – methodological commentary

Our teleological exposition looks very different from the expositions usual in commentaries. This is partly because of its different goal, since many of the questions the commentators ask would belong to causal exposition, and partly because of the different identifications of Paul's purpose and the nature of the text. The reader will notice, however, that our reading depends on the historical scholarship which also undergirds more traditional exegeses. It draws on that work differently because our questions are different.

We treated the two verses as a single claim to which The Apostle intends The Congregation to respond, not as exposition intended to be understood analytically. In the two kinds of writing and the two kinds of exposition appropriate to them, we see words working in different ways in the different kinds of communication. When the text is taken as theological exposition, we are usually dealing with concepts, which are complex. Our concept 'faith', for instance, has elements of intellectual assent, trust, the substance of the gospel, lived commitment. As far as we can see from the literature, Paul's and the Romans' concept 'πίστις' was similar, but with a larger element of faithfulness, which is more marginal to our 'faith' concept, appearing in phrases like 'keeping faith'. When we analyse Rom. 1.16–17 as theological exposition, we find that salvation is for all who believe, that righteousness is tied up with faith. This raises the question, What is faith? The answer is a substantial demonstration of the content and range of the concept. In contrast, when 'faith'/'πίστις' is used in a particular situation, there will be referents in the context to guide the response. When, in the situation we have indicated, The Apostle says παντὶ τῷ πιστεύοντι to The Congregation, they will hear this against the background of the debate about whether believing in Christ is all that is necessary for salvation, or Gentile believers must also become Jews. The appropriate response then is that 'faith' means believing in Christ. As listeners-in, we need to note that the contrast between (passive) believing and (active) obedience which has shaped our responses was not part of the context in which this was spoken and heard. Given our cultural distance from this text, we need to understand the first-century concepts in order to hear the words in their particular contexts accurately. When we come to the causal exposition, we shall be dealing with the underlying theology and shall need to explore the concepts.

The treatment of the term δικαιοσύνη θεοῦ in the teleological exposition is strikingly different from treatments in the mainstream debate. There, the presupposition that the text is some kind of justification account means that exegetes assume that the primary concern is with human righteousness. This is true even when the exegete stresses that the justification of believers is a revelation of God's righteousness.[1] Much of the debate about δικαιοσύνη θεοῦ starts from the assumption that the phrase refers, at least in part, to righteousness received by the believer. Because of our explorations in chapters 6–9, we see the term here as referring to God's own righteousness, making a controversial claim about it. Again, our response here is not to explore the concept of righteousness, but to see 'righteousness' in the light of the referents in the situation. The Apostle is talking about the righteousness of the God of the covenant and of the eschatological judge. The tests of his claim, then, are that God can be seen as faithful to the covenant, and righteous as judge. The latter involves being impartial and judging according to what people have done, saving Israel and condemning the wicked.

It may be objected that in the tradition and in Paul's usage elsewhere, δικαιοσύνη θεοῦ is God's saving power and has nothing to do with at least the negative side of judgement, condemnation and punishment.

---

[1] e.g. the commentaries of Barrett, Käsemann, Stuhlmacher.

If our reading proved to be inconsistent with Paul's usage elsewhere, we should have to think again. We are dealing with this text not in isolation from its historical context, but precisely as part of one of Paul's letters. On our method, however, we cannot apply this test at this stage. We must follow where the text takes us and only when we have completed the whole passage ask whether our reading is consistent with Paul's usage elsewhere, or whether it even throws new light on his usage elsewhere. This will be part of the testing of the teleological reading. For now, we merely note that interpretation of Paul's usage elsewhere is dominated by the kinds of presuppositions that we are questioning.

The objection that our reading is ruled out by the tradition requires an immediate decision. The tradition would provide common ground between The Apostle, The Congregation and The Conservative, so if our reading is inconsistent with it we must think again before we continue. Can the claim that in the case of God δικαιοσύνη refers only to saving action stand? In the tradition, δικαιοσύνη when applied to people covered a variety of activities, including righteousness in judgement. What constituted righteousness in judges among God's covenant people was determined by God's righteousness.[2] It is therefore very bold to claim that when δικαιοσύνη was applied to God it did not refer to God's role as judge, or referred only to part of it. There are texts in the tradition which show that righteousness terminology was used in connection with God's action as judge. In Greek texts, δικαιοσύνη and other words from the same root appear.[3] It is true that it could be described with other vocabulary,[4] but it is not true that right-eousness language was avoided.

Käsemann argues that δικαιοσύνη θεοῦ was an expression that Paul drew from the tradition.[5] This could be the basis of an argument against our reading if δικαιοσύνη θεοῦ were a fixed technical term with a specific meaning. Käsemann, however, does not argue on that basis but treats a wide-ranging sample of Paul's δικαι-vocabulary as part of his use of this expression.

Rom. 3.4–5; 2.5–11 reinforce the evidence that God's right-eousness was understood as including judicial righteousness. Since

---

[2] Ps. 72 (LXX 71).1–4; Deut. 1.16–17; Lev. 19.15.
[3] Ps. 51.4 (LXX 50.6); 98 (LXX 97).9; Wis. 12.12–22; 1 Enoch 38; Jub. 21.4; Pss. Sol. 9.4–5.
[4] e.g. 2 Baruch 44.12–15; 54.21; 1 Enoch 102–3; 4 Ezra 7.33–5.
[5] 'The "Righteousness of God" in Paul', 172.

Paul did not explain his terminology in those passages, it seems that he did not see it as surprising.

Rom. 1.17b ἐκ πίστεως εἰς πίστιν: We have taken this as an emphatic way of saying that God's righteousness is revealed in a sphere of faith. On our principle of preferring the reading which would be obvious to the hearer, we have taken the phrase with ἀποκαλύπτεται. Were the Romans intended to take it as one emphatic expression or as two separate phrases, presenting something like the basis and the goal of the revelation? In considering this, we remember that God's righteousness is being revealed in the gospel. How? Scholars have found a few parallels for the single phrase, with verbs and with nouns.[6] As one of these, the phrase would be emphatic. In favour of this reading are the facts that rhetorical stress is a proper part of preaching, and very appropriate here, and that there is nothing in the context to make a clear distinction between the two uses of πίστις. Against it is the fact that the emphatic phrases cited show some logic of progression. It makes sense to talk about going from strength to strength (Ps. 84.7 [LXX 83.8]) or from evils to evils (Jer. 9.2 LXX). It is hard to make similar sense of God's righteousness being revealed in the gospel in a progression from faith to faith.

If Paul intended two separate phrases to describe the way God's righteousness was being revealed in the gospel, the most likely explanation is that he intended it to be from the preacher's faith to the hearers'.[7] God's righteousness cannot be revealed in the gospel unless a believer preaches it, and there is considerable reference to preaching in the preceding verses. If that was Paul's intention, he might not feel a need to spell it out. In the context of The Apostle's claim, this is really another way of being emphatic about the necessity and sufficiency of faith. If he had intended to say that God's righteousness is revealed in the gospel from God's faithfulness to human faith, as Barth suggests,[8] that would be a major additional point. We should expect that he would have made it unambiguously and strongly, and that the idea of God's faithfulness would carry through to the ἐκ πίστεως of the Habakkuk quotation. There, however, the μου of the Septuagint version is missing.

---

[6] e.g. Käsemann, *Commentary on Romans*, 31.

[7] Augustine, *De Spiritu et Littera* XI.18. The recipient is usually expressed with the dative, but compare Rom. 8.18.

[8] *The Epistle to the Romans*, 41.

The phrase is too emphatic for us to suppose that it was a cryptic statement whose significance would become clear later. The preaching context does not allow for a major point to be made in a submerged way, and to remain submerged as it is developed. Accordingly, we have taken ἐκ πίστεως εἰς πίστιν as an emphatic way of underlining the fact that the revelation of God's righteousness in the gospel takes place in a sphere of faith, by one of the mechanisms we have outlined. Given our knowledge of Paul's language, listeners could take the phrase either way. In his own context, one reading or the other may have been obvious. We are happy with this conclusion, since we have identified the text as preaching. When it is taken as theological exposition, this becomes an explanation of last resort, 'mere rhetorical stress'.

Rom. 1.17c: In the Habakkuk quotation, we have taken ἐκ πίστεως with ὁ δίκαιος. In The Apostle's statement, ὁ δίκαιος here corresponds with those who receive salvation in Rom. 1.16, πᾶς ὁ πιστεύων. Thus, 'the one who is righteous by faith will live'. This is The Apostle's claim, and he presents the text as scripture support for it.[9] For The Congregation, the question of whether the phrase should be taken with ὁ δίκαιος or with ζήσεται is not critical. In the context of eschatological judgement, being righteous and living are virtually different ways of referring to the same verdict.

It is sometimes argued that Rom. 1.16–18 comprises a chain of clauses linked by γάρ, going back to Rom. 1.15, and that the chain should not be broken. Why, then, have we broken it when reading the text as belonging to a speaking–hearing context? At the beginning of the chain, the reasons for Paul's determination to preach in Rome have been given in Rom. 1.11–14 and taken up by the οὕτως of Rom. 1.15. In the chain that follows, attention is on the gospel Paul preaches. Towards the end, the Habakkuk quotation provides a minor conclusion, an aural and mental resting place. The γάρ of Rom. 1.18 begins the process of showing how God's righteousness is revealed in God's apparently questionable action.

Rom. 1.18–4.25 – overview

With the challenging claim of Rom. 1.16–17, The Apostle has awakened The Conservative's sense of his identity as part of Israel,

---

[9] Leenhardt (*The Epistle to the Romans*, 58) objects that this would require ὁ δὲ ἐκ πίστεως δίκαιος, but this is a quotation, not a freely formulated sentence.

and his difficulty in seeing how the God of Israel could save people simply on the basis of their believing the gospel, without reference to membership in Israel.

In making good his claim, he will have to deal with attitudes springing from The Conservative's self-understanding, and we shall be helped to see how he is doing this if we sketch out that self-understanding. The Conservative as narratee in the text is a flat character, not a whole person, and our sketch takes account only of his role in the preaching in the letter. Since he is a Jew (by birth or adoption), God is the point of reference for his identity. God is the God Israel knows in history, who elected Israel and is faithful to that election. Speak to him about God and you are talking to him about himself.

At the core of his problem here is something that we can perceive as a disjunction in his self-perception. To oversimplify, he sees himself before God as privileged, chosen, loved, a recipient of grace, and is in no doubt that that gracious action includes dealing with his sin, but over against Gentiles he sees himself as a member of God's holy and righteous people, who are separated from and favoured above the rest of the world, the Gentiles, ἐξ ἐθνῶν ἁμαρτωλοί (Gal. 2.15).[10] A clear example of this holding together of different self-images is offered by a comparison of the Hodayoth and the War Scroll from Qumran. While this is illogical, we recognize it as very human. The Conservative's expectation of the eschatological judgement is born of Israel's experience of oppression and suffering. God the righteous judge will vindicate God's righteous and oppressed people and punish their enemies.[11]

The root of his problem is not that Jews are good and Gentiles are bad, but that Jews are special to God and Gentiles are not. With this goes a view, perhaps not even conscious, that Jewish sin is different from Gentile sin, mere peccadilloes over against the blackness of a culture characterized by idolatry and sexual mores he finds abhorrent.

The thing in his new faith that threatens this image of God, people and judgement is not that he has accepted Christ as a sacrifice for his sins, but that the same sacrifice is being accepted by Gentiles for theirs and is bringing them into the church. If it brought them into Israel, he would have no problem. Christ

---

[10] See Wisdom of Solomon, e.g. chs. 5–19, Jub. 22.11–23.
[11] Daniel 7 is an early example.

crucified could be seen as the fulfilment of God's earlier means of dealing with sin within the covenant. The insistence that God's action in Christ is the same for Jew and Gentile *as Jew and Gentile* seems to wipe out Israel's distinctiveness, and with it Israel's election. This is what he cannot reconcile with his understanding of God's righteousness as including faithfulness to Israel. One thing The Apostle does is to bring The Conservative's recognition that he is a sinner to bear on his attitude that he is superior to, and rightly privileged above, Gentile sinners.

In dealing with the web of beliefs and presuppositions that shape The Conservative's identity and attitudes, The Apostle is not dealing with axioms identified as starting points for theological thinking. Rather, he is dealing with lifelong habits of mind and behaviour. The Conservative might not even be fully conscious of them. The Apostle has only words to use, but he needs to make them operate at the levels of mind, experience and attitude if he is to enable The Conservative to see his relationships to God and to Gentiles in a new light because of the Cross. This new thing he is offering is hard, but it is part of the obedience the gospel requires, and he is presenting it as good news.

We have noticed that The Conservative found the problem with The Apostle's preaching at the point where God justifies Jew and Gentile alike on the basis of faith, that is, when the Jew–Gentile distinction is over-ridden at the point of salvation. The Apostle's approach includes leading The Conservative to see the distinction over-ridden at the point of sin. Then God is dealing with sinful Israel, not with righteous and oppressed Israel. That is no new problem, as the prophets made clear.

We can now outline The Apostle's approach, remembering that his task is to establish for The Conservative that God's *right-eousness* is the saving power of the gospel that treats Jew and Gentile alike. That involves helping The Conservative to come to terms with important changes in his own idea of who he is as part of Israel. This means that The Apostle's theocentric discourse has a visible anthropocentric epicentre, but different from the one that liberated Luther.

In Rom. 1.18–3.20, The Apostle begins at the point of agreement about God's righteousness, the righteousness of God's wrath towards sinners. Thus he awakens The Conservative's judgemental attitude to 'Gentile sinners'. Then he leads on to the point where The Conservative has to see that his own axiom that God's judgement is just and impartial means that he as sinner deserves the same judgement (Rom. 2.1–11). The Apostle knows (from Paul's experience) that The Conservative will respond by grasping at Israel's special status: but what about the Torah? The νόμος, with its vital element the law of Moses, is the instrument of Israel's difference and the powerful symbol of God's election. Rom. 2.12–3.20 deals with this question. The Conservative is led to the point where he sees that the law does not make Israel different at the judgement, but places Jew with Gentile before God's judgement as sinner.

At this point it appears that Israel's sin has obliterated the Jew–Gentile distinction as far as judgement is concerned, and also that the only verdict the impartial judge can pass on anyone is Ἄξιος θανάτου (Rom. 1.32a). What has become of the claim that God's righteousness is saving power and that it includes the election of Israel, that is, includes God's righteousness as faithfulness to the covenant?

The Apostle shows that in the new gospel revelation, God's righteousness as impartial judge and saviour fulfils God's faithfulness to Israel in a way that breaks the bounds of Israel (Rom. 3.21–6). This leads on to an examination of Israel's election, showing that God's purpose in election is fulfilled in the gospel (Rom. 3.27–4.25).

It is worth noting here that in the teleological reading the traditional exegetical contrast between the revelations of God's wrath and God's righteousness disappears. The Conservative's question is about God's righteousness as eschatological judge, and he assumes that that includes righteous wrath, the proper judgement of condemnation on the sinner. *The Apostle is talking all the way through about God's righteousness.* There is a contrast. It is between the contradiction inherent in The Conservative's old way of understanding God's righteousness and the resolution of that contradiction by God's action in Christ. We shall see this working out as The Apostle's preaching unfolds.

Rom. 1.18–32 – teleological exposition

In chapter 6, we examined this passage to see whether it contributes to a demonstration that all have sinned. We concluded that there is no attempt to prove that anybody has sinned. Sin is a datum and the passage is about God's just judgement of wrath. This conclusion coheres with our reading of Rom. 1.16–17. Having elicited the question about God's righteousness, specifically God's righteousness as eschatological judge, The Apostle now takes up the issue of the righteousness of God's judgement. He begins at a point where everybody involved can agree. Using γάρ and a construction parallel with Rom. 1.17a, he takes up the claim he has already made, and begins his demonstration by presenting a picture of God's righteousness active in the condemnation of sin, as The Congregation believes it will be at the judgement. The core of what calls forth God's wrath is suppressing the truth (Rom. 1.18b). The Apostle does not say who does this, but characterizes it as the central sin. These people suppress the truth by rejecting the knowledge of himself that God has given them, and they are without excuse because God has made himself known. To refuse the knowledge of God is to refuse to give God glory and thanks (Rom. 1.19–21a). This refusal damages their own being, as their minds and hearts are darkened and they are made foolish, not wise as they think (Rom. 1.21b–22). God's first punishment is given with their sin. Their foolishness is expressed in the exchange of God's glory for idolatry (Rom. 1.22–3). The Apostle, The Congregation and The Conservative do not suppose that one may simply refuse God thanks and glory. The turning to worship of the mortal and created is an exchange, not a subsequent free choice.

God's judgement of wrath takes the form of giving them up to what they have made of themselves. The Apostle presents an appalling picture of widening circles of sin. The rhetoric is built around the repeated παρέδωκεν αὐτοὺς ὁ θεός (Rom. 1.24, 26, 28), and given its driving force by the interlocking of the individual vignettes through repetition ([μετ]ήλλαξαν, ἐν [ἐ]αυτοῖς, ἐδοκίμασαν – ἀδόκιμον νοῦν) and the binding effect of the cause and effect sequence. The justice of God's judgement, grounded in ἀναπολογήτους (Rom. 1.20b), is reinforced by the way the punishment fits the crime. The picture comes to its climax in the ultimate perversion, not only doing evil but doing it in flaunting defiance of God's known ordinance, and approving those who do it. They do wrong and see wrong done, and they call it right (Rom. 1.32). The sin of the ungodly and wicked is their punishment for giving to idols the glory and thanks due to God, but it is also their responsible action which brings upon them the final judgement, Ἄξιοι θανάτου (Rom. 1.32a). God's wrath is an activity of God's righteous judgement. Those punished are without excuse.

This picture is familiar to The Conservative. It is expressed in the language of Hellenistic Judaism's apologetic for its monotheistic faith and its attack on Gentile idolatry. It encourages him to respond, as he has always done, to a picture of God's wrath towards the Gentiles, towards 'them', not towards 'us', the Jews.

The Apostle has made The Conservative feel the security of his own presuppositions. Yet under the surface there is another current, if he is attuned to hear, or perhaps feel, it. The people on whom this judgement is pronounced are human beings, not Gentiles, and their identity is left vague. Idolatry appears as the root of all the other consequences of the suppression of the truth. Post-OT Judaism characteristically saw this as other people's sin,[12] but Rom. 1.23 describes the fall into idolatry in terms reminiscent of Israel's great sin of idolatry at Sinai.[13] At the same time, it seems to echo the story of the Fall, in which at least some Jews saw themselves involved,[14] and the language of Rom. 1.21b–22 echoes the LXX versions of Ps. 94 (LXX 93).11 and 2 Kgs. 17.15. The catalogue of sins in Rom. 1.30–1 is an example of the vice lists used in Jewish and church paraenesis. All this is part of The Conservative's background.

Rom. 1.18–32 – methodological commentary

Our teleological reading of this passage is controlled by conclusions about addressees and content. It is addressed to The Congregation, which has just been forced to ask questions about God's righteousness, with an eye to The Conservative, who is faced with a more specific question. It is about God's righteousness as judge who condemns sinners.

The Apostle's preaching is operating at two main levels. First, there is the level of argument. God is indeed righteous as eschatological judge who condemns people who sin by refusing God glory and thanks. Condemnation for the things they do when they act against their obligation to God is just (Rom. 1.19–21, 32). They are without excuse; they deserve death.

Reading this argument, we are struck by an apparent *non sequitur*. Rom. 1.19–20 appears to be modelled on the Hellenistic

---

[12] Wisd. 15; *b* Sabb 146a; *b* Yebam 103b; *b* Abod Zar 22b.

[13] Echoes of Ps. 106 (LXX 105).20; Jer. 2.11.

[14] See, later, 2 Baruch 54.19b; 4 Ezra 3.21–6; 7.48[118], and compare Rom. 5.12–14; 1 Cor. 15.21–2.

Jewish natural theology argument that God made himself known in creation and people who do not acknowledge God are guilty because they have not drawn the conclusion from the evidence.[15] When this is read with Rom. 1.21a, we find The Apostle arguing that God gave the revelation, and they knew, but they did not act on the knowledge. In causal exegesis we want to make sense of this argument as springing from a system of thought that we can accept as rational and credible, so we shall need to ask how Paul could have made it. In teleological reading, we need to highlight the claim and the logical gap. Clearly, The Apostle expects this line of argument to be acceptable to The Congregation and, since The Congregation is the implied audience, it is. In the causal exposition, we shall need to ask how Paul could make this assumption in addressing the Romans.

The second level at which the preaching is operating is that of suggestion and reminiscence that takes the overt argument down to The Conservative's presuppositions and feelings. This is achieved by the familiar language.

Rom. 2.1–11 – teleological exposition

Having elicited The Conservative's condemnation of 'them', the Gentiles, who are without excuse before the judgement (Rom. 1.20b) and worthy of death (Rom. 1.32), The Apostle begins speaking directly to him. He turns from what The Conservative thought was the climax of his picturing of God's righteous wrath with another διό: Διὸ ἀναπολόγητος εἶ, ὦ ἄνθρωπε πᾶς ὁ κρίνων (Rom. 2.1a). This further conclusion is a shock to The Conservative, but The Apostle goes on to demonstrate it. Just like the Gentiles, The Conservative is without excuse (Rom. 2.1; cf. 1.20). In condemning others, he condemns himself because he does the same things. The Apostle and The Conservative know that God's judgement on those who do such things is according to truth, just and impartial.

The Apostle continues remorselessly bringing out the effect of The Conservative's actual sin on his expectation that Israel will be justified when God judges impartially according to works. If The Conservative expects to do the things he condemns in Gentiles and escape God's condemnation, he is abusing God's patience and

---

[15] e.g. Wisd. 13.1–9; Sib. Or. III.8–45.

kindness, which are intended to lead to repentance, not to more sin. He is storing up for himself wrath on the day of judgement. Picturing that judgement, The Apostle expounds the tradition that God will give to each according to his works (Rom. 2.6; cf. Ps. 62.12 (LXX 61.13); Prov. 24.12; Sir. 16.14). Works are specified as good or evil, and are seen as resulting from the orientation of a person's life, either towards God's kingdom or in rebellion against God. The chiastic presentation stresses the correspondence of reward and punishment with works, and makes room for the repeated Ἰουδαῖος τε πρῶτον καὶ Ἕλλην (Rom. 2.9, 10), echoing Rom. 1.16. The Jew is first in punishment and in reward. This takes up the prophetic stress on Israel's responsibility as God's people (for example Amos 1.3–3.2). Rom. 2.11 is The Apostle's climax. It says to The Conservative, You believe that God is righteous and judges impartially according to works. According to your own belief, then, you stand before that judgement on the same terms as the Gentiles whom you judge. This cuts across The Conservative's presuppositions – and not just in theory. His judgement on the Gentiles has shown him up as one whose works deserve wrath and fury, tribulation and distress (Rom. 2.8–9).

Rom. 2.1–11 – methodological commentary

Our reading is controlled by the conclusion that The Apostle is addressing The Conservative. We notice his Socratic method. He does not tell The Conservative directly that he is doing what he thought The Apostle was doing in Rom. 1.16–17, holding together contradictory ideas. Rather he leads him through his own feelings and beliefs to a point where he runs up against something that starts to make him encounter his own contradiction.

It is very noticeable that The Apostle's point here turns on the statement that The Conservative does τὰ αὐτά (Rom. 2.1), yet he makes no attempt to establish this. If we were treating the text as theological exposition, we should ask how Paul could make this claim. For the teleological reading, we ask how Paul expected the charge to work. If The Conservative will retort that indeed he is not guilty of idolatry, sexual immorality and rejecting God, The Apostle's point will fail. If this were the case, Paul's point with the Romans would fail. Paul was an experienced preacher and pastor, and this letter was very important to him. Clearly, he expected that his words would carry conviction. Why? The Conservative believes that he will be saved at God's eschatological judgement not because of what he has done and refrained from doing but because Christ died for his sins. He does not need proof that he has offended against God. A person with as strong a sense of the righteousness of his community over against the rest of the world as a member of the Qumran community could still write,

> As for me, shaking and trembling seize me
>   and all my bones are broken;
> my heart dissolves like wax before fire
>   and my knees are like water
>   pouring down a steep place.
> For I remember my sins
>   and the unfaithfulness of my fathers.
> When the wicked rose against Thy Covenant
>   and the damned against thy word,
> I said in my sinfulness,
> 'I am forsaken by Thy Covenant.'   (1QH IV, 33–5)

Further, although the cap πᾶς ὁ κρίνων fits and he wears it, it also fits the community in which he formed his understanding of Israel and of God. Rom. 1.18–32 has brought that out by eliciting the judging response.

Rom. 2.12–29 – teleological exposition

The Conservative has always been comfortably familiar with the idea that there is no partiality with God (Rom. 2.11). The inference that Jew and Gentile will therefore be rewarded and punished equally and he will deserve punishment is simply shocking.[16] His response will be, But what about the Torah? Israel is marked off from the world around by God's gift of the Torah, the symbol of election. All his life The Conservative has experienced Israel's specialness in observing the Mosaic law. Surely all this makes a difference. Surely there is something amiss with the way The Apostle has been leading him.

The Apostle knew that this would be the question, and had planned it. Now he deals with it at length. His opening is virtually a summary statement of his response to The Conservative's objec-

---

[16] Sanders observes that the rabbinic literature asks questions within the confines of Israel's obedience. There is no systematic, or even consistent, treatment of Gentiles (*Palestinian Judaism*, 211–12).

tion: ὅσοι γὰρ ἀνόμως ἥμαρτον, ἀνόμως καὶ ἀπολοῦνται, καὶ ὅσοι ἐν νόμῳ ἥμαρτον, διὰ νόμου κριθήσονται (Rom. 2.12). For sinners, having the Torah makes a difference to the measure by which they will be condemned. It does not alter the fact that they will be condemned. Those who do the law will be justified, not those who hear it (Rom. 2.13 cf. Acts 15.21). He spells out for The Conservative what this will mean for Gentile and Jew.

He reminds The Conservative of the many times he has seen Gentiles doing things the law requires even though they do not have the law (Rom. 2.14). Their actions show that what the law requires is written on their hearts, so that their consciences and their thoughts will be witnesses at God's judgement (Rom. 2.15–16). The judgement will be through Christ, whom The Conservative has accepted as a sacrifice for his sin, and God will judge τὰ κρυπτὰ τῶν ἀνθρώπων (Rom. 2.16). These things The Conservative cannot see. God sees truly, and God's impartial judgement is just. Even though the verdicts are being determined by what people are doing now (Rom. 2.5), The Conservative cannot be so sure that he knows what they will be. The fact that Gentiles do not have the law does not put them at a disadvantage before God's judgement.

Now The Apostle turns to The Conservative's attitude to Israel's possession of the Torah. He has always seen this as making Israel special and privileged over against the Gentiles. The Apostle builds up a picture of The Conservative's self-perception. Simply because he is a Jew, he rests in the law and boasts in God. Knowing God's will, he can make right practical and moral judgements on the basis of the law, and so be leader, light, teacher to the benighted Gentiles (Rom. 2.17–20). At one level, this is a proper perception of Israel as God's elect, with her being determined by God and with the gift of wisdom to offer to the Gentile world. At another level, however, it is marred by the attitude to Gentiles. It matches the perception of the Gentile world that The Apostle evoked in Rom. 1.18–32, but is hardly compatible with The Conservative's perception of Gentiles he knows in real life (Rom. 2.14–16), or with his own acceptance of Christ's death for his sins. Here is a superior condescending to the benighted, not a recipient of grace who wishes to share the gift. Now The Apostle breaks off his sentence, and begins to drive home the contradiction between The Conservative's idea of what the Torah has made of him and the real-life effects of possessing it. His actual sin contradicts what he thinks God's election has made him.

The very fact that he boasts in the law causes his transgression to dishonour God (Rom. 2.21–3). The Apostle crowns his accusation with a text of scripture turned against The Conservative: τὸ ὄνομα τοῦ θεοῦ δι' ὑμᾶς βλασφημεῖται ἐν τοῖς ἔθνεσιν (Rom. 2.24). The prophets said this of dispossessed Israel (Isa. 52.5; Ezek. 36.20), but now it is unmistakably Israel's fault. The Conservative is most radically condemned διὰ νόμου (Rom. 2.12b).

But The Conservative has another defence. What about circumcision? God made the covenant with Israel, and is righteous as faithful to the covenant. 'No Israelite who is circumcised will go down to Gehinnom' (Ex Rab XIX.4). Again, The Apostle turns The Conservative's expectations upside down. He examines the principle of circumcision, showing the logical conclusion of insisting on God's impartial judgement. He states the principle. Circumcision counts if you do the law (Rom. 2.25a). In Rom. 2.25b he claims that the principle works in reverse. If you are a transgressor of the law, your circumcision becomes uncircumcision. He goes on remorselessly. That would work in reverse, too, would it not? If an uncircumcised person kept the law, his uncircumcision would be reckoned as circumcision (Rom. 2.26). In Rom. 2.27 he uses a logical future to state the startling result of this chain of logic. The law-keeping Gentile will be righteous and will judge the Jew who transgresses the law. In the light of Israel's sin and God's righteousness as judge, circumcision and the identity of the true Jew must be reassessed. The Apostle does this with a double contrast (Rom. 2.28–9). The true Jew is not one ἐν τῷ φανερῷ, but one ἐν τῷ κρυπτῷ. True circumcision is not ἐν τῷ φανερῷ, ἐν σαρκί, or γράμματι. It is περιτομὴ καρδίας ἐν πνεύματι. The Conservative should know this, since circumcision in the flesh is contrasted with circumcision of the heart in his tradition.[17] True circumcision is a matter of spirit, not of flesh. True circumcision and the true Jew are those recognized by God, who sees truly the things that are hidden from human observation (Rom. 2.16, 29). By now, The Conservative's image of God's holy and righteous people contrasted with the wicked Gentile world has gone, crushed by the recognition of the impartiality of the righteous judge and the practical realities visible to one whose own sin has been dealt with by the God of the gospel. The dividing line between God's people

[17] Deut. 10.16; 30.6; Jer. 4.4; cf. Jer. 9.24–5; Lev. 26.41; Jub. 1.23; Philo, *Mig.* 92; *Spec. Leg.* I, 304–5.

and not God's people is hidden in God's secret knowledge, and it seems unlikely that it will correspond with the division between Israel and not Israel.

Rom. 2.12–29 – methodological commentary

Again, the teleological reading is governed by the nature of the text. We notice particularly how our identification of the text as preaching and as directed first of all to The Conservative frees us from tensions generated by treating it as theological exposition.

In Rom. 2.14–16 there is a time shift, however κρινει is accented. Rom. 2.15 deals in the present with Gentile thoughts and consciences, but in Rom. 2.16, in the same sentence, these are active at the judgement, which is expected in the future. In our teleological reading, we recognize this fluidity. The close relationship between acts here and now and the outcome of the coming judgement allows The Apostle and The Conservative to blur present and future in their speech. The same blurring appears in Rom. 2.13 and Rom. 2.28–9, although it is not so noticeable because they are statements of principle. This is consistent with Paul's eschatology. In the Cross, the eschatological judgement has been brought forward into the present, yet it is still to be completed at the day of judgement. Romans belongs to this final time, with its sense of the imminence of the End (Rom. 13.11–14).

A second feature that is troublesome when we read the text as theological exposition is the presence of Gentiles who do the law (Rom. 2.14, 26–7), particularly since they are said to do it even though they do not obey the command to circumcise. Logically, circumcision is one of the commandments of the law and therefore Gentiles who by definition are uncircumcised cannot be said to keep the law. This text tells us that we are dealing with a discussion in which circumcision was thought of, at least sometimes, as separate from Torah observance. The same separation appears in Rom. 4.9–12 and is presupposed by Paul's insistence to the Galatians that anybody who accepts circumcision is bound to keep the whole law (Gal. 5.3). Circumcision and law-keeping are being considered as two marks of a Jew. We accept this as a feature of the text that we must respect.

In Rom. 2.14–16, The Apostle is not making a formal theological argument. Rather, he is directing The Conservative to the way his experience questions some of his ideas. Among the Gentiles he

knows are some who, by the standards of judgement outlined in
Rom. 2.7–10, must have as good a chance as he and other Jews he
knows will have. As long as we think in terms of theological
exposition, we shall not be free to recognize the character of the
text, which is directed very personally to The Conservative, his
experience and his attitudes. We note the inconsistency between a
blanket condemnation of Gentiles as a response to Rom. 1.18–32
and the recognition of the good qualities of some known Gentile
families. Even though it is illogical, it is common human experience
to find oneself condemning a category of people and excepting
known individuals.

φύσει, Rom. 2.14: Agreeing with Dunn's grammatical arguments,[18] we have taken φύσει with ποιῶσιν. The sentence is
ambiguous, however. If ὁ ἀναγινώσκων took it with μὴ ... ἔχοντα,
the same main point would be made. At the level of the teleological
reading, the difference is not critical.

Rom. 2.17–24: The thrust of this passage is that God is dishon-
oured because Israel sins while boasting in the law. This point is
made by the contrast between Jewish self-perception over against
the Gentiles and Gentile perception of Jews who sin. It is crowned
by the scripture quotation placed in the emphatic final position.
The anacoluthon has a dramatic rhetorical function.

If The Conservative can reject the charges implied in the questions of Rom. 2.21–2, The Apostle's argument will have lost its
persuasive force, yet the charges seem extravagant. How is this
rhetoric intended to work? The central charge appears in Rom.
2.23, and there is no problem about it. Inconsistency does not have
to express itself in dramatic ways to call forth harsh criticism,
especially of those who set themselves up as leaders and teachers.
Has it been over-illustrated? The Apostle (and therefore Paul's
discussion) proceeds on the assumption that the charges will carry
conviction. Since it is unreasonable to believe that all, or even a
considerable proportion, of the Jews were guilty of the crimes
enumerated, we must ask how this could be so.

This kind of rhetoric is part of the way such discussion was
carried on at the time. Stowers claims that Rom. 2.17–24 could
stand in for the characterization of the pretentious philosopher in
some Hellenistic literature,[19] and the epistle of Heraclitus to

---

[18] *Romans*, 98.
[19] *The Diatribe and Paul's Letter to the Romans*, 112–13.

Hermodorus describes the Ephesians in a way that cannot have applied to all of them: 'Give me an occasion for laughing in a time of peace when you do not wage war in court by using your tongues as weapons, and that after you have committed fraud, seduced women, poisoned friends, robbed temples, prostituted, been found breaking oaths, beaten your ritual drums, each one filled with a different evil.'[20] A good NT example of denunciation of a class of people whose actions were seen as belying their words is Matt. 23.1–36. Again, the charges cannot have applied to all.

The charges in Rom. 2.21–2 illustrate breaking God's commandments in ways that were particularly likely to cause Gentile blaspheming (Rom. 2.23–4), as Watson's citing of notorious individual cases shows.[21] All the items are paralleled in a list of crimes given by Philo: 'so that when he attempts to commit theft or adultery, murder or sacrilege or any similar deed, he should not find an easy path'.[22]

The services for Yom Kippur still include confession of such offences as robbery, violence, blasphemy, unchastity.[23] Gaster makes sense of this for modern American Jews by pointing out that the confessions are in the first person plural and concern purification of the whole House of Israel.[24]

Νόμος: In Romans, νόμος first appears in Rom. 2.12, and from then on it presents problems of understanding and translation. The term refers to the Torah, which includes the law of Moses. In the situation in which this letter was written, it was often represented by that law. This is because of its function in forming Jewish identity both within Israel and over against the rest of the world. Its sociological function as a boundary marker was a major factor in the problems faced by the young church.

In Rom. 2.12–29, the Torah appears largely as something that has to be done, that is, as the law of Moses, and as such it is the criterion of judgement. In Rom. 2.17–20, the statements are about the whole of the Torah, God's revelation. But again, the emphasis is on the Torah as The Conservative thinks of it in this context, primarily as the law. On the other hand, the real agenda here is The

---

[20] Malherbe, *The Cynic Epistles*, p. 203, no. 4.

[21] *Paul, Judaism and the Gentiles*, 113–15. See also Schenk's discussion of temple robbery: 'ἱερός κτλ', *TDNT*, III, 255–6.

[22] *Conf.* 163.

[23] *The Authorized Daily Prayer Book of the United Hebrew Congregations of the British Commonwealth of Nations*, 353–4.

[24] *Festivals of the Jewish Year*, 137.

Conservative's habit of seeing Israel as privileged by God's election. The main role of the νόμος in Rom. 1.16–4.25 is as symbol of God's election of Israel.

God's righteousness: The Apostle's concern in Rom. 1.16–4.25 is with the question of God's righteousness. The Conservative's perception of that needs to change. We note a shifting of focus through the discussion from Rom. 1.18 to Rom. 2.29. The Apostle begins by speaking directly about the righteousness of God's judgement. By the end, the focus has shifted onto The Conservative's perception of God's righteousness as judge of Jew and Gentile. The Conservative has been led to a point where he has to recognize that God's righteousness as impartial judge does not allow for a privileged place for Jews.

Rom. 3.1–8 – teleological exposition

By Rom. 2.29, it seems that God's righteousness as impartial judge leaves no room for Israel's election. What, then, has become of God's righteousness as faithful covenant partner with Israel? It seems that God can be righteous in one way or the other, but not in both. The Apostle and The Conservative have come to a point where it seems that Israel's sin makes it impossible for God to be righteous. There must be something wrong somewhere. The Apostle shows The Conservative that something is wrong with his presuppositions.

He leads The Conservative very carefully and very dramatically through this discussion, using questions and answers in the diatribe style of a teacher who wants to make sure that the learner will grasp a difficult point. In this case, the point is difficult because The Apostle is driving The Conservative hard into the dilemma created by his own presuppositions. He raises the question The Conservative will want to ask, and then uses more questions to make The Conservative think carefully about what lies behind the question in his own mind and in the debates he has been hearing.

Paul was able to use this technique because of the oral character of even a written letter. Ὁ ἀναγινώσκων would prepare the reading, and present it much more dramatically than modern liturgical readers usually do. The opportunities and constraints of our print-literate milieu would oblige one of us to use different techniques to present such an argument. The concrete context of the teleological reading helps us to identify whose question each one is, whilst we remember that this is not a real dialogue. The Apostle uses the technique to take The Conservative's doubts and problems seriously, but he asks and answers all the questions. There is no chance for The Conservative to contribute something that will undermine his intention.

Rom. 3.1: The Apostle voices The Conservative's question, τί οὖν τὸ περισσὸν τοῦ Ἰουδαίου ἢ τίς ἡ ὠφέλεια τῆς περιτομῆς; What is left of Israel's election?

Rom. 3.2: The Apostle gives his own reply: πολὺ κατὰ πάντα τρόπον. πρῶτον μὲν γὰρ ὅτι ἐπιστεύθησαν τὰ λόγια τοῦ θεοῦ. He insists that God's faithfulness to Israel is not set aside. Israel's first advantage is having been entrusted with God's λόγια. This shifts the focus from the Sinai covenant, characterized for The Conservative by the Mosaic law, to all God's address to Israel, including law, promise and prophecy. These commit God to Israel, *and place obligation on Israel* (ἐπιστεύθησαν). The Conservative has not been considering that.

Rom. 3.3: To make explicit the real issue, The Apostle asks a question of his own, one that goes to the root of The Conservative's problem about God's faithfulness (Rom. 3.3a): τί γάρ; εἰ ἠπίστησάν τινες ...; Israel's unfaithfulness has raised the problem. Now it can be properly formulated (Rom. 3.3b): μὴ ἡ ἀπιστία αὐτῶν τὴν πίστιν τοῦ θεοῦ καταργήσει;

Rom. 3.4: The Apostle gives the only answer possible for The Conservative: μὴ γένοιτο. In ordinary covenants, a betrayed partner might consider himself released from his obligations, but the chosen people know from experience that God's faithfulness is not bound to Israel's. Still speaking as the voice of The Conservative, The Apostle offers scripture support for μὴ γένοιτο, spelling out the experience of history: γινέσθω δὲ ὁ θεὸς ἀληθής, πᾶς δὲ ἄνθρωπος ψεύστης, καθὼς γέγραπται·

> ὅπως ἂν δικαιωθῇς ἐν τοῖς λόγοις σου
> καὶ νικήσεις ἐν τῷ κρίνεσθαί σε.

Even if the situation were worse than suggested and everyone in Israel were false, God would still be true. The quotation from Ps. 51.4 (LXX 50.6), which The Conservative certainly affirms, shows the dilemma that results from wanting to make God's righteousness as faithful covenant partner exclude God's righteousness as judge who condemns the guilty when Israel is guilty. The sin of the sinner actually shows God's righteousness. The sentence of condemnation is the righteous response to the falsity of the covenant partner. Because of Israel's sin God will be acknowledged as righteous in the law-suit with Israel, righteous precisely as the judge who passes the proper sentence of condemnation.

Rom. 3.5: By forcing this answer, The Apostle has opened the way for a still sharper challenge. The next question is his own: εἰ δὲ ἡ ἀδικία ἡμῶν θεοῦ δικαιοσύνην συνίστησιν, τί ἐροῦμεν; μὴ ἄδικος ὁ θεὸς ὁ ἐπιφέρων τὴν ὀργήν;

He qualifies this question by saying that it is a merely human one; it really voices an opposition question: κατὰ ἄνθρωπον λέγω.

If God gains from Israel's sin, is it fair to punish the sinner? The Conservative might not want to put it like that, but that is the only logical ground on which sinful Israel could still want God to save Israel and be just at the same time. This logic is a travesty of God's righteousness and of Israel's experience.

Rom. 3.6: Speaking as The Conservative, The Apostle supplies the only answer possible for him: μὴ γένοιτο.

He justifies this with another shared axiom: ἐπεὶ πῶς κρινεῖ ὁ θεὸς τὸν κόσμον;

The judge of all the world is just, and God's justice includes visiting wrath on sinners.

Rom. 3.7–8: The Apostle goes on to work out this false logic as far as it will go, in a caustic *reductio ad absurdum* – which is not so absurd, after all, since it runs into a real charge brought against Paul: εἰ δὲ ἡ ἀλήθεια τοῦ θεοῦ ἐν τῷ ἐμῷ ψεύσματι ἐπερίσσευσεν εἰς τὴν δόξαν αὐτοῦ, τί ἔτι κἀγὼ ὡς ἁμαρτωλὸς κρίνομαι; (Rom. 3.7).

But if you object to being judged on the ground that your sin has enhanced God's glory, the next step is only a positive formulation of the same principle: καὶ μὴ καθὼς βλασφημούμεθα καὶ καθώς φασίν τινες ἡμᾶς λέγειν ὅτι ποιήσωμεν τὰ κακά, ἵνα ἔλθῃ τὰ ἀγαθά; (Rom. 3.8). 'And should we (as we are slandered and as some say that we say) do evil that good may come?' The Apostle goes past the negative answer he has invited, condemning the τινες who want to draw so patently false a conclusion from the Pauline preaching.

The Apostle has forced The Conservative into a cleft stick. He has given voice to The Conservative's objections to what has been said so far, and shown that there must be something wrong with them. They run into contradiction with axiomatic truths; they lead to blasphemy. There must be something more to be said.

Rom. 3.1–8 – methodological commentary

Basic to this teleological reading of Rom. 3.1–8 are our recognition of the nature of the text – The Apostle is in charge, Paul is preaching with authority to lead a co-operative audience into new truth – and Stowers' work, showing clearly that the diatribal question and answer constitute a positive teaching technique[25] rather than a defensive tactic. The difficulties some people had with Paul's preaching are taken seriously, but Paul was not allowing the questioners to set the terms of the discussion. He did that.

Contemporary literature provides examples of the technique The Apostle is using here. The most useful are in Epictetus' *Discourses*, because not all of them are fake dialogues like this one: II.24.1–10 is an example of his questioning of another person; II.9.2–7 an example of the teacher giving both the questions and the answers. In II.12.5–13 he describes Socrates' use of the technique. Its use here continues The Apostle's basic approach of leading The Conservative to recognize his own presuppositions and start to question them.

With this reading, we have found that the unsatisfactory outcome of the questioning is intentional, not something that has to be condemned, excused or smoothed over. The Conservative will need to find a way of coming to terms with the dilemma into which his presuppositions have led him. He will need this resolution for his peace of mind and way of life, because he has to find solid ground to stand on once more.

λόγια, Rom. 3.2: We take the broad sense because the original idea of oracles does not refer to any particular content, while the context involves the covenant in some sense, with stress on responsibility rather than privilege. With this stress The Apostle was taking up a hint in Rom. 2.8–10. Part of his correcting of the question that was being discussed in the church was to balance the privilege of election with the responsibility it entailed. The Conservative's questionings suggest that the former had been much more in evidence than the latter.

ἐν τῷ κρίνεσθαί σε, Rom. 3.4: We have accepted Wilckens' argument for the middle: the double formulation with ἐν (where with κρίνεσθαι as passive ἐκ or ἀπό would be expected) and the parallelism between νικήσεις and κρίνεσθαι, which suggests par-

---

[25] *The Diatribe and Paul's Letter to the Romans*, e.g. 76–7, 182–4.

allel descriptions of God's role.[26] Yet if half the Romans took it to refer to God being put in the dock and the other half to refer to God as judge, all of them would hear that God is justified in the sight of Israel as the result of a legal process. The difference is not critical for The Apostle's discourse.

Rom. 3.8: The fact that The Apostle has the initiative rules out readings with one question running from Rom. 3.7, since there is no reason for the change of subject. The piling up of separate questions serves the rhetoric better. The reading adopted, taking μή with ποιήσωμεν, and treating ὅτι as redundant but prompted by λέγειν, avoids reading the τί of Rom. 3.7b into Rom. 3.8, which does not suit the sequence of separate questions.

Rom. 3.9–20 – teleological exposition

The Conservative is having a hard time. The Apostle has convinced him that Israel's sin means that God can be just as eschatological judge or as Israel's saviour, but not both. He has then led him into the affirmation that Israel's experience shows that God is both faithful to the covenant and just judge of the world, and God's faithfulness is not dependent on Israel's. The conversation is about what this means for Israel at the judgement. The Apostle puts one more of The Conservative's questions, and then answers it:

> Question: You said we are no better off than the Gentiles at the judgement. Now you say that God is faithful to the covenant even when we are not. Are you saying after all that we Jews are preferred (προεχόμεθα)?
> Reply: Not at all (οὐ πάντως). (Rom. 3.9a)

Divine faithfulness does not mean that Jews will receive preferential treatment at God's just and impartial judgement. The Apostle goes on to show The Conservative what it does mean.

He begins with the reason he gives for οὐ πάντως. What has been established in Rom. 3.1–8 does not overset what was being recognized before it, that Jews and not just Gentiles are under sin. The charge of being under sin does not admit of degrees of guilt. One either is or is not in bondage. That has wiped out the difference that The Conservative hoped that having the law would make. The Apostle repeats the catch-phrase Ἰουδαῖός τε καὶ Ἕλλην, this time

---

[26] *Der Brief an die Römer*, I, p. 165 and n. 439.

without πρῶτον, emphasizing the exact equality (Rom. 3.9b).[27] Then he presents a battery of scripture texts to support the charge. The wording of the charge is about exact equality, and the texts seem to apply to everybody. A listener-in might hear all this as being about everybody, but The Conservative is not a listener-in. He hears in the 'everybody', as The Apostle intends, a further repudiation of the idea that Jews might be an exception. He does not need to be convinced about 'Gentile sinners', but he does need to be convinced about Israel. The Apostle makes his point explicit when he says that the law speaks to those within its domain, so that every mouth (Jew as well as Gentile) may be stopped and the whole world (Jew as well as Gentile) be answerable to God the judge (Rom. 3.19). The Conservative thought that having the law was going to mean that at God's righteous judgement righteous Israel would be justified (cf. Rom. 3.20a), but Israel's sin means that what the law does bring is knowledge of sin (Rom. 3.20b), as The Apostle's quotations have just demonstrated.

The Apostle has led The Conservative to confront the contra-dictions in presuppositions he has never before articulated and scrutinized. He has been afraid that an eschatological judge who justified believing sinners without distinguishing between Jew and Gentile must be unfaithful to the covenant with Israel. The Apostle has shown him that by his own criteria, the righteous eschatological judge is impartial and must treat Jew and Gentile alike. His objections really depended on the assumption that Israel would come to judgement as God's righteous and oppressed people. The Apostle has pushed the problem back to Israel's sin. On The Conservative's presuppositions, God could be righteous as eschato-logical judge only if Israel deserved the verdict Δίκαιος, and the law, the instrument of election, has shown that this is not the case. The eschatological judge seems to be in a dilemma. Either his righteousness as impartial judge must cancel out his saving right-eousness, with its connection with righteousness as faithfulness to Israel, or else he must do the unthinkable (Rom. 3.5–6) and save at the expense of impartial justice. It seems that human sin can nullify God's righteousness. The Apostle has claimed that in the gospel the righteousness of the judge is saving power for Jew and Gentile, and includes faithfulness to elect Israel (Rom. 1.16–17).

---

[27] The reading of A is best explained as an insertion on the model of Rom. 1.16; 2.9, 10.

Rom. 3.9–20 – methodological commentary

Rom. 3.9a: This verse offers a real challenge to our principle of preferring the most obvious reading of a difficult text. We must work out first what the text is, and then what is the most obvious way of reading it.

Most editors and commentators accept the most difficult reading, τι ουν προεχομεθα ου παντως. Dahl, O'Neill[28] and Dunn[29] accept the otherwise unattested reading of P, τι ουν προεχομεθα. After a thorough review of the textual evidence, Dahl concludes that 'the textual history leaves room for the possibility' that the P reading is older than the text usually accepted.[30] Beyond that, all three arguments rely on questions of meaning, and depend on the context of the justification account. Not being convinced by these arguments, we accept the difficult reading, which is well attested. Accepting ου παντως, we accept also the Nestle–Aland punctuation. A question with τί would not be answered with οὐ πάντως, and the position of γάρ is against separating πάντως from οὐ.

What is the most obvious way of reading this text? In correct usage, οὐ πάντως would have οὐ negating πάντως, and this can be taken to mean 'not absolutely'. The phrase occurs in 1 Cor. 5.10. Some commentators take the construction as correct and meaning 'not absolutely'.[31] This would mean that the Corinthians were not instructed to avoid evil-doers absolutely. In 1 Cor. 5.10–12, however, Paul is correcting their understanding of his earlier instruction. This favours the interpretation that he did not mean that they were to avoid the evil-doers of the world. Rather, they must avoid evil-doers among the brothers. This requires 'not at all', as do Epictetus' *Encheiridion* 1.5 and *Diognetus* IX.1. In 1 Cor. 16.12, Paul used πάντως οὐ for an emphatic negative, so his usage is not simply irregular. Thus, οὐ πάντως could be a qualified negative, although we have no Pauline example, or an emphatic correcting negative, for which we have a Pauline example. There are two questions about προεχόμεθα. Who are 'we'? The context, with The Apostle's address to The Conservative and the diatribe

---

[28] *Paul's Letter to the Romans*, 67–9.
[29] *Romans*, 146.
[30] 'Romans 3.9: Text and Meaning', 184–204, 192.
[31] e.g. Cranfield, *Romans*, I, 190; Vaughan, *Η ΠΡΟΣ ΡΩΜΑΙΟΥΣ ΕΠΙΣΤΟΛΗ*, 59.

form, identifies 'we' as The Apostle and The Conservative, believers who think of themselves as Jews. Should we take the verb as passive, middle or middle as active? The use of middle as active is not otherwise attested for this verb. As Lagrange observes, however, some of the text variants indicate that this was accepted by readers much closer to Paul than we are,[32] and our evidence is limited. As a middle, it would mean 'do we defend ourselves?'. This is ruled out by the immediate context. It would have to refer to the charge in Rom. 3.8, but this has already been swept aside. Further, Rom. 3.9b is offering a basis for οὐ πάντως, and the charge that all are under sin is not a ground for saying that the 'we' of Rom. 3.8 do not urge the doing of evil that good may come.[33] There is no philological objection to the passive, but the usage is scarcely attested. It is hard to say that there is an obvious reading of Rom. 3.9a.

What, then, is The Apostle saying to The Conservative with τί οὖν; προεχόμεθα; οὐ πάντως? Our interpretation takes the least objectionable meaning of προεχόμεθα, the passive. The meaning usually offered for it is, Are we excelled? In the context of mainstream interpretation, this has to be made acceptable as, Are we worse off? 'We' must then be 'we Jews', and the Jews must be worse off than the Gentiles, which is not impossible, but is difficult. We accept the reading offered by Olshausen,[34] Vaughan[35] and Liddon,[36] Are we preferred? This is a perfectly intelligible passive of a known Classical Greek use of the active. Text criticism on this verse has been done in the context of the justification-account reading. In that context, a reference to being preferred by God seems strained, and is open to the objection that it involves an unacceptable change in the subject of the verb. In The Apostle's dialogue with The Conservative, however, the natural question at this point is precisely one about God's preference. If The Apostle says that God will not favour Jews (Rom. 2.1–29) but then insists that God is faithful to the covenant even when Israel is not (Rom. 3.1–8), perhaps he will go on to say that God will give preference to Jews after all. Certainly The Conservative is entitled to ask the

---

[32] *Romains*, 68–9.
[33] Guerra's argument that it can be so read (*Romans and the Apologetic Tradition*, 70) requires the Romans to be listening for corollaries, not following the text as it is being read.
[34] *Der Brief des Apostels Paulus an die Römer*, 128.
[35] *Η ΠΡΟΣ ΡΩΜΑΙΟΥΣ ΕΠΙΣΤΟΛΗ*, 59.
[36] *Explanatory Analysis of Paul's Epistle to the Romans*, 64.

question, and The Apostle will want to make sure that it is asked and answered, not left as a possible source of confusion. We expect the answer, 'Not at all', and for the reason The Apostle gives in Rom. 3.9b. Thus, οὐ πάντως is functioning here as a correcting negative, as in 1 Cor. 5.10. It rejects a wrong understanding of something that has been said and leads on to its replacement with a right one. In the setting of a diatribal encounter between The Apostle and The Conservative, there is no problem with a change of subject. In the diatribe, 'we' is the 'we' of the conversation. In this passage, the exception comes in Rom. 3.8, where the change of reference is readily intelligible.

Rom. 3.21–6 – teleological exposition

The Conservative's dilemma focusses on the law as symbol of God's righteousness, God's constant electing grace and impartiality as judge. Seeing this righteousness in the framework provided by his previously unexplored understanding of the law, he has been led to an impossible point: Israel's unrighteousness cancels the possibility of God being righteous and the possibility of anybody being saved. That is not the truth of The Conservative's life in God. He has known Israel's God as faithful saviour, and in Christ he knows that Gentiles are being brought under God's mercy, too. His problem is not with that fact, but with the terms on which it happens.

The Apostle says, 'But now God's righteousness has been made manifest apart from the law, being witnessed to by the law and the prophets' (Rom. 3.21). The reference to the gospel is obvious. What The Apostle stresses is the relationship of the new revelation of God's righteousness (νυνὶ δέ) to the earlier one. It is apart from the law, the marker of Israel's specialness and the instrument of a judgement that no one deserves the verdict Δίκαιος. At the same time, the law and the prophets bear witness to it. That is, it is new action of Israel's God, in continuity with his former action. The Apostle is not preaching some new God. The God of the gospel has not abandoned what he was doing with Israel but fulfilled it. This is both reassurance and challenge for The Conservative.

In Rom. 3.22, The Apostle goes on showing the newness of the new revelation. God's righteousness is now manifest and effective through 'Christ faith', faith in Jesus Christ. So far, The Conservative has no problem. That is the new truth he has found in the gospel. Salvation is in Christ. 'For everyone who has faith', The Apostle continues. This picks up χωρὶς νόμου. He has returned to his starting point, but this time 'for all who believe' is not the root of a dilemma, as it seemed in Rom. 1.16–17, but a necessary part of the solution contained in God's action. If it is through faith in Christ, then it is for all who have such faith, Jew and Gentile. The Apostle goes on to show how this resolves The Conservative's dilemma: 'For there is no distinction, for all have sinned and lack the glory of God, being justified freely' (Rom. 3.22d–24a). This is the judgement and salvation that is the power of the gospel. The Conservative has not wanted to accept that there is no distinction in justification because he assumed that there was distinction in the matters of sin and the glory of God. The gospel confirms the law's judgement of condemnation, but adds to it the judgement of justification. There is no distinction between Jew and Gentile as sinners; there is no distinction between Jew and Gentile as receivers of the verdict Δίκαιος. God's righteousness is effective for all who have faith, solely on the basis of their faith, that is, in this context, without reference to their membership of Israel.

The Apostle goes on to remind The Conservative of what he knows about *how* God the righteous and impartial judge gives to sinners the verdict Δίκαιος. It is by an act of grace (τῇ αὐτοῦ χάριτι Rom. 3.24a), διὰ τῆς ἀπολυτρώσεως τῆς ἐν Χριστῷ Ἰησοῦ· ὃν προέθετο ὁ θεὸς ἱλαστήριον διὰ τῆς πίστεως ἐν τῷ αὐτοῦ αἵματι (Rom. 3.24b–25a). Something has been added to the righteousness of the just judge, something that corresponds to the righteousness of Israel's saviour. It has been added ἐν Χριστῷ Ἰησοῦ, that is, again, χωρὶς νόμου.

There is ἀπολύτρωσις in Christ by virtue of the fact that God set him forth as a ἱλαστήριον. Here is the just judge condemning sinners. Everyone who needs and accepts redemption that is in a ἱλαστήριον is receiving from the judge the verdict Ἄξιος θανάτου. Yet in this very act of condemnation, the judge is dealing with the sin of the sinner. Two aspects of sin appeared in The Apostle's earlier discussion, sin's power over the sinner, and the sinner's responsible action. Because they had known God and refused him glory and thanks, God had given them up, so that they sinned more and more, ultimately wilfully defying God (Rom. 1.19–32). Jew has no advantage over Gentile before God's judgement because all are ὑφ' ἁμαρτίαν (Rom. 3.9b). Through Christ's death, sinners are being set free from the power of sin that was preventing them from receiving the verdict Δίκαιος. This redemption is in Christ Jesus, whom God set forth as a ίλαστήριον. We listeners-in cannot be sure exactly what this term meant to The Apostle and The Conservative, but it is clear that a ίλαστήριον deals with the effects of sinning, guilt and ever deeper bondage. The Apostle has not hesitated to insist on the accountability of those who were given up to sin. Because of their wilful disobedience, they are ἄξιοι θανάτου (Rom. 1.32a). Since the law condemns Jew along with Gentile, the whole world is ὑπόδικος ... τῷ θεῷ (Rom. 3.19b).

Thus, in the one act which is proclaimed in the gospel, God has acted both as just judge and as saviour. The Conservative knows already that his faith in Christ is faith in the one who died for his sin, but he has not until now looked into his own expectation and seen the judgement in the light of the Cross. He was expecting that God would judge impartially according to works and recognize righteous Israel. Instead, God has been doing what he did so often for unrighteous Israel, bringing Israel back from sin. And now, in the gospel of the Cross, God is doing that in a way that breaks the bounds of Israel.

The Apostle's account of the How of God's saving action has been brief because none of it needed explaining. It did need to be put into its proper context for The Conservative with his old ideas. The Apostle turns now to deal much more fully with the Why. He spells out for The Conservative certain implications of the Cross. Why did God do it in this way? Precisely, The Apostle explains carefully, so that God may be seen to be righteous and may be righteous. In setting forth Christ as a ίλαστήριον God demonstrated righteousness in two respects. The first is 'because of the passing over of former sins in the patience of God' (Rom. 3.25b–26a). God revealed the righteous judgement of wrath against sin first by giving up the sinners. The result was that they sinned more and more, in defiance of God's known judgement that those who do such things are worthy of death. There was still a judgement to come, as The Conservative expected. 'The passing over of former sins' refers to the delaying of the final judgement in the patience of God. We can understand what this would say to The Conservative by looking at Rom. 1.24–2.11. He would not need to be reminded. In the Cross, the final judgement has come down on the sins that were committed before that event. Their offence has been dealt with through the ίλαστήριον. Thus, God is seen to be just as judge in dealing with those sins. The second respect is 'for the demonstration of his righteousness in the present time' (Rom. 3.26). The present is the time of the sending and receiving of the letter, the present for The Apostle and The Conservative. It is characterized over against the time of God's wrath by the fact that the ἱλαστήριον has been set forth, God's righteousness has been revealed in the new way, believing sinners are being justified. The purpose of all this is 'that he might be righteous even in justifying the one who believes in Jesus' (Rom. 3.26). The note of surprise in καί is not there because God was plunged into a dilemma by sin. It is there because The Conservative has been finding it so hard to believe that the gospel really does mean that God justifies on the basis of faith alone – and this should be reflected in Jew–Gentile relationships in the church. Ὁ ἐκ πίστεως Ἰησοῦ stands before God's judgement as a believer. That is all there is to be said about that person. Nothing else counts.

God, The Apostle has affirmed, is righteous and saving eschatological judge. God saves righteously through the new revelation of divine righteousness, apart from the law, a redemption which is in Christ and received by faith. He passes the judgement of justification by dealing with the sin in the very action that conveys the judgement to the sinner. Acting consistently with his former action with Israel, and thus showing himself to be Israel's God, he has broken the bounds of Israel.

This account has resolved The Conservative's dilemma. It has shown how the insistence on faith as all that is required for membership of the church arises from what God did in Christ. Far from showing God as unfaithful to Israel's election, it has proved to be the means of God's faithfulness. If this is right, The Conservative has been misunderstanding God's election of Israel. The Apostle goes on to show that this is so, and to show what is the proper understanding in the light of God's new action in the Cross.

Rom. 3.21–6 – methodological commentary

In reading this pericope we have reaped the harvest of our re-examination of its grammar and meaning in chapter 6. In the context of the whole, we have been able to see more clearly the nature of the question that was set over God's righteousness, and identify the way it is tackled. The result is a reading in which grammar and meaning cohere, and in which The Conservative's problem – that a God who justifies believers without reference to the Jew–Gentile distinction must be unfaithful to the covenant with Israel – is finally overcome.

Rom. 3.22, 26: διὰ πίστεως Ἰησοῦ Χριστοῦ; τὸν ἐκ πίστεως Ἰησοῦ: The teleological exposition reflects the conclusion that in each of these phrases the reference is primarily to the faith of the believer. God's righteousness is manifest and effective through faith in Jesus Christ for all who believe, not for Jews who believe and Gentiles who believe and become Jews. God is righteous even in justifying the one of whom there is nothing to be said but, This person believes in Jesus. Many scholars now hold that the references are primarily to the faith(fulness) of Christ. Although the proposal is much older, this case has been argued vigorously from the 1950s. The debate is remarkable for its inconclusiveness, since the grammatical/semantic, exegetical and theological evidence is all capable of being seen to support either case. Why have we not been persuaded by the arguments for the subjective genitive?

Essentially, this is because we and the participants in the debate are asking different questions. The case for the subjective genitive is argued on the assumption that the phrase under consideration is πίστις Χριστοῦ, that the focussing question is that of the nature of the genitive, and that the contexts in which Paul uses the phrase are all concerned with the role of faith in justification. We do not accept any of these assumptions. The usual procedure is to describe Paul's concept, decide whether Christ's or the believer's πίστις is uppermost in it, translate the phrase accordingly, and slot the result into each of Paul's expositions of justification by faith. We hold that the phrases have to be considered separately in their contexts, and a teleological reading can show the context to be more particular.

The phrases do form a group, and they all appear in what was apparently a continuing debate which surfaces in several passages in Paul's letters – Rom. 3.21–6; 4; 9.30–10.21; Gal. 2.15–4.7; Phil. 3.2–11. The problem was whether Gentiles who believed had to become Jews, and this takes different forms. These passages contain about half of all the uses of the πίστις–πιστεύω vocabulary in the extant letters. Πίστις often appears in the phrases ἐκ πίστεως and διὰ [τῆς] πίστεως, which are contrasted with such phrases as ἐκ νόμου and ἐξ ἔργων, and set alongside others with the same form, such as ἐξ ἐπαγγελίας and διὰ δικαιοσύνης πίστεως. In a few cases, ἐκ/διὰ πίστεως is qualified, usually with Ἰησοῦ, Χριστοῦ or both, but with Ἀβραάμ in Rom. 4.16. It seems

likely that this was a pattern of speech hammered out in the course
of the debates. Accordingly, we have asked not what Paul means by
πίστις Χριστοῦ, but what Paul was intending to communicate to
the church in question with the ἐκ/διὰ πίστεως phrase qualified
with a name of Christ. This formulation leads us to concur with
Hultgren's proposal that the genitive Χριστοῦ or variant is a
genitive of quality[37] – 'Christ faith' – and then to ask in each case
whether the genitive has a subjective or an objective nuance.

We have argued that the issue in Rom. 3.21–6 is not how people
are justified. The fact that God justifies believing sinners is part of
the common ground between The Apostle and The Conservative,
Paul and the Romans. The question is whether God can do that
righteously without requiring believing Gentiles to add something
to their faith in Christ. Accordingly, considering the text as
communication, we conclude that in these two cases the genitive of
quality has an objective nuance, faith in Christ. There is no
question of redundancy in Rom. 3.22, and the subjective genitive
reading is scarcely an option for Rom. 3.26 in the context of our
reading of the whole passage, which has the advantage at Rom.
3.26 of making good sense of the καί. The passage is part of a
debate in which we should expect πίστις to refer to the faith of
believers unless something else was clearly indicated by the context,
as in Rom. 3.3.

This does not mean that we have excluded Christ's faith(fulness)
from Paul's concept of faith, only that we have concluded that Paul
was not talking about it here. He was talking to the Romans about
the relationship between God's righteousness and the faith of
believers. In this discussion, Christ very properly has a completely
passive role. God set him forth.

Rom. 3.22: δικαιοσύνη δὲ θεοῦ διὰ πίστεως Ἰησοῦ Χριστοῦ
requires some verbal supplement for us to explicate it. Rom. 3.22
continues the sentence begun in Rom. 3.21, with δικαιοσύνη θεοῦ
repeated for emphasis. Διὰ πίστεως is the positive completion of
the negative χωρὶς νόμου. The verb in the context is πεφανέρωται.
This must carry over for listeners. The choice of διά with πίστις,
however, indicates that the manifest righteousness is not simply
open to view but being seen in action. We have therefore taken the
verbal connection to be 'manifest and effective'. By its nature,
God's righteousness could not be manifest without being effective,

---

[37] 'The Pistis Christou Formulation in Paul', 257.

and it is manifest in the gospel, to believers. As listeners-in, we can make the confirming observation that this is parallel with the structure of Rom. 1.16–17, although this detail could hardly be still in the minds of speaker and hearers.

Rom. 3.24–6: We have read The Apostle's preaching on the basis that it is an original presentation that relies on concepts familiar to The Congregation, notably to The Conservative. He is reminding The Conservative of what he knows about how God justifies believers for the sake of discussing why God does it through the Cross, and he selects the elements of his reminder accordingly. We have rejected the hypothesis that Paul modified a traditional formulation. If that hypothesis were correct, we should need to consider again what The Apostle is doing. Why have we rejected it? On what basis have we then understood the difficult terms?

First, we have found it unnecessary. The 'problems' that led to its formulation have not proved to be problems. Δικαιούμενοι is not an impossible disjunction,[38] but is properly related to πάντες (Rom. 3.23). On our reading it is thoroughly appropriate, since the participle links free justification, the new element of equality, closely with the two already established. The relative ὅν could come from a liturgical setting, but is perfectly natural in the sentence as it stands.[39]

Some of the words are said to be un-Pauline, notably ἱλαστήριον, αἷμα, πάρεσις. The only other use of ἱλαστήριον in the NT is Heb. 9.5, which is not comparable. Before we call it un-Pauline we should ask where else in the extant letters we might expect Paul to use it. Even when this passage is seen as one of several theoretical accounts of salvation through the Cross, it would be hard to find a close parallel where we cannot see good reasons for the choice of other terms. The reference to blood is part of the definition of Christ as ἱλαστήριον, and it is paralleled in Rom. 5.9, which is an extension of this discussion into its eschatological implications. Similarly, πάρεσις is to be accepted as Paul's because of its specific function in the discussion.

The style is sometimes described as oratorical or proclamatory. This is appropriate to the preaching situation and the subject-

---

[38] Wengst, *Formeln*, 87; with BDF §468; Sanday and Headlam, *Romans*, 85–6; Schlier, *Der Römerbrief*, 107; Kuss, *Römerbrief*, I, 114.

[39] Schlier (*Römerbrief*, 109) rejects the suggestion that the relative is evidence of a quotation.

matter. The objection to it arises from the unconscious identification of the text as theological exposition. The charge that it is overloaded is applied especially to the apparent doubling of δωρεάν with τῇ αὐτοῦ χάριτι, and to the insertion of διὰ τῆς πίστεως between ἱλαστήριον and αἷμα. In the teleological reading the former is not a doubling. For the latter, both 'faith' and 'blood' are important to The Apostle, and faith, being the point at issue, should come first. The main reason for the impression of overload is the wrong identification of the text as theological exposition of justification. That makes this passage an unsatisfying climax.

Käsemann finds verses 25 and 26 inconsistent,[40] but we do not. His position is an extreme expression of the problem of traditional justification readings that it is hard to make sense of Rom. 3.25b–26 when δικαιοσύνη θεοῦ is seen only as God's saving action.

The hypothesis of a pre-Pauline formula is weakened by the demonstration that it is unnecessary, and by the variety of reconstructions offered, but neither of these factors rules it out. We have rejected it on these grounds together with two more. First, The Apostle's proclamation is much more specific than Paul's explanation of God's saving action through the Cross in more traditional interpretations. It is therefore less likely that an appropriate liturgical formulation would have been available, while the text as it stands is appropriate to The Apostle's purpose. Second, we should not expect that quoting and modifying a familiar liturgical formulation in the course of a longer address would be an effective way of correcting people's theological understanding. If modern congregations are any example, such treatment of any formula sufficiently well known to serve the proposed purpose would be more likely to raise annoyance and hostility.

Δικαιούμενοι, Rom. 3.24a: We take this to mean 'being given the verdict Righteous'. That is the issue in The Apostle's preaching, which is the subject of our teleological reading. The further question of what Paul understood that it means to be justified belongs to causal reading.

Ἀπολύτρωσις (Rom. 3.24b), ἱλαστήριον (Rom. 3.25a): These terms The Apostle uses without explanation, obviously assuming that they are familiar. Whence that familiarity? Why have we interpreted them as we have? As terms belonging in the gospel

---

[40] *Commentary on Romans*, 99.

context, they could be familiar only through worship or teaching. Both have roots in Jewish tradition. Both are rich images, and would function as images in worship. In our teleological reading, we are trying to understand how they would function in the particular setting of The Apostle's preaching here.

Ἀπολύτρωσις means 'redemption'. The word would carry echoes of the Exodus and of sacral manumission of slaves. Redemption normally carries the idea of being bought out of bondage. When this text is read as theological exposition, this becomes an exegetical problem. For teleological exposition, the dilemma that has to be resolved through the action of the eschatological judge controls our reading. Those who stand before the judge are in bondage to sin, and redemption is redemption from that bondage. To follow what is being said, we do not need to know whether The Apostle and The Conservative, Paul and the Romans, thought of a price being paid or of God bringing Israel out of Egypt without paying any price to Pharaoh. Because the communication does not require this, it would be sheer accident if the information were available from the context. This is one practical consequence of the fact that the text is created by the author's intention.

In the mainstream debate, argument rages over the meaning of ἱλαστήριον. Again, the problems arise because Paul's account of the Atonement is being sought and he was not trying to give it. The few examples in the context literature do not give us a full picture of the concept ἱλαστήριον, but we know enough to follow what The Apostle is saying to The Conservative. A ἱλαστήριον deals with the effects of sin, guilt and ever deeper bondage, and that is why judgement in the form of a ἱλαστήριον can be a verdict of Δίκαιος on sinners who receive it. Exploring what more we can learn will help with causal exposition.

Πάρεσις, Rom. 3.25b: Against the line of interpretation following Kümmel's important article,[41] we have read 'passing over' not 'forgiveness'. Kümmel does not consider that he has proved on linguistic grounds that πάρεσις should be taken to mean 'forgiveness', only that it can very well mean that and this is the reading that makes sense in the context. This is because he understands the context as an account of God's saving righteousness, with no issue of theodicy. The main objection to 'passing over' is that it involves

---

[41] 'Paresis und Endeixis: Ein Beitrag zum Verständnis der paulinischen Rechtfertigungslehre'.

assigning to the patience of God a time that is before the time referred to in ἐν τῷ νῦν καιρῷ, and that time has been characterized as being under the wrath of God. Wilckens argues convincingly that the idea of a time in which final judgement has not yet come and people are storing up for themselves punishment or reward is part of the tradition.[42] It is taken up in the NT, including Rom. 2.4–10.

Rom. 3.27–4.25 – teleological exposition

The Apostle has shown The Conservative that God is indeed righteous in justifying believers on the basis of faith without distinguishing between Jew and Gentile. The good news of salvation through Christ at the final judgement is the fulfilment of God's faithfulness to Israel – not to righteous and oppressed Israel over against the Gentiles, but to unfaithful Israel, standing with the Gentiles before God's judgement. But there is more to the claim that Israel's election is not cancelled by the gospel. The Apostle now turns to helping The Conservative to see Israel's history in the light of God's new action in Christ, showing him that this apparently new thing was God's intention in the election of Israel.

In handling this issue, The Apostle is again moving close to the question of The Conservative's understanding of his own identity. He aims to lead him into a truer but different understanding. Because it is different, and it demands changes to deep-seated attitudes and cherished practices, it will not be easy to accept. Once again, he uses the question and answer technique that draws in the listener.

He raises the question of boasting. Boasting is the expression of the way The Conservative misunderstood the meaning of election and the gift of the Torah that symbolized it. 'Where, then' – in the light of God's action in Christ (οὖν, Rom. 3.27) – 'is boasting? It is excluded. By what kind of a law?' The Apostle suggests first the answer he provided earlier. The Conservative was forced to recognize that Israel's boasting over against the Gentiles was excluded by failure to demonstrate superiority in living out the law. Instead, the law set Israel with the Gentiles under God's judgement (Rom. 2.17–24; 3.9–20). [Νόμος] τῶν ἔργων (Rom. 3.27) would have been the answer if the question had been asked after Rom. 3.20, but now

The Apostle rejects it. In the light of God's action in Christ, boasting is excluded by a different kind of law, a law of faith. He defines this: λογιζόμεθα γὰρ δικαιοῦσθαι πίστει ἄνθρωπον χωρὶς ἔργων νόμου (Rom. 3.28). His definition provides a summary of the relevance of his previous point (Rom. 3.21–6) for the question he is now asking. He is making a wry pun on νόμος. The Conservative has been thinking of God's self-revelation in Israel's Torah in terms of the Mosaic law understood especially as commandment requiring obedient action. God's righteousness has now been revealed both χωρὶς νόμου and μαρτυρουμένη ὑπὸ τοῦ νόμου (Rom. 3.21), and the revelation has confronted him with a new 'law', the principle of justification on the basis of faith alone. The law of works excludes the boast Israel had thought she had; the law of faith excludes the possibility of having a boast. Now it is not Israel's failure that excludes boasting, but God's gracious action in Christ.

Furthermore, if The Conservative really believes that God is one, he should be able to see that this is only right. 'Is God the God of the Jews only? Is he not God of the Gentiles also? Yes, of the Gentiles also. If God, who will justify the circumcision on the basis of faith, really is one, he will also justify the uncircumcision through faith' (Rom. 3.29–30). The Conservative with his mono-theistic faith takes it as axiomatic that Israel's God is God of the Gentiles also. God's oneness has a consequence he must take to heart: the one God of both will treat Gentiles as he treats Jews, justifying on the basis of faith. This, The Apostle has shown, God does and does righteously (Rom. 3.21–6).

In the earlier discussion, The Apostle has shown The Conserva-tive that Jewish sinner is no different from Gentile sinner before God's judgement. Eventually, it seemed that there was nothing left of God's covenant with Israel, and The Apostle confronted The Conservative with some of the inconsistencies in his thinking (Rom. 3.1–8). Now, on the positive side, The Apostle has shown that justified Jew is no different from justified Gentile before God's grace. Again, The Conservative is troubled. Is there anything left of God's election of Israel? Once Israel's difference has gone, it seems that Israel's election has gone. Thus The Conservative faces again the vital question about God's faithfulness. The Apostle states it as sharply as possible: νόμον οὖν καταργοῦμεν διὰ τῆς πίστεως; (Rom. 3.31a).

This is a question about what 'we' do. It is not asking whether

God has made the law of no effect. It is asking whether 'we', the discussion partners, have reached a point in our engagement with the gospel where we are faced with this unacceptable conclusion. If so, 'we' are wrong and shall have to try again. The question is not just about the νόμος as the commandments, but about the whole Torah. The Torah shapes Jewish life and mediates the consciousness of being God's people. The law of commandments is a tangible symbol of this. Through keeping the commandments Israel is marked off from the Gentiles, and the commandments have forced up the issue sharply in the life of the church.

Having posed the question thus sharply, The Apostle negates it as sharply: μὴ γένοιτο· ἀλλὰ νόμον ἱστάνομεν (Rom. 3.31b). In preaching this gospel, we most certainly do not make the Torah of no effect. On the contrary, we establish it. We establish the Torah, the symbol of God's faithfulness and call. We do so by showing that it cannot provide a ground for boasting, a basis for expecting privileged treatment from God – which seems to be tantamount to taking away its role as instrument and mark of Israel's identity. If The Apostle can establish this claim, The Conservative's problems will be more than overcome. He will be able to see himself and the church as participating in the fulfilment of God's purpose. But can The Apostle establish it? The grounds on which he might do so could hardly be said to spring to mind without further prompting!

The Apostle invites The Conservative to look carefully at Abraham, beginning with a question that is challenging almost to the point of being offensive: 'What, then, shall we say? That we have found Abraham to be our forefather according to the flesh?' (Rom. 4.1). The Conservative will certainly want to give a strongly negative answer. As a Jew, he will find a conclusion that Abraham is forefather κατὰ σάρκα wholly inadequate. Jews do not revere Abraham simply because they are descended from him. What makes Abraham a figure to be reverenced is the fact that God made the covenant with Abraham. He is προπάτωρ. In him Israel is elect. As a Jew who believes in Christ, The Conservative will have other reasons for finding the conclusion unacceptable. If 'we', the 'we' of Rom. 3.31, have searched the scriptures and our hearts and the church's experience of God's action, and have found that for believers Abraham is *reduced to* being forefather κατὰ σάρκα, then election and the covenant have gone for nothing – and the God of the gospel is not the faithful God of Israel.

If The Apostle's claim (Rom. 3.31b) is to stand, the answer to the question should be, No, we have not found Abraham to be our forefather κατὰ σάρκα. The Apostle does not answer with μὴ γένοιτο. Instead, he comments on the question: εἰ γὰρ Ἀβραὰμ ἐξ ἔργων ἐδικαιώθη, ἔχει καύχημα (Rom. 4.2a). If Abraham has ground for boasting, he will be cut off from all whose failure to live up to the law excluded boasting (Rom. 3.27a), and he will be a witness against the 'law of faith' (Rom. 3.27b–28) which denies The Apostle and The Conservative any possibility of having ground for boasting. Their connection with Abraham will be reduced to physical descent, he will be forefather κατὰ σάρκα, and The Apostle's claim will fall.

The Apostle's comment is worded to allow the possibility that Abraham was justified on the basis of works. In that case he would be not only a witness against the 'law of faith' (Rom. 3.27–8) but also a witness for The Conservative's old idea of Israel's election (Rom. 2.17–20). If Abraham has ground for boasting, God started out in Israel's election by justifying on the basis of doing the law. His new action is then inconsistent with the Torah. He has been unfaithful to elect Israel. But The Apostle asserts that Abraham has no ground for boasting before God (Rom. 4.2b). Gen. 15.6 is the basis for that assertion, and he introduces it with a flourish to mark its importance: τί γὰρ ἡ γραφὴ λέγει; (Rom. 4.3a).[43] The scripture says, ἐπίστευσεν δὲ Ἀβραὰμ τῷ θεῷ καὶ ἐλογίσθη αὐτῷ εἰς δικαιοσύνην (Rom. 4.3b). Abraham has no ground for boasting because he 'believed God and it was reckoned to him for righteousness'. Is that unassailable ground for saying that Abraham has no καύχημα and so cannot have been justified on the basis of works?

In the context of Rom. 3.21–8, it would be. There, people have no boast through the law and, being justified on the basis of faith, are justified apart from works. Rom. 4.2–3 moves Abraham from being justified ἐξ ἔργων to being justified ἐκ πίστεως. But this distinction is part of the new gospel context The Apostle has been creating, the new context that has forced the question, νόμον οὖν καταργοῦμεν διὰ τῆς πίστεως; (Rom. 3.31a). In The Conservative's old context, things are different. Abraham's righteousness is closely connected with works, even with works of the law:

---

[43] In a few cases where a scripture citation is very important, we see Paul using a substantial introductory question like this – Gal. 4.30; Rom. 11.4.

For Abraham was perfect in all of his actions with the
Lord and was pleasing through righteousness all of the
days of his life.   (Jub. 23.10a)

ὑπήκουσεν Ἀβραὰμ ὁ πατήρ σου τῆς ἐμῆς φωνῆς καὶ
ἐφύλαξεν τὰ προστάγματά μου καὶ τὰς ἐντολάς μου καὶ τὰ
δικαιώματά μου καὶ τὰ νόμιμά μου.   (Gen. 26.5, LXX)

Moreover, Abraham's πίστις makes him πιστός, faithful, and this
is reckoned to him for righteousness:

Ἀβραὰμ οὐχὶ ἐν πειρασμῷ εὑρέθη πιστός, καὶ ἐλογίσθη
αὐτῷ εἰς δικαιοσύνην;   (1 Macc. 2.52)

He is seen in this light in the very context of the giving of the
covenant:

Ἀβραὰμ μέγας πατὴρ πλήθους ἐθνῶν,
καὶ οὐχ εὑρέθη ὅμοιος ἐν τῇ δόξῃ·
ὃς συνετήρησεν νόμον ὑψίστου
καὶ ἐγένετο ἐν διαθήκῃ μετ' αὐτοῦ·
ἐν σαρκὶ αὐτοῦ ἔστησεν διαθήκην
καὶ ἐν πειρασμῷ εὑρέθη πιστός·
διὰ τοῦτο ἐν ὅρκῳ ἔστησεν αὐτῷ
ἐνευλογηθῆναι ἔθνη ἐν σπέρματι αὐτοῦ,
πληθῦναι αὐτὸν ὡς χοῦν τῆς γῆς
καὶ ὡς ἄστρα ἀνυψῶσαι τὸ σπέρμα αὐτοῦ
καὶ κατακληρονομῆσαι αὐτοὺς
ἀπὸ θαλάσσης ἕως θαλάσσης
καὶ ἀπὸ ποταμοῦ ἕως ἄκρου τῆς γῆς.   (Sir. 44.19–21)

Accordingly, Gen. 15.6 *must be shown to be* ground for saying that
Abraham has no boast before God and thus was not justified on
the basis of works. The text is well chosen. Abraham's πίστις
appears in verb form: ἐπίστευσεν, he believed. Further, the word
of God that he believed was the promise of innumerable seed.

The Apostle goes on to build on the advantage. In the matter of
reckoning righteousness, he separates faith from works: 'Now for
one who works, the reward is not reckoned as a matter of grace,
but as a matter of obligation' (Rom. 4.4). In that case he has earned
his reward and has a claim on the giver. He is like the Jew, whoever
he was, who expected God to vindicate righteous and oppressed
Israel. This is the case of the one who has ground for boasting. 'But
to the one who does not work but trusts in the one who justifies the

ungodly, his faith is reckoned for righteousness' (Rom. 4.5). This is the case of Abraham, the reckoning of Gen. 15.6. In Rom. 4.6–8, The Apostle supports this with a quotation from Ps. 31.1–2a (LXX). It speaks of the blessedness of those to whom righteousness is reckoned apart from works as the blessedness of those whose sins the Lord does not reckon, again placing Abraham with the believers of Rom. 3.21–8. God began with Abraham as he intended to go on with believers in Christ.

The Apostle has made his case for saying that Abraham has no ground for boasting, so that 'we' have not reduced him to being forefather κατὰ σάρκα (Rom. 4.1) and thus made the Torah of no effect (Rom. 3.31a). He is not, however, aiming for that merely negative point, so he goes on immediately with the rest of his answer. The nature of Abraham's forefatherhood does not depend simply on Abraham, but also on the nature of his seed. The next step (οὖν, Rom. 4.9a) is to ask whether this blessing is on the circumcision (which can be taken for granted) or also on the uncircumcision. He directs attention again to Gen. 15.6, the basis of the argument, summarizing the relevant point rather than repeating the whole verse: λέγομεν γάρ· ἐλογίσθη τῷ Ἀβραὰμ ἡ πίστις εἰς δικαιοσύνην (Rom. 4.9b). Thus, he equates Abraham's πίστις with his believing, and directs attention again to the reckoning of righteousness. In Rom. 4.10, he draws the conclusion very carefully. He does not simply give the answer, but takes The Conservative through a question and answer process that gives him no chance to miss the point. Πῶς οὖν ἐλογίσθη; (Rom. 4.10a). The possible alternatives are set out, and only then is the conclusion drawn, first negatively and then positively. Abraham's faith was reckoned to him for righteousness when he was in a state of uncircumcision, not of circumcision, and he received the sign of circumcision as a seal of the righteousness that he had while he was still uncircumcised (Rom. 4.10b–11a). It happened this way so that he should be father of the uncircumcised who believe, so that their faith will be reckoned to them for righteousness, and father of the circumcised who are not only circumcised but walk in the footsteps of the faith our father Abraham had while uncircumcised (Rom. 4.11b–12). Abraham's story interprets the symbol of circumcision.

The Apostle can now say, We have found Abraham to be our forefather not κατὰ σάρκα but κατὰ πίστιν. He has not, however, finished with his question. He asked it for the sake of demonstrating that this gospel establishes the Torah (Rom. 3.31). Abraham's story is The Conservative's story, and there is more to explore.

'For (γάρ) the promise to Abraham and his seed that they should inherit the world was not through law but through the righteousness of faith' (Rom. 4.13). That is, the seed had to be seed on the basis of faith to match the nature of the promise, for if only those who were seed on the basis of law were heirs, faith would have been emptied – so why justify Abraham on the basis of faith? – and the promise brought to nothing (Rom. 4.14). This is because the law works wrath, as the discussion of God's righteous judgement has shown painfully clearly (Rom. 4.15a; 2.12–3.20). The promise operates in a different framework (Rom. 4.15b). It is because of this reality of fallen human life that the promise is on the basis of faith, so that it is a matter of grace (Rom. 4.16a). Promise is not by definition separate from law. There is such a thing as a conditional promise: 'I will give you this land if ...'. God's promise is not conditional, because to be capable of fulfilment it must rest on God's grace alone.

Not only did the seed have to be defined by faith to match the promise, but the promise had to be by faith to match the seed. In Abraham's story, the seed to whom the promise was made were themselves children of promise. That promise made Abraham the father not just of numberless descendants (Gen. 15.5; 22.17) but of many nations (Rom. 4.17a; Gen. 17.4–6; Sir. 44.19a). So The Apostle says that it had to be by grace to be firm for all the seed, not only those who were seed on the basis of the law, but also the 'faith seed' of Abraham, the father of us believers, Jew and Gentile. This fact cannot be stressed too much in the face of The Conservative's lifelong presuppositions. Abraham is the father of us all, according to the authority of scripture and through the promise in scripture. He is the father of us all in the sight of God in whom he believed, who gives life to the dead and calls into being things that are not. The Conservative can recognize that God as Israel's[44] and also as the God of those who believe in Christ (Rom. 4.17b).

Believing Abraham is father of the seed defined by faith, and he became father through his faith (εἰς τὸ γενέσθαι, Rom. 4.18). The Apostle describes this faith. Abraham believed in hope against hope, and he did not weaken in unbelief when he considered the

---

[44] cf. Philo, *Spec. Leg.* IV.187; 2 Baruch 48.8; Joseph and Aseneth 8.9. Käsemann cites the second of the Eighteen Benedictions (*Commentary on Romans*, 121).

human realities of the situation, which put the fulfilment of the promise beyond human hope (Rom. 4.19).[45] Rather, he trusted God's promise, not wavering in unbelief, but being strengthened in faith. 'Giving glory to God and being fully persuaded that what he has promised he is indeed able to do' (Rom. 4.20b–21) is almost a parallel pair. In believing, Abraham was giving glory to God. Abraham's faith glorifies God by acknowledging him as God. *Therefore*, says The Apostle, it was reckoned to him for righteousness (Rom. 4.22). This completes the exposition of Gen. 15.6. The important thing about faith is that it gives glory to God. It acknowledges the God who gives life to the dead and calls into being things that are not.

The Apostle has shown in the story of Abraham and his fatherhood a tightly woven web of action and promise which demonstrates overwhelmingly that God intended from the beginning that Israel's election should be fulfilled, through faith, in blessing on both Jew and Gentile.

Beginning to turn from The Conservative to direct address to The Congregation, The Apostle goes on to relate the story to the church's situation. 'It was reckoned to him' was written not only because of him, the central human character of the story, but also for our sake, to whom it is going to be reckoned (Rom. 4.23–4a). That is, the statement was written for this new group of people to whom faith is going to be reckoned as righteousness. Their faith is in 'the one who raised from the dead our Lord Jesus, who was given up for our sins and raised for our justification' (Rom. 4.24b–25). It is in Abraham's God, who has fulfilled the promise to Abraham and his seed. Why did they need the statement? Not simply to reassure them that faith is all they need, but to show them that the God whose new action in Christ calls forth their faith is indeed the God of Abraham and can be trusted. Rom. 4.25, with its poetic balance and credal ring, provides a conclusion satisfying for The Conservative and pointing again to the foundation of the whole matter, and of the church's life, God's action through Christ.

By asking about the nature of Abraham's forefatherhood and developing the answer through his exposition of Gen. 15.6, The Apostle has shown that the gospel of salvation for all who believe

---

[45] Accepting that οὐ is not to be read. With Metzger, *A Textual Commentary on the Greek New Testament*, 451; Ziesler, *Romans*, 133; Wilckens, *Der Brief an die Römer*, I, 276, n. 895.

establishes the Torah in the very process of making Jew and Gentile equal before the grace of God. This is the fulfilment of the purpose for which God elected Israel, the bearers of the promise given to Abraham. The Conservative can live out his new faith in the confidence that in doing so he, too, will be giving glory to God.

Rom. 3.27–4.25 – methodological commentary

The teleological reading shows again the effect of recognizing that this is a pastoral text, created in particular circumstances. Again, we have been reading it as address to The Conservative as representative of particular people facing the problems of living out the gospel they have received. Again, we are recognizing that these believers still think of themselves as Jews and Gentiles. The framework within which the familiar terms are working is created not by the general distinction between Jew and Gentile, but by these particular Jews and Gentiles living together in the community of faith. Read in this way, the passage appears as a unity, with a coherent and important contribution to make to the whole of Rom. 1.16–4.25, and to Paul's purpose in the letter.

This awareness of the particularity of The Apostle's address shows in the treatment of several exegetical problems. In the concrete context of the discussion so far we identified the καύχησις of Rom. 3.27 as the boasting of Jew over against Gentile rather than boasting as the opposite of faith as a human attitude to God. Similarly, we understand νόμος not by asking after the meaning of the concept in this passage but by looking at the reference of the term in each of its uses. Thus, a law of works is Israel's Torah misunderstood as in Rom. 2.17–20, while a law of faith is God's action summarized in Rom. 3.28. In Rom. 3.31, the referent is not obvious, and we turn to the immediate context and the context of the letter so far. Again, we trace the way the discussion of the promise in Rom. 4.13–18 is focussed on the history of this promise. The Apostle argues that the promise had to be through faith and the seed had to be defined by faith. He shows this by reference to what happened, not by discussing the nature of promise in relation to law and faith. For instance, we understand the statement that the law works wrath by reference to the earlier discussion, rather than by seeing it as a statement about the nature of law.

Rom. 3.28: The γάρ shows this sentence to be the ground for the assertion that boasting is excluded by a νόμος πίστεως. It is a summary of the content of Rom. 3.21–6 as it affects this question. The Apostle summarizes the anthropocentric pole of his argument about how God is righteous in justifying believers.

Rom. 3.29–30: We have accepted the view of Stowers[46] and Hays[47] that εἴπερ should be given its proper conditional force and the construction read as elliptical. Hays' ellipsis of the verb in the apodosis is preferable to Stowers' treatment, which retains the nuance that the one God will treat the two groups alike. Our teleological exposition has opened our eyes to the possibility of a reading that sees God treating Gentiles as he is known to treat Jews. This suits Paul's sentence structure better, and relates closely to the way the question was posed. The Apostle did not ask whether God is one, but whether Israel's God is not also God of the Gentiles. He is dealing with The Conservative's problem that God does not distinguish between Jewish and Gentile believers. This is an intra-church question.

Rom. 3.31–4.3: The challenge is to make sense of the logical connections.

Given the role of the Torah as the symbol of God's election of Israel and the focus of Israel's identity as God's people, we can see in general terms why Abraham would be discussed to establish that the gospel does not make the νόμος of no effect (Rom. 3.31). This is a specific form of the problem that if Paul's gospel cuts the church off from Israel, it has cut away its own basis. It is at Rom. 4.2 that we as listeners-in feel that The Apostle and The Conservative have moved off into a debate in which we do not participate. The implication of the link formed by γάρ, the direction of the discussion, and The Apostle's statement that Abraham does not have ground for boasting before God seems to be that if The Conservative wants to say that Abraham was justified on the basis of works, he will have to say that Abraham has ground for boasting, and that will force him to conclude that Abraham is forefather κατὰ σάρκα. It is clear from the text that if Abraham was justified on the basis of works and therefore has ground for boasting, he will be cut off from all who have no ground for boasting – who, according to Rom. 3.27–8, would be both Israel with the mistaken understanding of her election, and believers in

---

[46] *The Diatribe and Paul's Letter to the Romans*, 164–7, esp. 166–7.
[47] 'Abraham', 84–5.

Christ, Jewish and Gentile, who are justified on the basis of faith apart from works. What has that to do with Abraham being τὸν προπάτορα ἡμῶν κατὰ σάρκα? For The Apostle and The Conservative as believing Jews, it would reduce their connection with Abraham to physical descent. Then he would be forefather κατὰ σάρκα. We can examine the text and work that out. Romans was dictated and meant to be heard: the most attentive listener could hardly be expected to go through such a process. We therefore presume that the letter was operating in a context in which a listener would be able to follow without having to think it out step by step. We need to identify that context.

Here and in Galatians, we have snippets of the debate about whether Gentiles who believed the gospel had to be circumcised. As Barrett argues, at least one approach to the question was to argue that believers receive the promise made to Abraham and his seed, and must therefore be seed of Abraham.[48] Paul's position was that being a believer in itself made one seed of Abraham because Abraham was reckoned righteous on the basis of believing in God. Abraham would then be forefather κατὰ πίστιν. An opposing position was that to be eligible to receive the blessing through believing, one must belong to the seed of Abraham, the covenant people, either by birth or by proselytism. Abraham would then be forefather κατὰ σάρκα. That debate provides the necessary context for these few verses. Our identification of it is vindicated by the fact that it yields a reading of the whole chapter as a coherent and persuasive presentation of the call of Abraham as the one in whom the covenant and election were given. It can be seen again in the discussion of the promise in Rom. 4.13–17. In Rom. 4.13, ἡ ἐπαγγελία ... τὸ κληρονόμον αὐτὸν εἶναι *κόσμου* indicates that Paul was not giving an exegesis of Gen. 15.7, 18–21; 17.8, where the inheritance of the land, ἡ γῆ, is promised. Rather, he was referring to the promise as it was understood in this debate, as a promise that could be and was being fulfilled to Jewish and Gentile believers. It was being held together with the promise in Gen. 12.3; 22.18 of blessing for all the nations through Abraham. We can see this in Gal. 3.6–4.7, and Rom. 4.23–5. It represents a development in the understanding of the promise, so that the eschatological blessings constitute the inheritance. Such a development can be glimpsed in some other Jewish literature. The promise becomes a

---

[48] *Freedom and Obligation*, 22–5.

promise of the whole earth (Sir. 44.21b; Jub. 22.14; 32.19) and, further, the idea of promise is associated with the blessings of the righteous at the End (4 Ezra 7.119; 2 Baruch 44.13–15; 51.3; 57.1–3; 59.2).[49]

Rom. 4.1: 'What, then, shall we say? That we have found Abraham to be our forefather according to the flesh?' This reading is not new,[50] but a case still needs to be argued for accepting it.

The reading of K *et al.*, τι ουν ερουμεν Αβρααμ τον πατερα ημων ευρηκεναι κατα σαρκα, has no significant support in the modern debate. It is suspiciously easy, since it takes the anarthrous phrase κατὰ σάρκα with εὑρηκέναι, smoothing the grammar. The reading of πατέρα instead of προπάτορα appears to be a substitution of the familiar term for a rare one. It is difficult to explain the other readings from it. The loss of εὑρηκέναι in the B reading could have been a copyist's slip, but there is nothing to prompt it. There is no apparent reason for correcting either grammar or sense by placing it before Ἀβραάμ. Further, this reading is open to all the objections to having at this point an unanswered question about what Abraham found.

It will be convenient to consider together the readings of B *et al.*, τι ουν ερουμεν Αβρααμ τον προπατορα ημων κατα σαρκα, and of ℵ *et al.*, τι ουν ερουμεν ευρηκεναι Αβρααμ τον προπατορα ημων κατα σαρκα. There is considerable support, especially Western, for the latter with πατέρα. While this can be rejected with some confidence, we have let it remind us that Paul may have chosen the unusual term to stress Abraham's role.

The two major readings can be punctuated and understood as follows:

B *et al.*

> 1. τί οὖν ἐροῦμεν Ἀβραὰμ τὸν προπάτορα ἡμῶν κατὰ σάρκα;
> What, then, shall we say about Abraham our forefather according to the flesh?
> 2. τί οὖν; ἐροῦμεν Ἀβραὰμ τὸν προπάτορα ἡμῶν κατὰ σάρκα;
> What then? Shall we call Abraham our forefather according to the flesh?

---

[49] See Byrne, *Reckoning with Romans*, 94; 'Sons of God' – 'Seed of Abraham', 157.

[50] Recently, Hays ('Abraham', 81–3), citing Zahn; Elliott, *The Rhetoric of Romans*, 158–9; Cranford, 'Abraham in Romans 4'.

ℵ *et al.*

3. τί οὖν ἐροῦμεν εὑρηκέναι Ἀβραὰμ τὸν προπάτορα
ἡμῶν κατὰ σάρκα;
What, then, shall we say that Abraham our forefather
according to the flesh has found?

4. τί οὖν ἐροῦμεν; εὑρηκέναι Ἀβραὰμ τὸν προπάτορα
ἡμῶν κατὰ σάρκα;
What, then, shall we say? That we have found Abraham
(to be) our forefather according to the flesh?

In terms of grammar and style, a case can be made for each of
these.

Numbers 1 and 3 take κατὰ σάρκα adjectivally. Strictly speaking,
this requires the article, but in Rom. 9.3 the phrase can only be
intended adjectivally. The objection is not insuperable.

Some scholars find the construction in Number 1 difficult. For
Wilckens, it is intolerable without περί.[51] On the other hand,
Sanday and Headlam offer John 1.15 (οὗτος ἦν ὃν εἶπον) as a
parallel,[52] and Schlatter interprets it as a perfectly good Greek
question with the advantage of not requiring an answer.[53]

Number 2 seems to be a straightforward use of a verb of saying
with two accusatives, and is recognizable, diatribal style.

For Number 3, Hays objects that the perfect εὑρηκέναι would
need to be explained, since what long-dead Abraham found would
normally be expressed with an aorist.[54] On the other hand,
Abraham is very much alive in the ἔχει of Rom. 4.2.

Number 4, which we accept, is rarely considered. It has the
advantages of retaining 'we' as the subject, following Rom. 3.31,
and of allowing τί οὖν ἐροῦμεν to function in diatribal style.
Diatribal style suits the context, but this consideration is not
decisive. Paul's use of ἐρῶ as a kind of logical future in the dialogue
style of Romans is very flexible.[55] On the other hand there is no
other example in the extant letters of its use in dialogue simply as
the opening of a substantial question. (Rom. 8.31a is simply an
expanded τί οὖν ἐροῦμεν;) There are several examples in Paul's

[51] *Der Brief an die Römer*, I, 260–1.
[52] *Romans*, 99.
[53] *Gottes Gerechtigkeit*, 159.
[54] 'Abraham', 80–1.
[55] Rom 3.5; 8.31; 9.19, 20; 11.19.

letters of εὑρίσκειν used as in this verse – to find somebody to be something – with εἶναι not expressed.[56] The construction is described in BDF §396: 'In classical Greek the complement of verbs of ... saying which indicate the content of the concept or communication, is formed to a great extent by the infinitive. If the subject is the same as that of the governing verb it is not expressed.' Dunn objects to applying this to Rom. 4.1, saying that an accusative and infinitive construction at the beginning of a sentence with the accusative unstated 'would be rather odd'.[57] This objection would carry weight in the case of an ordinary, independent sentence, especially in writing. Here, however, we are considering a mannerism of diatribal speech in a text that was spoken and intended to be heard. The two sentences comprise one sense unit. The same can be seen in the English. 'That we have found Abraham to be our forefather according to the flesh' is intolerable as an independent sentence in written English, yet the two sentences together constitute spoken English so normal that the meaning is accepted without the hearer, or even a reader, noticing the grammar. If Paul had supplied the ἡμᾶς, he would have produced an excessive stress analogous to, although not as heavy as, the one that would be created in English by, 'What, then, shall we say? Shall we say that we have found ...?'

Thus, considerations of grammar and style do not exclude any of the possibilities offered by the B and ℵ readings. We turn to textual and exegetical considerations. The ℵ reading is the better attested. Further, it is hard to explain the rise of the other two readings from B. The best line of explanation is that εὑρηκέναι was supplied as clarification and then moved because the intended clarification was not understood, but if the scribe read the B text as two questions it is hard to see why the clarification was wanted, and if he read it as one it is hard to see what εὑρηκέναι would clarify. The other two readings can be explained from the ℵ reading as independent alterations, the loss of εὑρηκέναι being scribal error arising from the similar beginnings of ευρηκεναι and ερουμεν, and its repositioning being an effort to correct a difficult text.

On the basis of the argument so far, the reading of ℵ *et al.* should be accepted. To choose between the two ways of punctuating it, we

---

[56] The closest are 1 Cor. 15.15; Gal. 2.17. Hays ('Abraham', 82) cites these and several which have a predicate adjective.
[57] *Romans*, 199.

turn to exegetical considerations. How is the question functioning in the context? That is, why does it arise, how is it answered, how does the answer contribute to the discussion as a whole? What is the point of κατὰ σάρκα? Within the mainstream debate, the one-sentence form is widely preferred, not to the two-sentence form (which is rarely considered) but to the one-sentence form of the B reading. It is accepted as the better-attested and more difficult reading, and exegetes make the best of it.

Familiarity has dulled our awareness of the magnitude of the problems it brings. With this reading, Paul's procedure is remarkable for its extraordinary ineffectiveness as communication, particularly in the oral setting, and for its uniqueness. Nowhere else in the extant letters does he proceed as he would be doing here. With the one-sentence reading, he poses a critically important question (Rom. 3.31a), rejects it with a claim that is worthless unless it is immediately substantiated (Rom. 3.31b), and then asks a question that has no obvious relevance to the preceding claim and contains a throw-away phrase (κατὰ σάρκα) that is controversial enough to distract most of his audience from what he is about to say (Rom. 4.1). An answer to the question might reveal its relevance, but instead of providing one he goes on with a discussion which is only tangentially relevant and from which the audience could have deduced an answer (if they were still interested!) by the time it was well developed (Rom. 4.5). A little later, he takes up the issue raised by the throw-away phrase, showing that it was inappropriate (Rom. 4.9–12).

Solutions have been proposed for some of these problems. The most widely accepted solution to the problem that the question is not answered is Michel's suggestion that it operates by allusion to the Septuagint expression εὑρίσκειν χάριν, which applies to Abraham in Gen. 18.3.[58] This has the advantages that grace is an important concept in the context and that the allusion method can be allowed to supply the answer with the question. On the other hand, it is hard to see any reason why the incident in Gen. 18.3 would be so much in the forefront of Paul's mind as to shape his question. The fact that the phrase is common in the Septuagint still leaves us with an unsatisfactory explanation, especially as the concept of grace is not explicit in the discussion that led to the question of Rom. 3.31a. When we assume that Paul's mind was

[58] *Der Brief an die Römer*, 161.

occupied with the attempt to engage the Romans, it seems extremely unlikely. Again, there is no other instance in the extant letters of a question that depends on allusion either for its intelligibility or for its answer, let alone for both. This solution occurs to a reader after long study of a puzzle. For our effort to elucidate what Paul was intending the Romans to hear, it is a counsel of despair. Black's proposal that there could be an allusion to Sir. 44.19 (οὐχ εὑρέθη ὅμοιος ἐν τῇ δόξῃ) is offered in the context of his despair.[59] Allusion to ἐν πειρασμῷ εὑρέθη πιστός (Sir. 44.20; 1 Macc. 2.52) is even less helpful.[60] It is not impossible that these echoes might have been in Paul's mind, or even that one or two of the listeners might have picked up one of them, but they do not offer an explanation of what Paul was intending to communicate.

Another approach is to propose alternative translations of the question. Black considers a Hebraism, 'What then shall we say befell Abraham ...?'[61] Dunn offers, 'What did Abraham find to be the case ...?'[62] ('What, then, shall we say that Abraham our forefather according to the flesh has found to be the case?') These share the virtue of the one-sentence form of the B reading. They do little more than introduce Abraham. On the other hand, they are not obvious readings of the Greek for ὁ ἀναγινώσκων, they are not effective introductions to what follows, and they do not account for κατὰ σάρκα.

A few exegetes, notably Schlatter, have recognized the importance of κατὰ σάρκα at this point.[63] In Paul's usage, σάρξ has various connotations, not all of them pejorative. His use of κατὰ σάρκα, though, is always limiting. In this category are the two references to Christ (Rom. 1.3; 9.5), and the reference to Jews as brothers κατὰ σάρκα (Rom. 9.3 cf. 1 Cor. 10.18). In the discussion in Galatians about who are heirs of Abraham and the promise, the phrase is set over against both promise (Gal. 4.23) and Spirit (Gal. 4.29). The other uses are less directly related to this issue, but also have negative overtones, some even polemical: Rom. 8.4, 5, 13; 1 Cor. 1.26; 2 Cor. 1.17; 5.16; 10.2, 3; 11.18. This evidence reinforces the view that in the context of Rom. 3.27–4.25, the phrase is not a merely neutral reference to physical generation. At least, it places

---

[59] *Romans*, 75.
[60] *Ibid.*, 75; Dunn, *Romans*, 199.
[61] *Romans*, 74.
[62] *Ibid.*, 198.
[63] *Gottes Gerechtigkeit*, 159–60.

limits on Abraham's fatherhood; at most, it already carries the implication that gospel and covenant are incompatible – and that means that God is not faithful. (This paragraph is an example of looking up a word in the context literature. The evidence helps us to bridge the two-millennia gap between us and Paul, but for teleological reading it can be used only in the context of the evidence of the text being read. In this case, it checks and supports the reading we developed in the context of The Apostle's address to The Conservative.)

In the light of this exploration, the two-sentence punctuation demands serious consideration, even if the one grammatical/ stylistic objection against it could stand. We have argued that it does not. Our teleological reading shows it yielding sense that makes the whole of Romans 4 a coherent contribution to The Apostle's purpose in Rom. 1.16–4.25. The chapter is seen as providing a proper answer to the question of Rom. 3.31. If the B reading is correct, its two-sentence form would function in the same way.

Rom. 4.12: We accept that τοῖς is not to be read with στοιχοῦσιν. The fact that the τοῖς stands and has not generated text variants challenges all our readings of the sense of the passage, and any reading that would accommodate it deserves attention. Cerfaux's carefully argued attempt to do this[64] involves a spiritualizing of circumcision at this point and an argument that Gentile Christians are superior to Jewish Christians. He makes a case for this in terms of the wider context of Paul's thought as he understands it. It seems extremely unlikely in the immediate context because there are no indicators visible to us that would mark the change to spiritual circumcision and it is no part of Paul's aim in Romans to argue that believers in Christ are the true circumcision (cf. Phil. 3.3; Col. 2.11). In favour of accepting τοῖς as an error, even in Paul's dictation of the complex sentence, is the placing of οὐκ ... μόνον.

Rom. 4.13: The γάρ can have its full logical sense only if the nature of Abraham's fatherhood, and therefore of his seed, is being shown to be necessary because of the nature of the promise.

Rom. 4.16: The argument comes perilously close to being circular: the fact that the seed had to be ἐκ πίστεως to match the nature of the promise of the inheritance runs into the fact that the

---

[64] 'Abraham "père en circoncision" des gentils'.

promise of the inheritance had to be ἐκ πίστεως not only because it could not be fulfilled if it were ἐκ τοῦ νόμου, but also because it had to match the promise that Abraham would be the father of many nations (Rom. 4.17a). All that saves it from circularity is the fact that the seed promise is independent action of God. This demonstrates the consistency of God's intention and action.

11

TESTING THE TELEOLOGICAL READING

We have tried to trace what the implied author is saying to the implied audience, and especially to the narratee, in Rom. 1.16–4.25. Before we can offer that as our reading of what Paul was intending the Romans to hear, it must pass the tests we established in chapter 9.

1. It must account for all of the text,[1] making sense of it as coherent communication accessible to the intended audience, and overcoming the intractable problems we identified in chapter 2.

2. It must function as part of the whole meaning of Romans. It must work as the first step of the preaching we hypothesized in chapter 7, accommodating the passages not obviously related to the Jew–Gentile issue, or correct our hypothesis. It must be compatible with the justification theology as a related element of meaning in Rom. 1.16–4.25, or demonstrate very convincingly that we were wrong in believing that the tradition of exegesis has not been a tradition of eisegesis.

3. It must *either* be something we can accept that Paul could have said in the situation *or* force us to ask reasonable questions about our understanding of the situation and/or of Paul.

Test 1 – making sense of all of the text

The teleological reading has made sense of all of the text as speech with its quality of linearity. There is no point where the listening Romans could not reasonably be expected to follow, and listeners are helped by such things as introductory questions, question and answer sequences, the use of familiar ideas, and interaction with their experience. The three major problems which appeared insoluble in a justification reading have disappeared.

---

[1] For this important concept, see above, pp. 42–3.

Rom. 1.18–3.20 was not intended to convince the Romans that everybody is a sinner needing rescue from God's condemnation. The Apostle was aiming to lead The Conservative to see that his presuppositions would not hold. Paul must have had to learn that himself, and it is reasonable to suppose that he would make this case for the Romans. Some of them would be like The Conservative; others would relate to it differently. The problem of righteous Gentiles in Romans 2 disappears, and Rom. 3.1–8 fits into the discussion as a forceful confrontation with a basic problem.

The imbalances in the whole passage and in Rom. 3.21–6 have disappeared with the recognition that the text is not exposition but pastoral preaching and that it is not a justification account but is addressed to people whose life problems are involved in the question of God's righteousness. Rom. 3.21–6 is not an over-compressed account of the Atonement. The mismatch between grammar and meaning disappeared when we assumed that Paul meant what he said, and drew on new historical knowledge to make sense of the key role of οὐ γάρ ἐστιν διαστολή.

Our teleological reading has passed Test 1.

Test 2 – making sense as part of the whole

What is the role of the justification account in the whole meaning of the text? The problem was not how God can justify sinners, but how God can be righteous in justifying believing sinners on the basis of faith without reference to the Jew–Gentile distinction. Accordingly, justification through faith is not the answer to the question and the goal of the discussion but the source of the question and therefore a major presupposition of the discussion. This explains why readings which assume that Paul was intending to give a justification account come so close to accounting for the text but always run up against the problems we noticed. The justification theology has a role in the meaning of the text as presupposition. This is parallel to the role of the household structure as sociological presupposition in the Herbert text we examined in chapter 4.

Can we see the teleological reading as the first major step in Paul's preaching of the gospel to the Romans in their situation? We concluded that his purpose was to help the Roman believers to share and live out his view that the gospel demanded mutual acceptance of Jew and Gentile in Christ.

A classic problem with Romans is that if the main theme is taken to be justification and its consequences, Romans 9–11 tends to fall away, while if God's faithfulness is seen to be the primary concern it is hard to account for Romans 5–8. Does the discipline of the teleological reading help us to see a fully coherent whole? We must do this at the level of the teleological reading.

The first stage of the preaching is God's action, which has past, present and future dimensions. Rom. 5.1–11 is the eschatological climax of the account of God's action in Rom. 1.16–5.11. God will come in judgement. Through Christ and the Spirit, believers live in the present time of suffering in peace, courage and love, having the sure hope of final salvation. The Apostle is taking time for The Congregation to rest and rejoice in the great certainties of their faith.

If The Apostle is preaching the gospel to The Congregation as calling Jew and Gentile to welcome one another in Christ, there are two major issues outstanding. The Torah as scripture has been fulfilled, but what about the Torah as the law of Moses? It seems to have no place. Why did God give it? What are believers, Jew and Gentile, to do about it? What about the charge of antinomianism? Again, what about Israel? If the gospel fulfils God's election of Israel, why is Israel not responding? Is God abandoning Israel? For the Romans and for Paul, these were not theoretical questions about God's quality of faithfulness or righteousness, or about justification. They were difficult, divisive practical issues in the living out of their response to God's grace in the gospel. They are taken up as the preaching continues, but they do not simply determine its content. This is not lecture or apologia, but preaching. The gospel controls the content; the problems help shape the preaching because they are important to believers.

Having grappled with God's action, The Apostle deals with life under the gospel (Rom. 5.12–8.39), the questions of Israel and the church (Rom. 9.1–11.36), and paraenesis (Rom. 12.1–15.6). Rom. 15.7–13 is conclusion and climax.

In Rom. 5.12–8.39, The Apostle deals with the questions about the Torah. He puts them in the context of God's victory over sin and death through Christ, and the way believers respond to this in their living. His aim is to encourage responsible, hopeful obedience to the gospel in a church which will be able to see the law not as rejected but as fulfilled in life in the Spirit. The language of the powers is suited to dealing with life in Christ as necessarily involving struggle and suffering, with the certain hope of God's love and victory.

Rom. 5.12–21 sets the scene, a battleground on which the victory has already been won through God's overflowing grace in the human obedience of Christ. The powers gained access to human life through human will and action (in Adam), and continue to do so (Rom. 5.12d). Compared with its power as an issue in the church, the law's role here is small and ambivalent. It shows sin for what it is, reckonable as transgression, and increases transgression, with the result that grace abounds more and more. The law slips in on the Adam side, a power that is overcome. Yet it seems to have a fifth-column role on the Adam side, making sin vulnerable to the power of God's grace.

Having established this ground, The Apostle proceeds by asking and answering some major questions. In Rom. 6.1–7.6 he considers the accusation and temptation of irresponsibility in life under grace. He begins with a question that could arise from Rom. 5.20, 'Shall we continue in sin that grace may abound?' Rom. 3.7–8 shows that this represents an accusation against Paul's gospel. It also represents a temptation, either to be irresponsible or to take refuge in law. The answer is that the question is nonsensical. Those who are baptized into Christ died to sin with him in order to share his life, life lived to God (Rom. 6.2–10). The Congregation are to understand themselves accordingly (Rom. 6.11), and yield their members not to sin but to God (Rom. 6.12–13). Rom. 6.14 offers a secondary basis, the assurance that this is possible because sin will not rule over them because they are not under law (which operates 'in Adam', where sin and death rule) but under grace (which rules 'in Christ'). Rom. 6.15–23 examines the nature of believers' freedom and the choices they face. They have been rescued from slavery to sin to become slaves of righteousness. Whereas the former pays the wage of death, the latter offers the gift of life, in Christ. In Rom. 7.1–6, The Apostle explains how it is that they, as believers, are no longer under the law. They have died to it in Christ in order that they may be Christ's, bearing fruit for God, slaving in the newness of the Spirit.

The discussion has been turning to the questions of the relationships among sin, law and Spirit. In Rom. 7.7–8.17, The Apostle deals with the relationship between sin and law, with the roles of flesh and Spirit. In the process, he offers an explanation of the role of the law, and disposes of the charge that Paul's gospel rejects it.

He takes the worst case first. Is the law sin? The answer is that the true nature of the law is not affected by the fact that sin used it to get a grasp on The Apostle (using himself as representative for all). It shows up sin for what it is. The next possibility is the suggestion that the good law brought about death. Rom. 7.13–25 considers who actually is the culprit. The conclusion is that sin takes advantage of the weakness of the σάρξ to prevent The Apostle (representative, again) doing the good law he knows. Rescue is needed, and it has come from God through Christ. Rom. 7.25 sums up the situation in which salvation and Spirit are to operate. In Rom. 8.1–8, The Apostle explains that God has overcome sin in the flesh through Christ as sin-offering, so that believers might fulfil the proper requirement of the law as they walk in the Spirit. Rom. 8.9–11 shows The Congregation that this includes them as the life-giving Spirit dwells in them, and Rom. 8.12–17 shows that they, as Spirit-led, are freed from the σάρξ and are heirs of the promise of salvation.

Rom. 8.17–39 deals with the suffering that comes to believers, both imposed from without and given with the command to be slaves of righteousness. Suffering is worth while because shot through with the sure hope of the fulfilment of God's purpose of salvation. This parallels the eschatological climax of the first part of the preaching, in Rom. 5.1–11, and moves again to triumphant assurance.

In Romans 9–11, The Apostle discusses Israel's failure to respond to God's fulfilment through Christ of the call of Abraham. Again, there is not a simply theoretical discussion, but a real response to the meaning of this question for the life of the church, specifically the church in Rome. This has two faces, the pain of a Jewish believer such as Paul, and the temptation for Gentiles who do not have roots in Israel's history to feel superior. Listening to the letter, some of them may feel that they stand apart from the radical overhaul of Jewish identity which the gospel demands. Especially in Rome, where Jews have come back into a church that has had some time to grow in relative freedom from the problems The Apostle has been facing, it may be easy to look down on the doubts and questionings of Jewish fellow-believers struggling with them. So The Apostle works out again the way God's faithfulness is not overcome by Israel's failure.

He evokes his grief for fellow-Jews who are not entering into their inheritance as God's elect (Rom. 9.1–5). Working from scripture, he then shows that this is not an indication either of God's failure or of Israel's displacement. Rather, it will be the means by which God's election of Israel is fulfilled in blessing for the Gentiles and salvation for all Israel.

First he traces the pattern of God's dealings with the seed of Abraham – election was always a matter of God's choosing some and therefore not others, so that it might indeed be a matter of grace, not of human deserving (Rom. 9.6–18). It may be objected that God should not then find fault because the human being is powerless to resist. The Apostle responds negatively by saying that people may not answer back to God, and then positively by suggesting that the whole process is part of the mystery of God's mercy. New people of God are being called from among the Gentiles and the Israel of the promise is, as scripture suggested, only a remnant (Rom. 9.19–29).

The second step is to show that Israel's present state is the result of culpable failure to recognize and submit to God's righteousness as it is revealed in Christ, the goal of the law they have misunderstood. Their scripture shows the rightness of the gospel way, and the gospel has been proclaimed to them. Their present state is described already in Isaiah's prophecy (Rom. 9.30–10.21).

This raises more explicitly the problem that was evoked but not allowed to stand in Rom. 9.1–6: God has not rejected his people, has he? The Apostle answers this by showing how God answered Elijah when he asked that question. There is the remnant kept by grace, and the hardening of the others is in God's purpose (Rom. 11.1–10). Through Israel's disobedience mercy has come to the Gentiles, and that mercy should stir Israel to emulation. The story should also show the Gentile believers that they and their faith depend on Israel and they also are subject to the kindness and the severity of God. In relation to their Jewish fellows, The Apostle calls them not to patience or to charity, but to humility. They, too, are dependent on mercy and could be cut off because of pride or unbelief (Rom. 11.11–24). The close of the passage is a celebration of the eschatological mystery. The hardening of Israel was for the sake of the all-embracing mercy of God, and in the end that will mean salvation for all Israel (Rom. 11.25–32). In the face of the mystery, adoration is called forth (Rom. 11.33–6).

In Rom. 12.1–15.6 The Apostle comes to the specifics of Christian living. Judging by the wealth of paraenesis in the NT letters, this would have been expected. Again, the needs of the

Romans and the pressures of the Jew–Gentile problems shape the preaching. Picking up earlier emphases, The Apostle exhorts The Congregation to live in the light of God's mercies (Rom. 12.1–2) and the imminent Parousia (Rom. 13.11–14), and presents love as the fulfilling of the law (Rom. 13.8–10). While all the ethical injunctions are appropriate for them, the treatment of attitudes to civil authorities may have been peculiarly appropriate, since the emergence of the churches had been accompanied by trouble, and there is evidence of problems over taxation.[2] The paraenetic section is dominated by discussion of one of the most difficult areas in a life where Jew and Gentile came together in Christ (Rom. 14.1–15.6). What, in actual practice, do you *do* about food laws and holy days? The Apostle does not tell The Congregation to eat or refrain, celebrate or refrain, but offers strong guidance for their handling of the problems. Believers are to respect one another as servants in Christ of the same God, not usurping God's judgement but making room for everybody to act according to conviction. The strong, having greater freedom, are to accept the weak, and all must consider others' good. This is grounded in Christ's own action, and the goal is life in harmony for the glory of God.

On this reading of the letter body, Rom. 15.7–13 is a lovely conclusion and climax to the whole. We saw in chapter 7 that such a reading is in harmony with the letter frame.

There has been an unnoticed assumption in much discussion of Romans that it must be *either* an account/preaching of the gospel *or* a treatment of a particular problem. Our study has shown the letter as a preaching of the gospel *shaped by* the Jew–Gentile problems. Some parts do not address that issue directly, but are part of putting it in the gospel perspective and helping hearers to respond.

Our teleological reading has passed Test 2.

Test 3 – making historical sense

Is our teleological reading something we can accept that Paul would have said to the Romans in the situation we identified? Or does it force us to ask reasonable questions about our under-standing of the situation and/or of Paul?

---

[2] J. Friedrich, W. Pöhlmann and P. Stuhlmacher, 'Zur historischen Situation und Intention von Römer 13, 1–7'.

At the level of general content, we can accept it. The pastoral problem and the interpretation of God's action are consistent with a debate then in progress, as Galatians and Philippians 3 show. Luke's later account of Paul's meeting with James in Jerusalem (Acts 21.17–24) indicates that the issue was important enough to become part of the history of the church. It is a good case for Paul to have put in that situation, and the procedure of going back to the gospel is characteristic of the Paul we see in the letters. 1 Cor. 1.18–31; 8; Gal. 2.16–4.7; Phil. 2.4–8; Rom. 14.1–12 are examples. It does force us to ask reasonable questions about our under-standing of Paul's thought and his pastoral method.

The current debate on δικαιοσύνη θεοῦ in Rom. 1.16–4.25 is dominated by the assumptions that the term is to be understood identically throughout Paul's opus and that it refers to the right-eousness of the justified, recognizing in some way that this is not separable from God's own righteousness. Rom. 3.5 is a clear exception. In the teleological reading, δικαιοσύνη θεοῦ refers throughout to God's own righteousness as it is seen and understood in God's dealings with people. It does not refer to the righteousness of the justified. On this basis, we have a teleological reading which coheres around a question about God's own righteousness.

We noted in chapter 10 that objections against our interpretation could be raised on the basis of tradition, which we ruled out, or of Paul's own usage, which we reserved for later examination. While the subjective genitive reading is not unique,[3] it is unusual. We submit that this does not rule out our teleological reading.

The contexts in which the term is seen to be used differ between the mainstream and the teleological readings. It is natural for δικαιοσύνη θεοῦ to be understood as 'God's righteousness' in a struggle to resolve a problem about God's righteousness. The new reading therefore appears as a proper step in understanding in the light of our current historical knowledge. This usage makes the term appear as a normal genitive construction rather than as a (semi-)technical term, so that the reading of the genitive need not be the same for every occurrence in the Pauline corpus. Would the others make sense if Paul's usage were consistent in this way? In Rom. 10.3, ὑποτάσσω would be an odd word to use for receiving a gift, but the idea of submitting to God's righteousness is a brilliantly succinct description of what, according to Rom. 3.24–6,

---

[3] e.g. Williams, 'The "Righteousness of God" in Romans'.

is involved in justification through Christ, as well as being appropriate to the immediate context. In 2 Cor. 5.21, Christ was made something he is not, sin, in order that people might become something they are not, the righteousness of God. The double metaphor makes good Pauline sense if we take it to mean that in the Cross God's judgement falls on Christ as one whose being is determined by the power of sin, and therefore falls on believers as those whose being is determined by his own just and saving righteousness.

Our reading accounts very satisfactorily for Paul's use of ἡ ἐκ θεοῦ δικαιοσύνη in Phil. 3.9 and σοφία ἡμῖν ἀπὸ θεοῦ, δικαιοσύνη κτλ. in 1 Cor. 1.30, where he was talking about the righteousness of the justified.

The question of the relationship between God's own righteousness and the righteousness of the justified belongs to the causal reading. For now, I have shown that the unusual reading of δικαιοσύνη θεοῦ does not invalidate the teleological reading.

The teleological reading produces a radically new impression of Paul as pastor and letter-writer. The Paul of mainstream exegesis is a penetrating thinker, but a poor communicator. We have found a pastor and preacher who brought a profound understanding of the gospel to bear on practical questions of life in Christ, who said what he meant in ways that touched his hearers' experience and understanding, even actively helped them to change. Can we account for this difference?

The discipline of the historical-critical method requires that Paul's texts be taken seriously as letters, and exegetes normally assert that what they conclude the text means is what they believe Paul was saying to the Romans. Käsemann's commentary offers a clear example. He considers that the letter is for a Christian community which needs a high degree of theological understanding.[4] Käsemann's Paul is not writing to the Romans about their situation, but about the human condition. He is expecting them to recognize their situation as a particular manifestation of it. Thus, in Rom. 3.19 the Jew becomes the exemplar of the pious person.[5] He is the example chosen because he is culturally relevant, but the point at issue is his mistaken piety, not his Jewishness.

Further, Käsemann's Paul expects from the Romans a high degree of analytical skill. They would have to exercise this at

---

[4] *Commentary on Romans*, 34.
[5] *Ibid.*, 87.

lightning speed as the text was read to them. For instance, they would need to identify the presupposition which makes sense of a radical and otherwise disjointed shift in the argument at Rom. 3.4:

> This can only mean that the covenant violated by the people is still maintained from God's side. Now the argument does not continue ... in such a way that Christ has become a servant of the circumcision to confirm the promises made to the fathers and thereby to confirm God's covenant faithfulness to Israel. In a most remarkable way the problem is extended to every human being and to God's trial with the whole world. *This makes sense only if the faithfulness of God to Israel is a special instance of his faithfulness to all creation.*[6]

The justification account that Käsemann's Paul sends to the church at Rome would be suitable for a high-level theological seminar or, better still, a learned journal. Of course a commentary must explain much that would be obvious to first-century believers, and the material necessarily seems more difficult to us than it would to them. Of course the Romans would be expected to reread the letter, think and talk about it. Nevertheless, it is a letter, and if Paul was even minimally competent as communicator, listeners should have been able to follow through at a first hearing, even if details and implications might be missed. If Käsemann is right, this letter demands that they identify unstated connections and presuppositions at high speed, and think at the level of abstraction involved in seeing the Jew as the pious person rather than themselves or the Jews listening with them in a situation where Jewishness was an issue. Such a capacity for abstract thinking normally exists only in a tiny fraction of a population. Where would one find such a congregation today? If the Romans were so different from most modern congregations, what made the difference? Or was Paul after all an insensitive and unsuccessful communicator through whom the Spirit nevertheless founded all those churches?

Of course, not all commentators find Paul's text as opaque as Käsemann does. Nevertheless, exegeses within the justification-account framework virtually all show Paul giving a lecture about the human condition and expecting the Romans to think of the

---

[6] *Ibid.*, 81–2, my italics.

agonizing problems of their church life as examples of it, not as issues in their own right.

Our teleological reading would make great demands on the Roman listeners because it brings out and challenges presuppositions which might not have been noticed, even. On the other hand, it treats them directly and concretely. It deals with real Jews and real Gentiles. It takes up live issues. The speaker's skills and opportunities are used to engage and help hearers. If Paul was presenting that, he could reasonably expect to be understood.

How is this new Paul revealed? We separated the tasks of understanding the text as something Paul wanted to say and understanding it as expression of his thought. To understand a letter as communication, the exegete must concentrate on this one text, without referring constantly to the whole corpus, and must give priority to understanding it as address. In doing these things, we asked radical questions about the nature of the text, and thereby formed a new view of the kind of thing we are reading. In other words, when we read the text as communication, we found that Paul was a very effective communicator. Given his record as a successful missionary, this view of him has much greater historical probability than the traditional one. We can now see that the traditional one is a function of exegetical interest in Paul's thought at the expense of his communication.

This is not to say that mainstream exegetes are wrong. We do not wish to discard the variety of rich encounters with the text, but to point out the distortion imposed on our picture of Paul by single-strand exegesis on the basis of the one question, What does this text mean?

Our teleological reading has passed Test 3.

Test result

The teleological reading has passed our tests, so we can now use it as a framework for the causal reading and offer it to the debate as our best answer to the question, What was Paul intending the Romans to hear when this passage was read to them?

12

THE CAUSAL EXPOSITION OF ROMANS
1.16–4.25

In this book we are developing a new kind of historical-critical reading of Rom. 1.16–4.25. In the teleological reading developed and tested in chapters 6–11 we made sense of the text in terms of Paul's purpose in creating it. We gave our best answer to the question, 'Where was it going *to*?' Since it is part of a letter, we had to read it as coherent communication. In this chapter, we complete our exegesis with the causal reading. Our aim is to make sense of the text in terms of Paul's thought from which it arose. This time our question is, 'Where was it coming *from*?' We need to read it as arising from a coherent pattern of thinking.[1]

We seek access to this pattern of thinking by examining theological presuppositions which are visible in the text. In chapter 4, we saw that the extract from *The Country Parson is* Herbert's account of the way the Parson rules his household. There is a visible sociological presupposition, the household structure. Rom. 6.1–11 *is* Paul's explanation of why believers cannot sin that grace may abound. There are visible presuppositions – the nature of baptism, the concepts of being in Christ and living to God. Rom. 1.16–4.25 *is* Paul's preaching about how God is righteous in justifying believers. Now we look at two visible presuppositions, the theology of justification and the Creator–creature relationship.

These are significant patterns in Paul's thought. In this causal exposition, we shall examine them, their interrelations, and the interactions between them and what Paul was intending to say. This will deepen our understanding. It will also enable us to show how Paul's preaching is generated partly by the presuppositions and how the form in which the presuppositions appear in the text is controlled by what he was intending to say. Because causal exposition is concerned with the thinking from which the preaching arose,

---

[1] On making sense of a text, see pp. 42–3.

it involves reading this text in the context of the Pauline corpus. This is in contrast to the teleological exposition, where we must restrict our attention to the text in hand. Here we are disappointed. Our study makes Romans look so different from the letter we thought we knew that we are forced to ask whether the other letters might also look different. We shall therefore draw on material outside our text only where we can be reasonably confident that we are dealing with very characteristic patterns of thought or action. The causal exposition of a text provides contributions to studies of the writer's thought. Our contributions will be limited by our limited access to the wider corpus. This has the very serious disadvantage that it will not be possible to include in this book an example of a full causal exposition, but it has the advantage of disciplining us to the text we are reading, which is the focus.

As with the teleological reading, we shall be working alongside the mainstream debate, not within it. We are asking questions in a different framework, and direct engagement with the debate would pull us into its familiar framework and away from our unfamiliar task, thus distorting the causal reading.

For our causal reading, we have some parameters already set. The first is provided by the teleological reading. In chapters 3–4 we saw that a text is generated partly by patterns of thought in the author's mind and partly by her intention, what she wants to communicate. The author will not describe the generating patterns, but they will be visible in the text to some extent. They control its content to a significant extent and its form to some extent. On the other hand, the extent to which and the form in which they are visible in the text is controlled by the author's intended communication. The teleological reading has elucidated Paul's intended communication. This frees us to concentrate here on the thought patterns, the theological presuppositions. It also shows us what communication was shaping the forms in which we find them. We know now that we are reading pastoral preaching, not an exposition of ideas. This means that we shall not expect to find straightforward accounts of the presuppositions. Our knowledge of the nature and detail of the intended communication will help us to understand them.

The other pre-set parameters arise from ourselves as readers. We come to the text as heirs of a rich tradition of interpretation, and this affects our perception. Specifically, we are bringing from chapter 2 our question about the role of the justification ideas in the text. Coming from a debate in which it was assumed that Paul was giving a didactic or polemical account of justification by grace through faith, we are turning to a new task. We are seeing the text not as exposition but as pastoral preaching. We are not trying to understand the justification account as what Paul was intending to say, but trying to understand its role in what Paul was intending to preach about God's own righteousness and its implications for believers. We hope to clarify our understanding of the theology and deepen our understanding of the text by doing so.

How have we moved from the former to the new perception of the text?

First, we made it possible by examining ourselves as readers and clarifying what it is that we want to know. This helped us to develop the technique of separating our major interests, dealing with Paul's intention and communication in the teleological reading and with his thought in the causal reading. That allowed us to divide the load of detailed work and to sharpen our questions, so that Paul's preaching came clear for us. Our examination of the nature of the text and the techniques of the teleological reading contributed significantly.

Further, in chapter 4 we took account of the fact that texts contain more than authors intend to communicate, and identified factors which draw readers' attention to other elements of meaning. Cultural distance from the text can mean that later readers' attention is attracted to elements of meaning that were secondary or submerged for the addressees. Later readers may bring to the text questions other than those it was created to answer. We noted that for biblical texts the long history of intensive study makes these factors particularly potent. We can now see how they have operated in traditional justification readings of Rom. 1.16–4.25.

How were they operating in that case? If our teleological reading is an element of meaning genuinely contained in the text, why has it not been discovered before? In chapter 3, we identified some general cultural and scholarly factors helping to direct attention to the secondary element of meaning: exegetes' concern with Paul's thought rather than his communication, the preference for causal over teleological explanation in our culture, and the misleading identification of the text as exposition. We can now add the particular factor that the question of God's faithfulness and right-eousness so important to the church of the fifties quickly became a dead issue. By the second century, there were already different questions about Jewish–Christian relations, as the term 'Christian' shows. Justin Martyr's *Dialogue with Trypho* is a clear example. This meant that Paul's question was not being asked, so his answer was not noticed.[2] It has been possible to recover it only by stringently disciplined detective work in the context of recent studies of the emergence of Christianity from its Jewish matrix.

On the other hand, for virtually the whole history of historical-critical exegesis in Western biblical scholarship the passage has been read as if Paul were dealing with the question of how sinners can be acceptable to a righteous God. I am arguing that this has directed attention not away from the text but away from the element of meaning that represents Paul's intended communication. This has been possible because the theological presupposition of the preaching provides a valid Pauline answer to the later question.

That is why the justification reading with all its variations has been so durable. It relates to an element of meaning that is close to the surface of the text, and thus comes close to accounting for all of the text. It does not offer a perfect fit, and we have seen in chapters 2 and 6 that some of the failures are critical. The fact that exegetical attention has been focussed on Paul's thought to the exclusion of any effective concern with his communication helps to account for the lack of any felt need to look beyond the justification framework. This arose only recently, because study of the Torah in first-century Judaism forced some of the points of misfit into uncomfortable prominence.

The justification theology as presupposition

We begin the causal exposition, our effort to trace in the text some of the theology from which it sprang, by considering justification.

In chapter 2, we proposed that we should test an hypothesis that in Rom. 1.16–4.25 Paul was doing something other than giving the Romans a justification account, but that justification was important for what he was trying to do. In chapters 3–4, we examined the workings of both texts and exegetes to develop the teleological plus causal approach to historical-critical exegesis. This provided a more specific hypothesis: that the justification thinking might be a presupposition of what Paul was intending to say, present in the

---

[2] cf. Beker, *Paul the Apostle*, 75 on the early loss of understanding of Paul's letters in their own situation.

text as a by-product of his intended address to the Romans. The teleological reading has given us our view of what Paul was intending to do. He was intending to remove a barrier to proper Jew–Gentile relationships in the church by helping believers to recognize that God was indeed righteous in justifying believing sinners without reference to their membership in elect Israel. In doing this, he discussed the status of Jewish and Gentile sinners and rehearsed the 'How' of God's justifying action for the sake of explaining the 'Why'.

Whether it is identified as a presentation of the doctrine of justification or as an account of the gospel in justification terms, the good news in Rom. 1.16–4.25 is normally seen to be that God justifies believing sinners by grace through faith. The foil to this is that human beings cannot justify themselves by doing what God requires. All have sinned; all need grace; God gives gracious justification to all who believe. There is no other requirement. Here, we shall call this pattern of thought Paul's justification theology. Our causal exposition will help us to check whether this particular formulation reflects accurately the traces of the theology which we find in the text.

We notice immediately that the statement of the justification theology is a statement in universal terms of the problem that brought the text into being. Paul's solution to the problem of whether Gentiles who became believers had to become Jews was a conclusion from God's action in the Cross. God's action was justification of all who believed, therefore belief alone was the human response required. When that view was put into practice, it caused practical problems about how Jew and Gentile could live together in Christ, and the theological problem of how God could be righteous if he acted in a way that seemed tantamount to abandoning the election of Israel. At both levels, the problem focussed on the Torah as instrument of election. The Torah, the νόμος, enters into the meaning of the text not as an element of the justification theology, but as an element of the situation in which it was being put into practice.

In sharp contrast, readings in the mainstream debate see gracious justification not as the problem but as the solution. Why? The text offered the answer to Luther's agonized sense of being unable ever to satisfy the righteous demands of the righteousness of God. The answer he found in Rom. 1.17 is that God gives the righteousness he demands. The gift is received by believing, not deserving. One becomes righteous in God's sight not by achieving righteousness through effort (works, works of the law) but by receiving it through faith.[3]

We may schematize this reversal:

(1) God's gracious justification of believing sinners is the *source* of the problem Paul was discussing as he created the text: How can God be righteous in our eyes [his and the Romans', believers of his time] if he justifies believing sinners simply on the basis of their believing, without reference to the Jew–Gentile distinction that he created in electing Israel?

(2) God's gracious justification of believing sinners is the *solution* to the problem that exegesis following Luther brings to the text Paul created: How can we [human beings] be righteous in God's eyes, since we are not able to create that righteousness by our own efforts?

We can formulate the reversal in another illuminating way. The element of the justification theology that poses the problem changes.

(1) In Luther's situation, sin is the problem and it draws a great deal of theological attention.

(2) In Paul's situation, grace is the problem, and sin is a background datum. The theological attention sin draws is focussed on the double question of God's judgement and Jewish believers' self-understanding.

Luther is not to be held responsible for all the exegetical developments that flowed from his work, but the contrast we have delineated is central to the argument of this chapter. For brevity, we shall refer to this stream of exegesis as the Luther tradition.

This shift in emphasis changes the theological and the anthropological problems. In exegesis in the Luther tradition, the driving problem is anthropological, the problem of how human beings as human beings can be acceptable to God. The Jew–Gentile distinction is a cultural factor defining the detail of that question. God's grace is the solution to the human problem, but it can be seen to generate a problem about God's righteousness. How could God be

---

[3] Preface to the Wittenberg edition of his Latin writings, 336–7.

God if he justified believing sinners without dealing with their sin? That would be calling black white, and God would cease to be God. Atonement through the Cross answers that problem. In the letter situation, the driving question is about God's righteousness, since Paul's proclamation of grace seems to carry the implication that God must fail in righteousness as faithfulness to the covenant. The problem about God's righteousness is central, not secondary, and it is a different ethical question. Here, the anthropological problem is not how human beings can be acceptable to God – that has already been solved – but how Jew and Gentile are related to one another under God's unconditional grace.

Our first answer, then, to the question of the way the justification theology functions as theological presupposition of Paul's preaching in Rom. 1.16–4.25 is that it lies outside the text as the problem that generated it. The difference between Paul's and the Luther tradition's problems makes us ask whether further exploration may force us to modify the formulation of the justification theology with which we began.

There is a second-level answer to our question. The justification theology also functions as presupposition in the preaching. In exploring this, we shall be beginning to deal with our question, What is the form in which the justification theology appears as presupposition in the text?

In chapter 4, we saw that in Rom. 6.1–11 two interconnected elements of meaning are clearly visible. Rom. 6.3–11 contains the fullest discussion of baptism in the extant letters. It is there because Paul was drawing on the Romans' understanding and experience of baptism to show them why believers cannot continue in sin so that grace may abound. In Rom. 3.21–6, also, he was drawing on a known idea and experience in dealing with the point at issue.

Two elements of the justification theology appear in Rom. 3.23–4a, sin and gracious justification: πάντες γὰρ ἥμαρτον καὶ ὑστεροῦνται τῆς δόξης τοῦ θεοῦ δικαιούμενοι δωρεὰν τῇ αὐτοῦ χάριτι. In Paul's preaching, this is the ground for οὐ γάρ ἐστιν διαστολή in Rom. 3.22d. That is, it is not something that has to be proved, but a datum from which something else can be proved. Οὐ γάρ ἐστιν διαστολή is critical, because it is the ground of εἰς πάντας τοὺς πιστεύοντας in Rom. 3.22c, and that is the point towards which Paul has been driving. God's righteousness, manifest and effective through faith in Jesus Christ, is effective for *all* who believe, not for Jews who believe and for Gentiles who believe and become Jews.

Paul's first step in showing this was to point to the church's experience. All have sinned; all are being justified freely by God's grace. The πάντες clause, universal in form, is true of all believers, and the statement is being made to point out to the conservative Jewish believer that Jewish believers are no different from others. In Rom. 3.21–6, the other element of the justification theology, faith, is separated from this statement. It appears as the means by which grace becomes effective for the believers. Faith to some extent defines grace, by stressing its character of gratuity and by showing how the ἱλαστήριον is brought to bear on sin. There is no possibility here of any suggestion that the faith justifies the believer. Its instrumental character appears clearly in the long chain between grace and faith: τῇ αὐτοῦ χάριτι διὰ τῆς ἀπολυτρώσεως τῆς ἐν Χριστῷ Ἰησοῦ· ὅν προέθετο ὁ θεὸς ἱλαστήριον διὰ τῆς πίστεως. In Paul's preaching, faith was central to the driving problem, the problem of whether faith alone or faith plus conversion to Judaism was necessary for the final justification of the Gentile believer. It was essential but not central to the understanding of God's action that supplied the answer. The centre was God's grace in the Cross.

The point of Rom. 3.21–6 was that justification of sinners by grace through faith is the activity and the demonstration of God's righteousness, not a theological error that impugns God's righteousness. The church's experience that believers were sinners justified by God's grace was interpreted to help make that point. So far, the justification theology as explicit presupposition appears as a statement about believers consonant with believers' experience and with the preaching of the gospel. It is not a statement about sin, grace and faith as theological concepts or universal realities.

In Rom. 1.18–3.20, the sin of the people under discussion is a datum from which Paul made his case about Jew being in the same position as Gentile before God's righteous judgement. Again, it functions as a presupposition because the believers' experience cohered with the gospel as it was proclaimed.

In Rom. 1.18–3.26, elements of the justification theology function as direct presuppositions of some of the discussion. In Rom. 1.16–17 and Rom. 3.27–4.25, it is a more distant presupposition.

The single claim of Rom. 1.16–17 is that salvation through the gospel is indeed for all who believe *because* God's righteousness is revealed in it in a sphere of faith. God's new action fulfils the word of Israel's prophet, and includes Israel's election. The justification theology lies behind this as the interpretation of God's action that leads to the claim. Accordingly, establishing the claim involves some indirect spelling out of the theology.

In Rom. 3.27–4.25, God's former action with Israel, in the call of Abraham and the gift of the Torah, is viewed through the lens of God's new action, in Christ. Once this light is cast on it, it becomes clear that God's purpose in the election of Israel was something that can be described in terms of the justification theology.

This discussion seems to come close to saying that the justification theology is both presupposition and conclusion of the preaching in Rom. 1.16–4.25. Did Paul, then, beg the question? He did not. His justification theology was the problem that gave rise to this particular preaching of the gospel. He was demonstrating that the problem was not a problem at all, but life-shaping divine truth. The critical question is, A problem for whom? The unconditional grace that broke the bounds of Israel was a problem for some of the existing servants of this God. The process of the preaching was to refocus the problem, facing up to the way their self-understanding, their lifestyle and even their God were called into question, and showing this as a proper and fruitful process. Such a process does not end until the whole of the letter is being lived out.

Having looked at the way elements of the justification theology function as presupposition of the preaching, we can now formulate a more general answer to our question, What is the form in which this presupposition appears *in* the text which arose, in part, *from* it? On the evidence so far, we can say that Paul's presupposition was that all of the people to whom and about whom he was talking were sinners justified by God's grace on the basis of their believing in Christ. The people to whom he was talking were the Roman believers. What definition can we offer of the category of people about whom he was talking? We can safely say that he was talking about the believers of his time. He himself is included in what The Apostle is saying to The Conservative. His greeting and thanksgiving establish the Romans as part of the whole church, and the statement of what God was doing in Christ (Rom. 3.23–5a) is clearly about the way God deals with believing sinners, whoever they may be.

Key terms and underlying events

We can deepen our understanding of key terms in this passage, and thus of Paul's thinking as it underpins the preaching, by exploring another feature of the text. It is an interpretation of a series of events. By adding that deeper understanding to what we have already learnt, we shall put ourselves in a position to consider whether the statement of the justification theology with which we began, a philosophical-dogmatic statement about all human beings, is a fair statement of Paul's theology of justification as we can discover it in this passage.

The key terms as we discuss them in exegesis and theology are sin, justification, righteousness, grace, faith. They are represented in the text by ἁμαρτία, ἁμαρτάνω, ἁμαρτωλός and some of the uses of verbs like πράσσω (e.g. in Rom. 2.1–2); δικαιοσύνη, δίκαιος, δικαιόω, δικαίωσις; χάρις; πιστεύω, πίστις. Again, we are limited to what we can learn from this passage, so that our results will not be full studies of Paul's concepts, but contributions to such studies. We saw in chapter 11, however, that Paul's account of God's action continues to Rom. 5.11. We must take account of the event element of Rom. 5.1–11 to avoid distorting our understanding of the events. It provides the eschatological conclusion to the sequence.

The central event is the crucifixion of Jesus of Nazareth. It appears in the text as a happening already interpreted. The crucified Jesus is Jesus Christ whom God put forth as a means of dealing with sin through faith, by his blood, a means of salvation by redemption. As this event is preached as God's saving action (δύναμις ... θεοῦ ... εἰς σωτηρίαν, Rom. 1.16) human beings encounter God's final judgement, brought forward into history. The event preached is revelation of God's own righteousness, and as such (γάρ, Rom. 1.17a) the judgement is power for salvation for everyone who believes.

As far as this text is concerned, the interpreted happening is a datum. The question of how it came to be so interpreted therefore lies outside our discussion. We simply note that the preaching of the Cross presupposes both the Resurrection and the recognition of these events as God's saving action (as in Rom. 4.25). There is no good news in the verifiable fact that a man called Jesus was crucified. For the purposes of Paul's theology, events are happenings that have been understood, and the gospel events are understood as action of the God of Israel. That is how God revealed his righteousness.

The judgement of the Cross is a judgement which is at once condemnation and salvation. The sinner who by believing the gospel is brought under that double judgement is saved from one state into another. The state from which the believer is saved is described with the phrases ὑφ᾽ ἁμαρτίαν (Rom. 3.9) and ὑπόδικος ... τῷ θεῷ (Rom. 3.19b), the latter describing the consequence of the former (cf. Rom. 1.32). The state into which the believer is saved is described with the phrase δίκαιος ἐκ πίστεως (Rom. 1.17). In Rom. 5.1–11 we see δικαιωθέντες ... ἐκ πίστεως (Rom. 5.1), and the certain hope contained in πολλῷ ... μᾶλλον δικαιωθέντες νῦν ἐν τῷ αἵματι αὐτοῦ σωθησόμεθα δι᾽ αὐτοῦ ἀπὸ τῆς ὀργῆς (Rom. 5.9). The state of salvation into which the believer is brought thus appears as definitive but not final. That is, God's judgement through the preached Cross decides the believer's destiny, but there is still the eschatological judgement to come. The events obviously involved in this account are the crucifixion, the preaching, the believer's hearing and believing, and the eschatological judgement, an event that is still to happen but is certain.

What can we learn from Rom. 1.16–4.25 about what Paul understood that it means to be a sinner? Our best starting point is the term δόξα. It appears as follows:

Rom. 1.21–3

διότι γνόντες τὸν θεὸν οὐχ ὡς θεὸν *ἐδόξασαν* ἢ ηὐχαρίστησαν, ἀλλ᾽ ἐματαιώθησαν ... φάσκοντες εἶναι σοφοὶ ἐμωράνθησαν καὶ ἤλλαξαν τὴν *δόξαν* τοῦ ἀφθάρτου θεοῦ ἐν ὁμοιώματι εἰκόνος φθαρτοῦ ἀνθρώπου καὶ πετεινῶν καὶ τετραπόδων καὶ ἑρπετῶν.

Rom. 2.6–10

ὃς ἀποδώσει ἑκάστῳ κατὰ τὰ ἔργα αὐτοῦ· τοῖς μὲν καθ᾽ ὑπομονὴν ἔργου ἀγαθοῦ *δόξαν* καὶ τιμὴν καὶ ἀφθαρσίαν ζητοῦσιν ζωὴν αἰώνιον ... *δόξα* δὲ καὶ τιμὴ καὶ εἰρήνη παντὶ τῷ ἐργαζομένῳ τὸ ἀγαθόν ...

Rom. 3.7

εἰ δὲ ἡ ἀλήθεια τοῦ θεοῦ ἐν τῷ ἐμῷ ψεύσματι ἐπερίσσευσεν εἰς τὴν *δόξαν* αὐτοῦ, τί ἔτι κἀγὼ ὡς ἁμαρτωλὸς κρίνομαι;

Rom. 3.23–4a

πάντες γὰρ ἥμαρτον καὶ ὑστεροῦνται τῆς *δόξης* τοῦ θεοῦ δικαιούμενοι δωρεάν ...

Rom. 4.20

εἰς δὲ τὴν ἐπαγγελίαν τοῦ θεοῦ οὐ διεκρίθη τῇ ἀπιστίᾳ
ἀλλ᾽ ἐνεδυναμώθη τῇ πίστει, δοὺς *δόξαν* τῷ θεῷ ...

In Rom. 5.1–11, Rom. 5.2

καυχώμεθα ἐπ᾽ ἐλπίδι τῆς *δόξης* τοῦ θεοῦ.

Basically, there is some lack in relation to δόξα in connection with sin, and some restoration in connection with believing and being justified. Study of the δόξα language shows that the events of the passage are events in Paul's story of the relationship between the Creator and humanity as creatures of the Creator. This relationship defines the terms. Two strong verbal clues start our study. The people who by their wickedness suppress the truth do it by not glorifying or thanking God even though they know God (Rom. 1.18, 21). Abraham's growing strong in faith and trusting God involves – or even is – giving glory to God. That is why faith was reckoned to him for righteousness (Rom. 4.20–2). The second clue is the reminder of Adam in the δόξα statements of Rom. 1.23; 3.23. In later developments of the Genesis stories, Adam at the Fall lost the glory of God which had been reflected in his face.[4] With justification is given the hope of the glory of God (Rom. 5.2). These clues together suggest that the sin of which the sinners are guilty and which holds them in bondage is the sin of Adam. It involves the breaking of a relationship which may be partially described with the phrase 'giving glory to God'. Salvation would then consist in the re-establishing of this relationship, so that God is given glory and the believer is given the certain hope of the glory of God. We begin our exploration of this idea by examining the echoes of earlier tradition in Rom. 1.18–32.

As we saw in chapter 10, this is not an argument by allusion. Nevertheless, a number of scholars have noticed numerous echoes of the Wisdom of Solomon, especially chapters 13–14, and of the Fall story.

There are very strong resemblances in both language and content to Wisdom 13–14. Closer examination shows, however, that we are not in Wisdom's thought world. The arguments about the knowledge of God are radically different. In Wisdom, the evidence is there in creation and people should deduce the Creator. In Romans, God is known but denied recognition. In both cases, idolatry follows. In Romans, it is an inevitable exchange for the

---

[4] Gen Rab XI.2, XII.6; Apoc. Mos., esp. chs. xx, xxi.

worship denied the Creator, and idols are seen as a poor exchange, mere images of things God created. In Wisdom, idolatry arises in the hiatus resulting from failure to deduce God, and the idols are seen as the worthless and powerless work of the worshippers' own hands. In both cases, evil and social disruption follow. In Wisdom, they are caused by idolatry; in Romans, παρέδωκεν αὐτοὺς ὁ θεός shows them as God's punishment. The Romans account is far more strongly relational.

At the verbal level, the Genesis echoes are slighter than the Wisdom ones. In the context of the presentation of God as Creator, the language of Rom. 1.23 is strongly reminiscent of Gen. 1.20–6 (LXX), where God creates τετράποδα, ἑρπετά, and πετεινά, and also creates ἄνθρωπον κατ᾽ εἰκόνα ἡμετέραν καὶ καθ᾽ ὁμοίωσιν. Further, the wilful exchange of glory and its consequences reminds us of the Fall. Closer examination of the structure and sequence of events reveals that we are in the world of the Fall story. We are dealing with different literary forms. The myth of Creation and Fall is story; the preaching in Rom. 1.18–32 can be analysed as argument. Nevertheless, both speak of a series of things that happened in a chain of cause and effect.

The human being is related to God by an initiative of the Creator requiring an appropriate creaturely response. In Genesis, the initiative is the command not to eat from the tree of the knowledge of good and evil; the appropriate response is to obey. In Romans, the initiative is God's gift of the knowledge of God; the appropriate response is to give glory and thanks. In each case, the creaturely response is refused, in Genesis by eating the fruit, in Romans by not giving glory and thanks. In the act of refusal, the human beings damage their own being. Adam and Eve recognize and are ashamed of their nakedness, and they hide from God. The rebels of Romans 1 become futile and foolish, with darkened minds. So far, refusal of the creaturely response carries with it its own punishment. In addition, God punishes the sin. The curses on Adam and Eve bring trouble into life, and their banishment from the Garden is separation from the tree of life. In Romans, God gives the sinners up to what they have made of themselves. In both cases, the outcome is widening circles of sin and the disruption of human community (Gen. 4.2b–16; 6.1–5; 11.1–9; Rom. 1.24–32).

The shared creation setting and the parallel sequence of significant events strongly suggest that the ἀσέβεια and ἀδικία of Rom. 1.18 are the sin of Adam. Supporting this argument are the general observations that human beings appear to suffer as heirs or bearers of the sin of Adam in Rom. 5.12–14 and 1 Cor. 15.21, 22, and that the future hope of Rom. 8.19–22 has elements of reversal of the Fall. More particularly, it explains why πάντες ... ἥμαρτον in Rom. 3.23 is underlined with a reference to lacking the glory of God.

There are differences between the Genesis and the Romans stories. The most important is that there are God-given signs of hope in Genesis, the acts of God's mercy. Adam and Eve are given proper garments, Cain is given a protective mark, the beginnings of a new world are saved out of the flood, and the call of Abraham is the promise of a new unity after the scattering of the sinners of Babel. In the pronouncement of the righteous wrath of God on sinners, there are no signs of hope. Hope now lies outside human history, in God's new action in Christ.

This examination suggests that Paul understood sin as turning away from the relationship of dependence and gratitude towards God for which humanity is created. This affects the human being, now not able to function properly, and God, now not acknowledged as God and therefore not allowed to be God in relation to the creature. Ὑφ᾽ ἁμαρτίαν in Rom. 3.9 shows this as a condition of life, not simply the nature of particular actions.

We can now comment on two particular questions.

In the teleological reading, we noticed a logical gap in the argument of Rom. 1.19–21. Apparently, there was a natural theology argument that people should have deduced God from God's self-revelation in creation, but their sin was described as refusing the knowledge of God that they had. We can now see that the knowledge of God mentioned in Rom. 1.19, 21 is the relationship of dependence and gratitude given with creation.[5] This would explain the ἐν of Rom. 1.19. Then the rest of creation bears supporting witness to the Creator (Rom. 1.20). The γάρ of Rom. 1.20, however, seems to be part of a logical sequence, so we still feel a logical gap. This is at least partly because we live in a world where atheism as belief that God does not exist is a widely accepted option. In a world where the nature of the divine rather than the existence of the divine was open for widespread disagreement, it is easier to see how Paul and the Romans could feel no problem.

---

[5] This text has generated much discussion. My interpretation is close to those of Hooker ('Adam in Romans 1', 299), Käsemann (*Commentary on Romans*, 41–2) and Ziesler (*Romans*, 77).

We have moved a long way from the older formulation of the problem of sin in Rom. 1.16–3.26 as the inability to establish one's own righteousness by doing what God requires. For Paul, sin does not consist in failure to keep the law. Rather, that failure shows the underlying problem. This is consistent with the role of the law in the teleological reading as a measuring stick.

How did Paul see God's action in the Cross dealing with sin, the broken relationship and consequent darkened minds and defiant deeds? Looking at the events, we see that here 'grace', 'faith', 'righteousness' and 'justification' come into play. The broken relationship does not leave the sinner loose in the cosmos, but in bondage. This is represented most explicitly in the text by παρ-έδωκεν αὐτοὺς ὁ θεός (Rom. 1.24–8) and ὑφ' ἁμαρτίαν (Rom. 3.9b). It is pictured in Rom. 1.21b–23. God deals with this situation by an act of redemption – ἀπολύτρωσις (Rom 3.24b). The believer is rescued from bondage back into relationship with God. This relationship is created by the means of redemption, [Χριστὸς Ἰησοῦς] ... ἱλαστήριον διὰ τῆς πίστεως (Rom. 3.25a). Christ is ἱλαστήριον by his sacrificial death (ἐν τῷ αὐτοῦ αἵματι, Rom. 3.25a). In that action, God creates a relationship of faith responding to grace. He makes a righteous person of the sinner, and gives the sinner justification, the verdict Δίκαιος.

What did Paul understand was involved in God justifying and human beings being justified? This question is framed to correspond with Paul's discourse. Although he had the noun δικαίωσις at his disposal, he usually used the verb. This fits the fact that he was preaching about happenings. There are active forms of δικαιόω with God as subject in Rom. 3.26, 30; 4.5, and passive forms with people being, or not being, justified in Rom. 2.13; 3.20, 24, 28; 4.2. (In Rom. 3.4, God is to be justified. This is recognition of a righteousness that exists, not one that must first be created.)

In the judgement context, δικαιόω is a juridical term. It refers in this preaching to the giving of the verdict Δίκαιος. What is involved in giving and receiving that verdict through the Cross? First, sinners are justified. This contravenes the standard of righteousness for judges in Israel, but that is no problem in this preaching. God justifies *believing* sinners, and the question was not *whether* but *on what terms* God is righteous in doing so, with reference to the covenant with Israel. The believing sinner who is justified through accepting a ἱλαστήριον is receiving and acknowledging God's judgement on him as sinner, Ἄξιος θανάτου (Rom. 1.32a). The fact that that verdict comes not as a pronouncement but in the form of a ἱλαστήριον means that the guilt and power of sin are overcome, as we observed in chapter 10. Further, the person who accepts a ἱλαστήριον is coming to God the judge as a believer, that is, in the creaturely attitude of dependence and trust. Thus, the judgement itself creates the relationship of human faith responding to God's grace. It does this by virtue of its nature – it is a ἱλαστήριον διὰ τῆς πίστεως. (The placement of the two participial phrases with ἱλαστήριον is a syntactic oddity. Since both are anarthrous, one would expect to take them with the verb, but they are placed with and conceptually related to ἱλαστήριον. Christ's death happened and is ἱλαστηριον because of God's purpose and action, so προέθετο and ἱλαστήριον in Rom. 3.25a are themselves very closely linked.)

The relationship of human faith responding to God's grace is a relationship created by God's initiative which requires an appropriate creaturely response. This is the pattern of the Fall story (God's initiative in a command, with the response of obedience) and of Rom. 1.19–21 (God's initiative in giving knowledge of God, with the response of giving glory and thanks). In Romans 4, Paul showed that God's intention in the call of Abraham was that Jew and Gentile should be related to God by faith. Again we see God's initiative and the appropriate human response. Abraham's faith is response to God's grace – the promise (Rom. 4.3; Gen. 15.5; Rom. 4.18–21), τὸν δικαιοῦντα τὸν ἀσεβῆ (Rom. 4.5). The promise is necessarily a matter of grace (Rom. 4.16). In his gracious action, God appears as Creator, and he is so described in Rom. 4.17b. Abraham's faith as response to the grace of the promise epitomizes the dependence and trust proper to the creature: παρ' ἐλπίδα ἐπ' ἐλπίδι ἐπίστευσεν (Rom. 4.18a). He believes that God can perform the promise even when human resources are dead (Rom. 4.19) and an act of creation is needed, giving life to the dead and calling into being things that are not. With this faith Abraham gives glory to God. This brings us back to the relationship between creature and Creator in Rom. 1.19–21, and this time the relationship is complete.

Thus, through the Cross God provides a ἱλαστήριον διὰ τῆς πίστεως that redeems from bondage to sin. It does this by dealing with the guilt and power of sin and in the process creating the relationship of human faith responding to God's grace. God creates the proper righteousness of the creature, and vindicates his own righteousness. God is acknowledged as God, and this establishment of the Creator's right and power is necessary to the very existence of the creature's righteousness. The human creature is free from bondage to sin only when God is given glory and thanks, that is, treated as God. Accordingly, any one of those described as δικαιωθέντες (Rom. 5.1) can also be described as ὁ δίκαιος (Rom. 1.17).

We can now see why Paul would not have any requirement added to faith for membership in the church. The relationship created by justification through a ἱλαστήριον διὰ τῆς πίστεως would be destroyed.

We can also see two reasons why the expiation/propitiation/ Mercy Seat debate over ἱλαστήριον is so inconclusive. First, the text is not an Atonement account, even an over-compressed one. For Paul's concern here, the Atonement is a datum, and whatever debate there had been or was about it in the church at the time is not under consideration. Second, our Atonement account debate presupposes that this passage is dealing with a contrast between God's saving righteousness and God's condemning wrath, but the teleological reading does not show this contrast. We have seen that the ἱλαστήριον makes righteous people out of sinners, partly by virtue of the fact that it is itself the judgement of condemnation. As far as the believing sinner is concerned it does not avert the wrath, but transforms it.

This brings us to Paul's terms χάρις and πίστις/πιστεύω. Χάρις is God's. Besides God's dealings with Abraham, it is represented in this passage by the action described in Rom. 3.24–6, and by the gift the sinners rejected, knowledge of God (Rom. 1.19–21). The utter gratuity of grace, its creative power and disturbing character are underlined by the description of God in Rom. 4.5, τὸν δικαιοῦντα τὸν ἀσεβῆ.

In the teleological reading, we found that in Rom. 1.16–4.25 πίστις refers to believing in Christ, since that was the disputed point for the people to whom Paul was preaching. Correspondingly, the functioning of the noun πίστις in this passage is usually controlled by the verb πιστεύω. Rom. 1.17 follows from Rom. 1.16, and the discussion in Rom. 3.23–6 spells out εἰς πάντας τοὺς πιστεύοντας (Rom. 3.22c). Abraham's πίστις is defined by his believing. Only God's πίστις appears independently of this pattern (Rom. 3.3–4). What content can we give to πιστεύειν as we explore the patterns of thought revealed in the passage? It means 'to take

God at his word' rather than simply 'to give credence to'. This shows clearly in the case of Abraham's believing in Gen. 15.6. In Gen. 15.5 God makes him a promise, and he believes God. Again, believing is a matter of relationship. The believer's faith consists in believing God's word as it is spoken, accepting God's address, and continuing to rely on it. Believing in Jesus means believing in him as the one in and through whom God acts (Rom. 3.25a; 4.24–5). This discussion deals only with the aspects of Paul's understanding of faith that are visible in this passage. Because he was preaching here about God's righteousness, our view of his thought through this text does not include the matter of faith in relation to the lordship of Christ.

In exegesis in the Luther tradition, the theocentric pole of the problem of righteousness is often seen as an issue of how God can righteously justify sinners simply because they believe. The problem of sin is failure to meet God's righteous requirements. This context makes it easy, especially in popular theology, for God's grace to appear as the solution – to that extent, an emergency measure. Then faith can easily become an alternative work, an attainable condition that God set when human beings failed to attain justification by meeting the demands of the law. The Cross can be seen as a way of satisfying the demands of justice, so that God is not guilty of calling black white. This worst-case scenario is not representative of serious modern scholarly interpretation of Rom. 1.16–4.25. The view that attempting to justify oneself by works is in itself sinful means that grace is not simply an emergency measure, for instance. Similarly, even when δικαιοσύνη θεοῦ is taken to refer primarily to the righteousness of the justified, God's righteousness is still seen to be revealed in the justification of sinners.

The worst-case scenario highlights some problems of interpretation within the traditional framework, and reminds us of their impact on much contemporary faith and preaching.

The preaching and the pattern of thought we have found in the passage show a different view of God's action through the Cross. Grace is not a response to sinners' failure to be righteous, although God in grace deals with that failure. Rather, God's grace is the ground of human righteousness. Faith is not a precondition for a Δίκαιος verdict, or simply the means of receiving a gift of righteousness. It is one essential part of human righteousness, the other being God's grace. Thus, the believer receives the verdict Δίκαιος, and God is righteous in justifying the one who believes in Jesus

(Rom. 3.26). God's righteousness in the Cross is not meeting an abstract requirement of justice. God acts as righteous eschatological judge and as saviour, vindicating his own righteousness and creating the righteousness of the believer. If righteousness is conduct in conformity with a norm, the norm here is the Creator–creature relationship, which includes the encounter of faith with grace and, inseparable from that, the proper being of both Creator and creature. This proper being is reflected in the language of the passage: God's δικαιοσύνη stands independently, while the human being is δικαιωθείς/δίκαιος ἐκ πίστεως; God's πίστις stands independently, while the human being's πίστις is defined by believing.

Again, this text offers only a partial view of Paul's thinking. Because the preaching concerns God's righteousness in giving the verdict, the character of life being lived under the judgement of justification is not included, nor is the cluster of ideas associated with Paul's ἐν Χριστῷ.

Re-examining the justification presupposition

We have studied the justification theology as the direct presupposition of Paul's preaching in Rom. 1.16–4.25 and deepened our understanding by exploring it as arising from events – the Fall, the Cross, the preaching of the Cross, believers' response, God's justification of the believers, the Abraham story, and the expected eschatological judgement. Have we found evidence that Paul's visible presupposition – all believers are sinners being justified by God's grace – is a particular application of a universal theological statement that Paul could have made, the stuff of philosophy and dogma? This would be, All human beings are sinners who are offered justification through faith as a gift of God's grace. This would come close to the formulation of the justification theology with which we started this exploration. This question is formulated according to the constraints governing our study. We should need a study of the whole Pauline corpus to obtain a fuller view of Paul's thought on justification.

We begin by looking again at πᾶς in Rom. 1.16–3.26. In chapter 6 we asked what Paul was intending to say to the Romans with this πᾶς, and formed an hypothesis, substantiated by the teleological reading, that it is an example of one common usage of 'everybody'. The universal statement is made for the sake of the case under consideration. Attention is not on the general truth of the statement (which is taken for granted), but on its applicability to the speaker and addressee/s. Thus, the πάντες of Rom. 3.23 was saying something like, 'and that means you and me, conservative fellow-Jew. We are not an exception, different from Gentile sinners.' Now we consider the fact that the text can function in this way precisely because the speaker can assume that both speaker and addressee accept the general statement. This means that for causal study we can bring a different question to Paul's πᾶς, What are the limits of the 'all'? To what category does it refer? We have established that it refers to all believers, but there are hints that it goes wider, that we are getting a glimpse of a truly universal 'all'.

Πᾶς in Rom. 2.9, 10 and ὅσοι in Rom. 2.12 refer to the eschatological judgement, which was understood to be universal. There is another glimpse of this in Rom. 3.5–6. In Rom. 3.9–20 the argument is that the Torah adds sinful Jew to sinful Gentile, ἵνα πᾶν στόμα φραγῇ καὶ ὑπόδικος γένηται πᾶς ὁ κόσμος τῷ θεῷ (Rom. 3.19b). In the case of judgement, then, the category 'believers' is part of the larger category 'humankind'.

The teleological reading does not show whether or not Paul believed that the sinners of Rom. 1.18 included all humankind. Our causal study, showing sin as the sin of Adam, indicates that he did. This is consonant with Rom. 3.19–20.

In Rom. 3.24b–25a, Paul said that God set forth Christ as a ἱλαστήριον through faith, and so there is redemption in Christ. No limit is placed on who may receive this. Similarly, in Rom. 3.26, we find that God acted in this way so that he might be righteous even in justifying the person of whom there is only one thing to be said, This person believes in Jesus.

The underlying Creator-creature theology comes to the surface of the text in the δόξα references of Rom. 1.23; 3.23; 4.20. We need not move far outside Rom. 1.16–4.25 to find confirmation of these intimations of universality. Paul's statement of his missionary obligation in Rom. 1.14 establishes that he believed the gospel was for everybody.

This evidence shows that the universal statement, 'All human beings are sinners who are offered justification through faith as a gift of God's grace' is not simply one we can deduce from Paul's text. We have good reason to believe that Paul would have formulated it had the occasion arisen. It is not what he intended to say with any of the statements in the passage we are studying. It is one of the structural elements of his theological thinking that we see through the particularity of this preaching.

We return to the question of whether the formulation of the justification theology with which we began would need to be modified if it were to be a statement of Paul's view as we can see it in this passage. Our new universal formulation reads: 'All human beings are sinners who are offered justification through faith as a gift of God's grace.' The formulation with which we began our exploration was: 'God justifies believing sinners by grace through faith. The foil to this is that human beings cannot justify themselves by doing what God requires. All have sinned; all need God's grace; God gives gracious justification to all who believe. There is no other requirement.' We can restate this for clear comparison with our new formulation: 'All human beings are sinners who, being unable to justify themselves by doing what God requires, are offered justification through faith as a gift of God's grace.' The post-Sanders formulation 'by doing what God requires' replaces the older 'by works of the law'.

The parallel formulation highlights the extra phrase 'being unable to justify themselves by doing what God requires'. Its importance for exegesis in the Luther tradition is demonstrated by the way the RSV translators modified Paul's text at Rom. 3.23–4a *'since* all have sinned and fall short of the glory of God, *they are justified'*. Why is it missing in the new formulation? The teleological reading shows that Paul was not trying to persuade the Romans that they could not justify themselves and therefore needed the gift of grace. The phrase in the formulation derived from the Luther tradition reflects the perception that that is the function of Rom. 1.18–3.20. Is the insertion consistent with Paul's understanding of sin and justification as we have been able to trace it in this text?

Certainly Paul's understanding of the nature of sin means that the sinner cannot earn justification. Since he was starting from the presupposition that all believers are sinners justified by grace, he had no need to say so. In the passage, sinners are in bondage and must be rescued by redemption. On the other hand, the traditional formulation seems to allow the inference that there would be some theoretical or protological state in which human beings could attain righteousness by doing what God requires. A strong strand of exegesis in the Luther tradition holds that according to Paul the attempt to do this is in itself sinful. That underlines the relevant feature of the theology in Paul's preaching: doing what God requires is an effect, and therefore evidence, of being righteous, that is, properly related to the Creator as human creature. We saw that the extra clause leaves room for a view of grace as an emergency measure. To reflect Paul's thinking as we have been able to trace it here, the inserted clause should be removed from our formulation. If we were to attempt a formulation of Paul's justification theology as it can be traced in the whole Pauline corpus, we should need to reconsider this question.

The law

The law is not mentioned in either of our formulations of the justification theology. This is a long move from the view that Paul argued that human beings are not justified by works of the law and therefore need grace. It occurred because in our teleological reading of Rom. 1.16–4.25 we did not find the law playing such a role. This is consonant with the recognition that extant records of first-century Judaism do not show the Torah as a means of self-justification.

What role does the νόμος play in Paul's preaching in Rom. 1.16–4.25? How is it perceived? What can we learn from that about his thought?

In the context of the letter situation, the νόμος must be understood as the Torah, not (as in the Luther tradition until recently) as the principle of legalism, with the law used as a means of self-justification. In Rom. 3.27–4.25 it is seen in its fullness as God's revelation, including the law of Moses but also the history of God's dealings with Israel. It functions, in line with Rom. 3.21b, as witness to God's new action in Christ.

Rom. 1.18–3.20 is more difficult. Paul was dealing with the disjunction in The Conservative's self-understanding. He understood himself as a member of Israel, a sinful human being graciously accepted by God, but at the same time he understood himself as a member of Israel over against Gentile sinners, one of God's righteous people. The Torah, here primarily the Mosaic law in practice, was the instrument and mark of Israel's difference. In the debate with which Paul was dealing, it was virtually being hijacked for service of the element of superiority and favoured status over against the Gentiles. Having the law made Jews better and favoured at the judgement. It was in this way that the Torah came in as the first defence against the logical inference Paul was drawing from God's righteousness as judge. The inference was that God is impartial, therefore Jews who have the law are first in vindication and in condemnation. In Rom. 2.12–3.20, Paul dealt with the way the Torah was being hijacked for the service of Jewish privilege. He did it on Jewish terms, by showing that the criterion of judgement is doing the law (Rom. 2.12–13). This receives some positive description in Rom. 2.7 and some negative description in Rom. 2.8, 17–24. It does not appear as the scoring of good and bad deeds, but rather as a matter of attitude and the consistency of behaviour with belief. In effect, a person's actions are a measure of whether or not she is under sin. The Torah has this instrumental function in Rom. 2.12–13. To use it to bolster up the position of Jewish sinner over against Gentile sinner is to misuse it in a way that is itself sinful, and causes Gentiles to blaspheme against God (Rom. 2.23–4). The Jewish believer who tries that will find that the Torah itself places the Jewish sinner before God's righteous judgement of wrath on the same terms as the Gentile sinner.

The function of Rom. 3.20 in the preaching and in the pattern of thought is interesting. In the preaching, Paul pointed out as a matter of fact that through the law comes knowledge of sin (Rom. 3.20b). That is the ground for ἐξ ἔργων νόμου οὐ δικαιωθήσεται πᾶσα σὰρξ ἐνώπιον αὐτοῦ (Rom. 3.20a). That clause, in turn, joins with the application of the catena to provide the ground for Rom. 3.19b where the whole world, Gentile plus Jew, is arraigned before God.

Two comments are in order here. The practical assertion that through the law comes knowledge of sin coheres perfectly with The Conservative's self-understanding in relation to God, that he is a sinner graciously received, and the fact that he is a sinner has underlain the whole discussion. The issue has been, in effect, whether his sin is somehow less sinful than Gentile sin. The second comment begins with a question. Why have ἐξ ἔργων νόμου in Rom. 3.20a? This has been a key element in much exegesis in the Luther tradition. In the preaching, it is a summary way of referring to the criterion of judgement in Rom. 2.12–13, doing the law not hearing it. The statement ἐξ ἔργων νόμου οὐ δικαιωθήσεται πᾶσα σὰρξ (Rom. 3.20) denies a theological position which, as far as we know, does not belong in the theology of either Israel or the church of that time. On the other hand, The Conservative's attempt to use the Torah as a shield against God's judgement and the proposal that Gentile believers should be required to become Jews and therefore keep the law both come dangerously close to perverting the Torah in this way. In the latter case, this is less obvious in the proposition than it would be in practice, when proselytes accepted circumcision and took up the food and sabbath laws. The suggestion is that The Conservative (i.e. those people in the church whom he represents) is treating the Torah as if doing it is what makes Jews acceptable to God. He ought to know that law-keeping follows from acceptance and not vice versa; it is a Jewish response to God's grace as it has been given to Israel. Having said all that, we note that this is a turn of phrase characteristic of Paul's participation in this debate. It could be that a study of Galatians, in particular, would add to the understanding we have been able to derive from this passage.

In the older pattern of exegesis in the Luther tradition, Rom. 3.20 becomes a paradigmatic statement of the human predicament. It is a problem to which only divine grace offers a solution. Paul presented it as the outcome of The Conservative's false approach to the Torah as symbol of the election of Israel. It puts The Conservative in a true and proper position, and in fact amounts to a statement about God's grace.

The question of the nature and role of sin in Paul's justification theology is closely allied with the questions about the Torah. We can now see clearly that the problem of sin in relation to the Torah is not that it prevents human beings from justifying themselves by doing what God requires, which is defined and measured by the Torah. Rather, sin perverts even the gifts of God's grace, in this case the Torah, into possessions, into marks of deserving, even of achievement.

Review of the causal exposition

In this chapter we have been exploring Paul's thinking as we can trace it in Rom. 1.16–4.25, focussing on two theological presuppositions. They are ideas which had a large part in generating the preaching, the justification theology and the Creator–creature relationship. They have helped us to understand the preaching as springing from a pattern of thought that we can accept as rational and credible. They do not by themselves account for the preaching. The other major factor is Paul's intention to preach to the Romans in their particular situation.

We have also seen how Paul's intention to preach in the way he did has shaped the forms in which his presuppositions appear in the text. Two points warrant further comment. First, the exploration of the idea of sin played a large role in elucidating the Creator–creature ideas. This is not because it was critical, or even necessarily seminal, for Paul's thinking about this theologoumenon. The large role reflects the fact that that is where the evidence happens to be clearest and most extensive. This is the case because Paul needed to deal with the desire of some Jewish believers to see election in terms of privilege. Second, the role of the law is very much smaller in the theological sub-strata of the text than it is in the preaching. It has a large role in the preaching because of its significance in the church's problem. It seems that the problem had a large role in creating the theological thinking, too, but it drove Paul back to think about the action God took apart from the law.

For the causal reading there is no testing process parallel to the battery of tests applied to the teleological reading. The control function of the tests is partly replaced by the discipline of working with the teleological reading. In the practice of exegesis by the two-step method, further control would be exercised by the need to look for consistency or credible explanations of inconsistency throughout the Pauline corpus.

We have now completed our two-step exegesis of Rom. 1.16–4.25. It does not show the insoluble problems we identified with the justification-account reading. We have made sense of the text both as communication and as springing from a pattern of thinking that we can accept as rational and credible. We have found that Paul was not talking to the Romans about the justification theology, but that it has an important role in the meaning of the text. We have seen how the text was generated in part by some of Paul's theological ideas, and how the forms in which those ideas appear in the text are controlled by what he was intending the Romans to hear when it was read to them.

This causal reading has been subject to one important limitation. We have not been able to draw on the rest of the Pauline corpus to develop a fuller understanding of the underlying thought patterns. This limitation is given not with the two-step method of exegesis, but with the fact that this is the first experiment with it. Ideally, a two-step exegesis of one passage would be part of continuing study of all of Paul's extant letters by the same method, making wider knowledge available. Since we do not know how the other letters would appear if we applied to them the method we have begun to apply to Romans, we do not have that wider knowledge as a source. In the initial experiment, this has the advantage of illustrating the discipline of beginning with what we can see through the window of the text being studied. That would always have to be done.

At this point, it is worth considering some other readers of Paul's text. In the teleological reading we were seeking the element of meaning in the text that was what Paul intended the Romans to hear when it was read to them. This corresponds to what we should normally call 'the meaning' of a lecture or sermon, an address for a particular occasion. We now note that the Romans had Paul's address in the form of a text which they kept. Having listened and received the message, they could go back to the text again and again, and come to a fuller understanding. We can do the same if we have a copy of an address. The Romans' ways of doing this, and the questions and background knowledge they brought to it, would be different from ours. Again, if we are listening to a lecture by somebody whose mind we know well, we are likely to notice how she is drawing on a wider understanding to say what is to be said to this audience. Some of the Romans might well have been doing that when Paul's letter was read. Prisca and Aquila, for instance, could even have shared in the development of the theology. Our two-step exegesis does not involve an historical judgement that the Romans heard only what we found in the teleological reading and the theological substructure was a closed book to them.

We may also want to ask whether Luther got it wrong. If Luther had been an historical-critical exegete who, actually or ostensibly, wanted to know what Paul was saying to the Romans, then we should have to say that he did get it wrong. He would have had no chance of getting it right, since the historical information was not available. Luther was not an historical-critical exegete. The question he brought to the text led him, we can now see, not into Paul's preaching but into the underlying theology. The answer he found was a valid Pauline answer, and it was good news for the late medieval church in which he found himself, or at least for parts of it.

13

REVIEW AND CONCLUSION

In our study of Rom. 1.16–4.25, we have asked some fundamental questions and developed new exegetical attitudes and techniques. We now review these and consider the significance of their outcomes.

Rom. 1.16–4.25 – A new basic conception in continuity with the old

In chapter 2, we argued that the basic conception guiding mainstream exegesis of Rom. 1.16–4.25 is inadequate and needs to be replaced. We proposed testing the hypothesis that Paul was trying to do something other than give a justification account but the justification theology was important for whatever that was. We suggested further that if this hypothesis is correct, we could expect our conception of the passage to change in two major stages. In the first, we should see the passage as a justification account influenced by the different issue. In the second, we should have a new basic conception arising from a new understanding of Paul's intention. The changes resulting from study of the law questions could represent the first stage.

We have found that Paul was dealing with the question of how God could be seen to be righteous if he justified believers on the basis of their faith without reference to the Jew–Gentile distinction. He did this not as one giving an account, even a polemical account, of justification, but as one preaching the gospel to believers for whom this was a major practical issue. The justification theology is important for this preaching as the source of the question and therefore as a presupposition of much of the address to the Roman believers. Paul's answer to the question affirmed the justification theology. The two-step reading that yielded these results resolves the major problems that led us to formulate the new hypothesis, and accounts for the text more successfully than readings developed according to the old basic conception. It shows the law in a different light, especially by separating it from the definition of sin that emerges from Paul's discussion.

Our new basic conception does represent the second stage of the proposed two-stage change in our understanding, and so appears as an intelligible development in historical-critical study of the passage. The phrase Ἰουδαίῳ τε πρῶτον καὶ Ἕλληνι (Rom. 1.16b) is a textbook example. In traditional exegesis, Rom. 1.16–17 is the key statement of salvation through the gospel, righteousness through faith. Ἰουδαίῳ τε πρῶτον καὶ Ἕλληνι appears as an insertion that is hard to interpret. Dodd, for instance, could only say that Paul recognizes that the Jews did in fact receive the gospel first, according to God's will.[1] More commonly, it was seen either as pointing to the universal nature of the gospel over against the earlier special position of Israel, or as providing for the continuity of the plan of salvation. The first stage of the shift appears in exegeses that recognize the importance of the priority of Israel for the faithfulness of God. It is fully established in Ziesler's and Dunn's commentaries. Both still give the impression that the phrase is added in, but it is seen as seminal for important elements of the meaning of the letter.[2] When we explained Rom. 1.16–17 as Paul going to the heart of the issue of faith in the church and making the Romans ask questions, the phrase was both important and clearly integral to the whole. This represents the second stage of the shift.

This development is reflected in exegesis of the whole passage. Older exegesis saw it as exposition of justification, culturally conditioned by the Jew–Gentile distinction. More recently it has been seen as an account of justification that had a role in dealing with the impact of the gospel on the Jew–Gentile distinction. The two-step exegesis shows it as pastoral work, dealing with the new Jew–Gentile relationship created by God's gracious justification of believing sinners on the basis of faith alone.

A new historical-critical approach to Paul's letters

Our two-part exegesis tests not only our original hypothesis about this passage, but also the exegetical methods and emphases by

[1] *The Epistle of Paul to the Romans*, 9.
[2] Ziesler, *Romans*, 70; Dunn, *Romans*, 47.

which it was developed. Thus, the experiment has yielded an alternative reading of Rom. 1.16–4.25 and also an alternative historical-critical approach to Paul's letters. Whence this new approach? What are its special characteristics?

The new approach is unusual among alternative methods in that it arises from the problems and successes of mainstream historical-critical exegesis rather than being an application of a theory or technique imported from some other field. It arises from a convergence of the major questions raised in chapter 1 with the exegetical problems of Rom. 1.16–4.25 and other Pauline texts. A useful starting-point for examining it is the collapse of the basic tool question, What does this text mean?

Critical to the way we understand a text is the battery of questions, with their presuppositions, that we bring to it. Readers of this study will have noticed a continual spelling out of questions to be asked. This contrasts with mainstream exegesis, where the questions form a skeleton shaping the exegesis but not itself on view. The basic question is, What does this text mean? Its hermeneutical collapse is not bringing mainstream Pauline exegesis to a halt because it is assumed that the consensus of the debate, the basic conception of a text, *is* the answer. This corresponds to our observation in chapter 3 that the mainstream debate on Rom. 1.16–4.25 is being conducted with a consensus understanding that the whole is an exposition of justification. This approach involves the presupposition that there is such a thing as 'the meaning of the text', and its nature is self-evident.

In chapter 1, we considered the breakdown of that presupposition. This massive problem has proved to be a primary creative point in our work. It forced us to ask what we want from our encounter with the text. If the answer to such a question is not to be purely idiosyncratic, we must be able to turn to something other than the text for an answer. We received one answer from two sources. The Christian NT scholar's concern with Paul's apostolic testimony and the concern of the NT scholar per se with the text as one of Paul's letters both require that we ask what Paul was saying to the Romans. We can explore the text, as Paul's and as apostolic testimony, further by examining it as a source for Paul's theology and for a picture of him as pastor and as person. This answer kept us working with the understanding of meaning as governed by authorial intention. It was the recognition that we needed to find a new basic conception of Rom. 1.16–4.25 that made us re-examine the procedures and interests of mainstream historical-critical exegesis.

Mainstream exegetes ask, What does this text mean? What are they seeking? Interpreting the question by the answers given (the content and range of the debate), we find that they are seeking an understanding of Paul's thought as it comes to expression in the text. One of the clearest indicators of this is the criterion of coherence. In the mainstream debate, the measure of the coherence of one of Paul's letters is the coherence of the underlying thought. This may be sought at the expense of its coherence as communication. The question that we put first because of our concern with the text as Paul's and as letter, the question of what Paul was saying to the addressees, is in practice secondary. Having a transcript of what Paul was saying, mainstream exegetes ask what the text means and then say that their answer is what Paul was saying to the addressees. Thus, the two questions become forms of the one question. This process, however, depends on the presupposition that we are seeking *the* meaning of the text, and that this single entity is there to be found.

We have separated the two questions and reversed the sequence. We separated them on the ground that they will be different forms of the same question only if Paul was intending to give an account of his thought. In reading a collection of occasional, pastoral letters we cannot assume this. Accordingly, the questions must be asked separately. If in any one case the answers to the two prove to be the same, then in that case he probably was expounding his thought on the particular issue/s. When the questions are separated, each gives rise to other questions, some of them new to the debate.

We reversed the sequence of the two questions because Paul's intention is primary in the creation of the text, and gives it its nature. We are giving effective recognition to the fact that he was writing to people who were in situations and had problems, whereas mainstream exegesis, with its focus on Paul's thought, tends to see him addressing situations and problems. We saw this in Beker's work, vitiating his concern with the contingency of the letters, their occasional, pastoral character.

The separation and reversal of the questions gives its character to our new style of historical-critical exegesis of Paul's letters. It involves a teleological reading and a causal reading. It also gives rise to certain characteristic features. The most important of these are the redefined and more influential question of purpose, the characterization of the personae involved, the separation of coherence of thought and coherence of communication, the examination of the nature of the text, and the criterion of intelligibility.

The teleological reading of any letter (in principle, of any text) answers the question, Where was this going *to*? It involves reading the text in the light of its goal, the achievement of the author's purpose. The causal reading answers the question, Where was this coming *from*? It is concerned with the text as giving expression to the author's thought, and therefore as giving readers at least some access to that thought. In theory, it might be objected that this distinction is artificial because the two elements interact so closely. In practice, applying the distinction to Rom. 1.16–4.25 has freed us from trying to do too many things at once, and allowed us to see the text and Paul in a new light.

Because of the dominance of causal reading in the historical-critical search for '*the* meaning of the text', certain elements of the teleological reading that are essential to our whole understanding of the text are reduced or not considered. Giving them their due place has been important in giving us a new view.

The first is the question of purpose. In causal reading, purpose becomes an element of cause. Why did Paul write this letter to these people at this time? It becomes an introductory question, part of the preparation for detailed exegesis. In teleological reading, purpose is by definition central, and the question is a true purpose question: What response was Paul trying to elicit from the people to whom this letter was being sent? While the answers to the two questions overlap considerably, the difference of emphasis is critical for exegesis. In this study, it has been an important factor in our approach to the text as communication rather than as a network of ideas, and as pastoral speech rather than as exposition. The question of why Paul wrote this letter in these circumstances can be asked only when we know what we mean by 'this letter'. The true purpose question allows the possibility of questioning what we thought we knew about the letter.

The true purpose question involves a more sharply focussed concern with the addressees. They are considered not as a sociological grouping or a theological point of view, but as the intended recipients of this letter. We do not scour the sources for every scrap of information about the Roman church in the fifties in order to form the most detailed possible picture of the recipients of the letter. Rather, we examine Paul's text to see how he perceived his

addressees. Information about the church in Rome helps us interpret the evidence, since it helps us to establish the issues and the
setting; it does not control our picture of Paul's addressees. The
technique of identifying the personae involved – The Apostle, The
Congregation, The Conservative – is applicable to all the letters. It
may seem cumbersome, but we need the disciplines that will hold us
to the teleological reading. It is fatally easy to be drawn away into
the old global study of meaning.

In this study, the identification of the audience was sharpened by
two particular investigations. Examination of πᾶς in Rom.
1.16–4.25 led to the hypothesis, vindicated by the teleological
reading, that this πᾶς was referring to accepted general or universal
truth for the sake of the particular case in hand. It is not the
universal 'all' of philosophical-theological discourse, as is assumed
without investigation in mainstream exegesis. This discovery forced
us to consider audience more closely in chapters 7 and, especially,
8. The lack of direct address to the Romans in the passage and the
substitution of discussion with a dialogue partner led to the
identification and characterization of The Conservative. In this
respect, the passage is atypical. I have not found in the Pauline
corpus any other diatribal dialogues that shift the address like this
for so long.

In study of other letters, the sharply focussed purpose and
audience questions can modify our view. For instance, identification of opponents is widely seen as an important key to understanding Pauline letters. This takes account of the polemical
character of much of Paul's extant writing, but often at the cost of
its pastoral nature. Brinsmead's puzzled comment on Galatians
shows the problem involved: 'Thus the dialogical nature of Galatians stands out. It is a letter motivated by an intruding, offending
theology, yet it addresses the theology almost exclusively by addressing the congregation that has been 'bewitched' by the intruders.'[3]
In fact, Paul's purpose in Galatians needs to be differently conceived. It was to do everything possible to rescue the Galatians
from the temptation to accept circumcision. When his purpose is
understood on the basis of the conflict model, it is conceived as a
defence of the justification theology and/or an argument against the
opponents' case. This turns the Galatians into a jury. Something
similar although less striking occurred in our examination of

---

[3] *Galatians – Dialogical Response to Opponents*, 187.

Romans. Over against the tendency to see Romans as in some sense apologetic, we have seen Paul preaching to a committed and co-operative audience. In both cases, Paul's role as missionary and pastor is rescued from unconscious assimilation to the adversarial patterns of modern academic debate.

Awareness of the letter as address shows also in another important difference between causal and teleological reading. We noted that for mainstream exegesis coherence is the coherence of Paul's thought. That coherence question belongs to causal reading. It causes exegetes to read each of Paul's letters with one eye on the text and one on the rest of the corpus. There is nothing wrong with this. In our causal reading, too, the criterion of coherence is the coherence of Paul's thought. The severely limited discussion in chapter 12 shows how necessary is the context of the other letters for such work. On the other hand, when the only reading is causal, the function and character of the text as communication is distorted. The teleological reading is concentrated on the one letter and is concerned with coherence of communication. This shows the importance of separating the two questions and recognizing that they are complementary, so that both are necessary for full understanding and exposition.

An example of the difference created by focussing on the one letter is the treatment of Abraham in our teleological reading of Romans 4. There is recognition in the mainstream debate that the discussions of Abraham in Romans 4 and Galatians 3 are different and should not be assimilated to each other. On the other hand, one is still used to interpret the other, on the basis that Gen. 15.6 is a key Pauline proof-text for justification by faith, and that both passages are discussions of the role of faith in justification. We referred to Galatians in our study of Romans 4, not to learn about Paul's view of Abraham, but for help in defining the context of his discussion. This was part of the common ground between Paul and the Romans, and it does not show clearly enough in Romans itself. We used Galatians as a contemporary document to help establish the setting, as we might use Acts or Philo in another case. This helped us to examine Romans 4 in its own context and on its own terms. What we found was not an exposition of Abraham as a key example of justification by faith, but an exploration of Abraham's fatherhood, showing that justification of believers on the basis of faith without distinction between Jew and Gentile was the fulfilment of God's intention in the election of Abraham. Of course, no modern scholar can read one of Paul's letters except in the context of a picture of Paul derived from centuries of study of all of them. This does not invalidate the attempt to read them one at a time.

Recognition of the need for a teleological reading freed us for and directed us to careful consideration of the nature of the text. Causal reading in practice involves treating the text more as a network of ideas than as communication (although the latter is not simply missing from mainstream exegesis). Giving primary emphasis to the text as address to its particular audience led us to a study of first-century letters. The general results are applicable to all Paul's letters. They were all created in the speaking–hearing context for listeners. Therefore they all demand from us the appropriate responses, different from our responses to other texts on our desks.

Arising from concern with the text as communication, and sharpened by this study of first-century letters, is the criterion of intelligibility. It is a powerful factor in teleological reading. A general formulation is: Any proposed teleological reading should allow the text to fulfil the purpose for which it was created. Since Romans is a letter dictated for a listening audience, the text must be able to get the message across to its listeners at a first hearing. The debate does not recognize the criterion of intelligibility. So radically true is this statement that scholars generally find utterly incomprehensible any suggestion that a proposed reading of a passage cannot represent Paul's intention because his intended audience would have had no hope of recognizing it. I have heard an entire theological community, NT scholars included, burst out laughing at the suggestion that Paul's churches might have understood his letters. The burden of proof is therefore on the exegete who wants to use intelligibility as a criterion.

We argued in chapter 2 that a Paul whose letters were poor communication is an historical improbability. The Paul who emerges from mainstream historical-critical scholarship expressed his ideas and sent them to his churches. The ideas treated their issues. Apparently, he expected them to treat the letters the way scholars do, to take mysterious texts and pore over them until they yielded up their meaning. They had no tradition of interpretation to guide them, but neither did they have a two-millennia culture gap to cross. It is proper for us, who do have this gap to cross, to have to pore over the letters to get them to yield up their meaning. *It is not, however, proper to propose interpretations that would have forced Paul's churches to do likewise.* To us, the letters are scripture or the subject-matter of our discipline, so they have a claim on inordinate quantities of time and energy. To Paul's churches, they were not scripture, but messages he was anxious to convey in particular situations. Furthermore, he had (at least in some cases) to establish his claim on his readers' attention by the impact of what was being read to them. These are the reasons for insisting on the criterion of intelligibility in readings that claim to be what Paul was saying to his addressees.

That does not mean that the recipients of the letters would not have pored over them, too, and learnt more than they had first heard. It does mean that we must assume that Paul intended to say something comprehensible and directly responsive to their needs. We do not have to make Paul into a superman who always succeeded in what he intended to do, but we do need to allow that our problems of understanding are likely to arise from some failure on our part. One precept of historical-critical exegesis is that biblical texts must be taken seriously as human documents, not treated as direct divine revelation, beyond criticism. In avoiding this risk, we incur another. Exegetes may too easily be satisfied with readings which show the NT writers in a very poor light, and not be sufficiently insistent on allowing themselves to be challenged by the text.

The criterion of intelligibility is not used in the debate because interest is in Paul's thought rather than his communication. One reason for this attitude is that pastoral work in many modern Western churches is conceived in terms that are heavily psychological and sociological, and conditioned by a world view in which religion is a matter of private preference, a hobby, like golf or gardening. In our world, ordinary people do not usually understand themselves and their problems theologically. Theological language is for theological discourse. Generally, twentieth-century minds balk at the idea that when Paul talked to fellow-believers about sin, grace and being justified, he was talking directly to real people about their personal experience. If he is seen to be doing so, this means that he was interpreting and explaining it theologically. In the first century, Paul's language about grace and faith operated in a realm that has more in common with Luther throwing an ink pot at the Devil. In contrast, many present-day exegetes lived through the 'death of God' debate of the sixties, when it was often considered unreasonable to suggest that ordinary Christians should learn what 'sin' means, although nobody would have dreamt of suggesting that ordinary drivers need not learn what 'accelerator' means.

This situation creates a double block between scholars and Paul's texts. On the one hand, it seems unreal to move beyond Paul's ability 'to bring the gospel to speech in each new situation'[4] and ask what 'faith', for instance, would have meant in practice. On the other hand, the fact that Paul's terminology is in our world the specialist language of theology awakens in us inappropriate responses, just as the fact that we read the letters in printed books does.

We may again take the vocabulary and concept of faith as an example, and take the opportunity to look at another letter. In his article 'The Function of ΠΙΣΤΙΣ ΧΡΙΣΤΟΥ in Galatians', Taylor argues that Paul's use of πίστις is predominantly in juridical contexts, where he has to argue against the proposition that the law is the source of righteousness. In these discussions, πίστις and νόμος are contrasted on the basis of membership in the category of juridical language. In Galatians 3, Paul uses διαθήκη in the sense of will, not of covenant, as a way of explaining how God's benefits, including righteousness, come as a free gift through Christ and apart from the law to Jewish and Gentile beneficiaries on the same terms. Taylor spells out the terms, conditions and intended beneficiaries of the διαθήκη, showing that πίστις has a role in every aspect. He then explains the Roman *commissum fidei*, showing that its elements correspond to those of God's διαθήκη as discussed by Paul in Galatians. In his exposition, Taylor further explains, Paul uses πίστις to refer to the *fidei commissum* on which the διαθήκη depends (Christ's faithfulness) and, separately, to the trustfulness appropriate to the beneficiaries (Abraham's and the believers' faith). He sees the parallels between Paul's exposition and the Roman provision as so detailed that they can hardly be accidental. He therefore hypothesizes that Galatian law at least contained elements that would enable the Galatians to follow his argument. In this context, πίστις refers to Christ's reliability which fits him for his tenure in *commissum fidei*. Finally, a juridical understanding rather than an understanding of πίστις as faith in Christ yields a more intelligible reading of Galatians.

This approach is wholly conceptual. Taylor gives no attention to the concrete referents of Paul's terms in the Galatians' situation

---

[4] Beker, *Paul the Apostle*, 34.

and the history of God's dealings with humanity. Nor has he put himself in the Galatians' place. How were they supposed to know when Paul started this argument in Gal. 2.15 that he was using πίστις in this technical legal sense? The διαθήκη on which it all depends does not appear until Gal. 3.15, and then as a human analogy. The Paul we saw leading his Roman readers so carefully through the Abraham argument in Romans 4 does not match up with this Paul! This is a good example of Pauline exegesis that treats the texts as conceptual networks rather than as address.

Hays' book *The Faith of Jesus Christ* is very highly regarded. An example of his exegetical method also shows treatment of the text as a network of theological concepts. Examining the function of πίστις in the narrative structure of Paul's gospel, he sets out to explicate ἐξ ἀκοῆς πίστεως in Gal. 3.2.[5] He has in mind the tendency of Protestant exegesis to turn faith into a work, and is developing his ideas in contrast with the kind of position represented by Betz. His method is to examine in detail the meaning and function of πίστις in Gal. 3.2, 11, 22, and reinterpret Galatians 3 accordingly. Parallel passages to be used are Gal. 2.20; 3.26; Rom. 3.21–6. He is arguing that in the three texts Paul was not talking about the saving effect of believing, or about Jesus as the object of human faith. This tells us that he understands the context to be Paul's account of justification.

Having established the problem and the method, Hays begins with ἐξ ἀκοῆς πίστεως in Gal. 3.2. He tabulates the grammatical possibilities and the exegetical suggestions. He then looks at the other uses of ἀκοή in the letters commonly accepted as Pauline, Rom. 10.16–17; 1 Cor. 12.17; 1 Thess. 2.13. From study of these passages he concludes that ἀκοή means 'message: (what is heard)' rather than 'act of hearing'. Accordingly, he postulates this for Gal. 3.2, 5. He deals with the antithetical parallelism with ἐξ ἔργων νόμου by arguing that the two must be taken as 'indivisible meaning-units', and that a contrast between a human and a divine activity makes better sense than a contrast between two human activities as basis for God's action. He argues this case for Gal. 3.5, but not for Gal. 3.2. This leads him to accept 'message' rather than 'hearing' – not an unreasonable conclusion from the evidence he considers relevant and in the context he postulates. He then discusses the possibilities this leaves for πίστις, again considering some other verses. He concludes that, even if πίστις does mean 'believing' in some sense, the emphasis is on the message believed, and it is at least possible that it functions as a collective designation for 'that which is believed'.

Tackling his problem in this way, Hays handles the text as theological exposition and as expression of Paul's thought. He shares the assumption that we are dealing with Paul's apologia for justification through faith, and assumes that in Gal. 3.2–5 Paul was intending to talk about how God gives the gift of salvation to people. The evidence he considers relevant includes various other Pauline texts. He deals with the exegetical problems of this paragraph and the whole of Gal. 3.1–4.11 without ever offering a reading of the passage.

If we treat the text as address and apply the criterion of intelligibility, we tackle the interpretation of ἐξ ἀκοῆς πίστεως differently. First, Paul was not talking about the universal question of how God gives salvation to people. In the letter, he was making a strenuous effort to save the Galatians from succumbing to the temptation to add circumcision to their faith in Christ. He was talking to people who were in the process of making a momentous decision about what they should *do*. Should they add circumcision to their faith in Christ or continue as Gentile believers? In Gal. 3.1 he reminded them of the powerful preaching of Christ crucified that they had heard. Then he introduced his question in a way that underlined its importance and demanded an answer (Gal. 3.2a). That is, he engaged the Galatians in working this through with him. They were not to be mere auditors. The question took them back to the occasion (already evoked in Gal. 3.1) when they first heard and responded to the gospel, an experience that changed their lives. Twentieth-century Western exegetes, in a culture where (the aftermath of) Christianity is part of the order of things, easily forget how dramatic that was. The question asked about what *they did* on that memorable occasion when they received the Spirit. It was asked in the context of their need to decide what they were going to do now in relation to receiving the gift of God, eschatological justification. The question begins with the impossible alternative, which is something one does, works of the law. Set against it is ἐξ ἀκοῆς πίστεως. Ἀκοή is a perfectly ordinary word with several ordinary meanings. In the context of doing, it means 'hearing'. That corresponded to something they did on that memorable occasion. The Spirit came when they heard and believed, that is, heard with faith. Paul hammered that home with a series of questions to show just how fundamental it was, and how they should look to that experience when faced with this temptation.

The second question (Gal. 3.5) is about things that God does for them. Whereas the question about their conversion was put in terms of how they received God's action, the question about their continuing experience is put in terms of the basis on which God gives the things they are receiving. The same choice is offered. In this context, it is not at all ridiculous to ask whether God acts on the basis of something the Galatians are doing. This is not theory, but a question about what is happening and how they are participating in it.

What does 'faith' mean in these verses? We may sharpen the question: Does our reading have Paul convincing the Galatians that they can get God to do things for them by a mental act of believing rather than a physical act of circumcision? Taylor and Hays found that an appropriate way to express their concern.[6] This problem arises not from Paul's text, or even from Paul's thought, but from the later debate over justification by faith alone. That shapes the way exegesis in the Luther tradition conceives Paul's idea of faith. It is governed by the soteriological alternatives of faith *or* works of the law, believing *or* doing, receiving *or* earning. This leads to the kind of debate that is reflected in the contrast between Dodd's and Byrne's accounts. Dodd describes an 'attitude of pure receptivity in which the soul appropriates what God has done'.[7] Byrne argues that Christians are justified in Christ and Christ is justified on the basis of his work of obedience. 'God's gracious justification runs its full course in Christians in so far as they "remain within" and live out in their own lives the justifying obedience of Christ.'[8]

In writing Galatians, Paul was not faced with a question about the theology of justification, or with a choice between faith and works. He was helping the Galatians face the question of what they needed to do to be sure of receiving at the eschaton the salvation promised in the gospel, and the choice was between faith and faith plus works of the law. He reminded them that God had acted and was acting among them 'on the basis of' their faith, and that God justified Abraham because Abraham believed. How did he expect

---

[6] Taylor, ΠΙΣΤΙΣ, 75; Hays, *The Faith of Jesus Christ*, 140.
[7] *The Epistle of Paul to the Romans*, 56.
[8] *Reckoning with Romans*, 66.

them to understand the 'believing' terminology? The modern faith–works contrast was simply not on the scene. Their believing was not separable from God's action that created it, and not separable from the fact that it had turned their lives upside down, given them a new Lord, a new fellowship and new ways of living. Paul did not expect them to sort out some theological essence of faith as pure belief, or decide how far faith was separable from works. He was helping them decide whether to continue as they were or change their lifestyle, adding to their allegiance to Christ a responsibility to the law of Moses.

Similarly, we have argued that when Paul was talking about faith to the Romans in Rom. 1.16–4.25 the issue was faith over against faith plus membership in Israel. Again, the question of a theological essence of 'faith' was not at stake. For those people, faith and a new lifestyle were inseparable. This does not imply that the faith *or* works question is theologically invalid, or that Paul's texts will not yield a Pauline answer to it. If we read Paul's texts through that question we shall be led away from what he intended to say to his addressees, and risk misunderstanding the underlying theology.

These are the inappropriate sets of responses to which we refer when we say that Paul's letters are treated in the debate as theological exposition. Correspondingly, the life-settings of the letters are understood primarily in conceptual terms. A classic example is the debate over whether the opponents in Corinth were Gnostics or Enthusiasts. Such a question is necessary but not sufficient. Some help with recognizing the 'real-life' quality of the situations is coming from sociological studies, although these also tend to abstract from the texts in the direction of a modern academic discipline.

In sum, experience in our world tends to hide from exegetes the fact that Paul's letters were not 'doing theology'. Mainstream historical-critical exegesis with its inherited understanding of them as theology shows a strong tendency to treat them as networks of concepts, and to abstract general theology from his pastoral speech. The criterion of intelligibility has not been rejected. It has simply not been considered. Now that we have proposed it, we submit that it imposes itself. The primary characteristic of a letter is that it is communication. We say that Paul's letters were substitutes for his presence, and even opponents said that they were βαρεῖαι καὶ ἰσχυραί (2 Cor. 10.10). The criterion of intelligibility could be rejected only if it proved inapplicable in practice, if it were clear that Paul's letters will not make sense if we assume that they could be followed by listeners, without extensive exegesis. Our teleological reading may not command acceptance in every detail, but it has shown that Romans will make sense as communication, very powerful sense.

The criterion of intelligibility will exclude certain readings of what Paul said, but it does not mean that we reject all the theological wealth found by exegetes before us. The separation between teleological and causal reading allows the criterion of intelligibility to operate, and has the complementary advantage that we need no longer try to make the text 'say' all that we can learn from it. The separate causal reading allows us to acknowledge that in it we are studying this text in the context of the whole corpus for the sake of an understanding of Paul's thought. We recognize that he was not intending to give an account of his thought, but because his pastoral work was rooted in the gospel it gives us access to a great deal of his thought. This is a development from the mainstream approach to taking the letters seriously as letters and pastoral. There it is done by perceiving the material essentially as occasional rather than systematic theology.

Perceptions of the creation theology in Rom. 1.16–4.25 offer an example of the unnecessary constriction which arises from treating, What was Paul saying to the Romans? and What does this text mean? as two forms of the one question. Our study in chapter 12 shows the Creator–creature relationship as defining the nature of sin and of salvation, thus shaping the theology of justification. This theological insight is not new. It appears in various forms in scholarly study of Romans and of Paul's thought. Käsemann, for instance, expounds the newness of the gospel in this passage in terms of the extension of God's covenant faithfulness to faithfulness to the whole creation. We saw in chapter 11 how this distorts the text so that it cannot meet the criterion of intelligibility. The appropriate response is not to say that Käsemann is wrong. This insight is very important. It is to say that Käsemann's rich encounter with the text demonstrates the inadequacy of the traditional pattern of exegesis. Within that pattern, Barrett's treatment of the Creator–creature relationship is truer to the text as letter.[9]

Similarly, we argued in the causal exposition that the sin of which the sinners are guilty and that holds them in bondage is the

---

[9] *A Commentary on the Epistle to the Romans*, 81–2.

sin of Adam. Hooker's earlier proposal that Paul was talking about Adam in Rom. 1.18–32 aroused interest but did not become established in mainstream exegesis, at least partly because of the difficulty of arguing that as '*the* meaning of the text'.[10]

Accountability to NT scholarship

We have argued that a new historical-critical approach to Paul's letters is needed, developed it, shown it yielding helpful results with a key passage, and argued that its special features open up the texts to us in a new way. The study of Rom. 1.16–4.25 is recognizably part of the current debate on Romans, but methodological changes so fundamental and extensive create a difficulty for accountability. Any academic discipline is a communal enterprise. Scholars expect to be accountable to the scholarly community. In NT exegesis the normal form of this accountability is participation in the continuing debate *on its terms*. We questioned elements of the mainstream debate which are accepted presuppositions and therefore not discussed. This led us to formulate new key questions. As a result, neither our teleological nor our causal reading can be presented as a running engagement with other readings. It is vital that this should not be attempted, since its effect is to pull the detail of the two-step exegesis back into the framework of the mainstream debate, choking off the new enterprise before it has been considered on its own terms. Of course, this comparative isolation is not characteristic of the two-step method of exegesis. It is an inevitable feature of this first experiment with it.

We noted that changes in exegetical practice take place in continuity and discontinuity with the dominant patterns of their times. To present a new approach, one must concentrate on the new elements, thus emphasizing the discontinuity. This study nevertheless arises from the ongoing debate and I am very much beholden to it. The informed reader will have noticed strong elements of continuity. Some of these have already been mentioned. A few more examples may point up the continuity more clearly.

We argued that the issue in Rom. 1.18–3.20 is God's righteousness as judge. Paul was discussing it not as a question on a philosophical-theological agenda but as a problem believers faced with the gospel of justification for all believers without reference to

[10] 'Adam in Romans 1'.

their membership or non-membership in Israel. This reading over-comes the problems the passage poses when Paul is assumed to be trying to convince The Reader that all have sinned and therefore need grace. It allows us to see that sin is a datum in the passage, not in any sense the goal of the argument.

Barrett in his 1957 commentary explicates this passage, with a pre-Sanders view of the law, as demonstrating the human predica-ment of sinfulness and the misguidedness of any view that the law enables human beings to escape that predicament. He faces all the problems this poses. On the other hand, his exegesis is on the basis that 'before salvation can be completed, righteousness must be manifested. God, the righteous judge, must do righteous judgement in his court; and, in this court, man must secure the verdict, Righteous.'[11] Accordingly, when he concludes his discussion at Rom. 3.20, he describes the human predicament not in terms of human sin but in terms of the way God's righteousness as judge is manifested: 'As long, therefore, as God's righteousness is mani-fested and understood in terms of the law it must spell wrath. The only hope for man is that God should find some other means, beyond law and religion, of manifesting his righteousness.'[12]

It will be obvious that we share Barrett's view that Paul was talking about the eschatological verdict. It is also clear that our view that Rom. 1.18–3.20 is focussed on God's judgement rather than on human sin is a development from Barrett's position. This results from two major factors, Sanders' presentation of the role of the law in first-century Judaism, which has been a major factor in the continuing debate, and the new method of historical-critical exegesis, which sets the text in a different light.

Our whole exegesis clearly rests on assumptions about the apocalyptic framework of Paul's discussions and about the way righteousness is to be understood on the basis of Jewish tradition. These are a set of presuppositions widely accepted in the debate, and we have accepted them even while we were questioning major methodological presuppositions. If we had taken a more Bultman-nian view of the relationship between Paul and the Hellenistic world, for instance, the language would have appeared to be functioning somewhat differently.

Another example of continuity is provided by Dunn's assessment

---

[11] *A Commentary on the Epistle to the Romans*, 30.
[12] *Ibid.*, 71.

that Paul wanted to free promise and law from ethnic constraints for the benefit of a wider range of recipients.[13] This is a good analytic comment on Paul's pastoral work as it appears in the teleological reading. As an interpretation of what Paul was intending to do, it tends to impose a presupposition that he was writing theology. Dunn shows him doing it polemically. We saw Paul drawing on his theology for pastoral speech. Here the continuity is clear, and the discontinuity is created methodologically, by the new view of Paul's purpose and the nature of the text he created in fulfilling it.

The reader will be able to call to mind other examples of this kind of continuity. Always it comes together with discontinuity. Problems are redefined or disappear, and new questions arise. Accordingly, answerability to the current debate takes the form of very careful presentation of the general issues, explicit spelling out of questions, and very detailed accounting to Paul's text for the readings. In this context, two issues need further discussion: the testing of the readings offered and the discussion in chapter 2 of the danger of making Paul in our own image.

In chapter 11, we tested our teleological reading extensively before accepting it as a reasonable account of what Paul was hoping the Romans would hear when Rom. 1.16–4.25 was read to them. Only then did we use it as the frame of reference for the causal reading. Such testing does not appear in the mainstream debate. In practice, it is replaced by the exegete's decision to publish or not publish ideas, and by the processes of the debate. For the causal reading, no battery of tests is applicable. In this limited study their control function has been largely replaced by the discipline of working on Paul's thought in the framework of the teleological reading. In a full causal reading, we should also have the disciplines of working within the context of the whole corpus. In a full debate with two-step readings, the normal processes of academic debate would be established as well.

In chapter 3, it was asserted that most Pauline studies show Paul as a scholar writing for other scholars. He is seen as making the best possible argument, and seeking an assessment that his argument was good enough to establish his conclusion. Any action he hoped for would flow from that intellectual response. At that stage, only a series of apparently trivial examples could be adduced as

---

[13] *Romans*, lxxi.

evidence. The exegesis of Rom. 1.16–4.25 has shown the meaning
and ground of this assertion, making it more open to assessment. It
is revealed as a positive statement of the negatively stated claim
that mainstream historical-critical study fails to take with full
seriousness its own dictum that Paul's letters are *letters* and *pastoral*
and must be treated as such. We made two important moves in
treating them as letters. In chapter 8, we started from our knowledge of ancient letters and asked how this should affect our
reading. Usually, scholars assume that Romans contains a long
treatise section and seek a category of letter to accommodate this.
The other move was to make the purpose question truly teleological, forcing a closer study of the addressees as Paul saw them.
These moves also helped us to see the letter as the work of a pastor
in action. One other move has been critical to this. We worked on
the assumption that Paul was speaking with authority as pastor
and apostle, not with some deference or diffidence as apologist. In
doing this, we were taking Paul at his word.

Making Paul in our own image as scholar rather than allowing
the text its full pastoral impact is partly a result of underlying
questions. The key question that makes Paul in the image of a
scholar is, Against whom or what is Paul arguing? This is a key
question of Pauline scholarship.

The key question that allows Paul to emerge as a pastor is, To
whom was he speaking and what response was he seeking? This
question will not reveal a pastor if it is asked about a text in which
a scholar is trying to defeat opponents' arguments. It may be
objected that The Apostle's address to The Conservative in our
teleological reading is directed against the presuppositions inhi-
biting his relationship with Gentile believers. This is true, but by
itself it would constitute an inadequate and distorting account of
The Apostle's purpose and approach, which are positive, not
negative.

One cannot understand Paul's arguments without identifying his
problems, and these were often caused by opponents who were
putting conflicting points of view, even attacking Paul's preaching
and teaching. The 'against' question must be asked, but it must
always be subordinated to the true purpose question of teleological
reading. Otherwise, it imposes a presupposition that makes it
unlikely, if not impossible, that Paul will appear as pastor in the
way he does in our teleological reading.

Again, it may be objected that we have avoided making Paul in our own image as scholar only to make him in our own image as pastor. First-century Mediterranean pastors did not use twentieth-century Western psychology, and surely that is the source of a term like 'a disjunction in his self-perception', which we used in describing The Apostle's approach to The Conservative.[14] This objection invites several comments.

First, we observed that Paul did bring to light and strip away some assumptions that underpinned The Conservative's self-perception. We did not speculate on whether he thought of the process in the way a modern Western psychologically trained pastor might think of it. Paul raised issues such as the impartiality of God's judgement and the special gift of the Torah to Israel, and showed that they had been misunderstood. On the other hand, he did say σὺ Ἰουδαῖος ἐπονομάζῃ καὶ ἐπαναπαύῃ νόμῳ καὶ καυχᾶσαι ἐν θεῷ (Rom. 2.17) and τί οὖν τὸ περισσὸν τοῦ Ἰουδαίου; (Rom. 3.1a). It is difficult for twentieth-century Western listeners-in to get a grasp on these as address without using some such term as 'self-perception', even though we know that our understanding of a 'self' is different from Paul's and the Romans'. There is truth, then, in the suggestion that we have made Paul in our own image as pastor, but we have been aware of the question and taken care of the way this affects our reading. Thus, for instance, the full phrase about the Conservative's self-perception is 'something that we can perceive as a disjunction in his self-perception'.[15] The explication of this is related to clear textual evidence. It is therefore far less insidious than the unconscious making of Paul in the scholarly image that leads Conzelmann to talk about addressing the reader with surprising directness or Kelber to consider the significance of Paul's preference for letter as a literary form.[16]

Second, the admiration that the Fathers or Luther, for instance, sometimes express for Paul's pastoral awareness and approach finds little echo in modern commentaries. This contrast is pointed up by the agenda that Best finds relevant in his study of Paul as pastor.[17] Thus, a modern reader is particularly likely to perceive a concern with Paul as pastor as a peculiarity of the exegete.

Third, and most important, the question of the way in which and the extent to which we make Paul in our own image is a form of the

---

[14] Above, p. 123.
[15] Above, p. 123.
[16] Above, pp. 32–3.
[17] *Paul and his Converts.*

hermeneutical question of the role of the reader in meaning. We noted in chapter 1 that we now have different ways of conceiving of the meaning of a text. Is it contained in the text as what the author wanted to say? Does it inhere in the structures of the text, more or less independently of the writer's intention? Does it arise in the encounter between the reader and the text? We argued that in practice the model of meaning which is applicable depends on the nature of the text we are reading and what we want to do with it. We have acknowledged that Romans is a letter written as part of Paul's ministry and that we want to attend to it as his. This requires the model of meaning as contained in the text and in some sense governed by the author's intention. (It does not, of course, involve a judgement that the use of other models of meaning could not also be valid, for purposes to which they might be appropriate. That is a separate question.)

Our view of the text here and our goal for this exegesis preclude the use of the model of meaning as arising in the encounter between reader and text. It does not, however, negate the truths of that model. Without a reader, a writer's text is for ever locked up in silence. Only a reader can make it 'speak', and the reader must necessarily contribute to what she 'hears' it 'say'. Meaning cannot be sought in a letter like this as if it were a chemical compound which will be found to have the same composition whoever performs the analysis. No exegete, therefore, can avoid making Paul in her own image to some extent. That is one of the reasons why the continuing debate is necessary. It also means that we should be aware of what we are doing. For this, the work in this book has two advantages. First, we have been forced to ask questions that are not usually made explicit and that focus attention on ourselves as exegetes: What do we want to achieve? What kind of text do we think we are reading? How should that shape our approach to it? Second, good use of historical-critical principles relates us to the text in such a way that we are as open as possible to be challenged by it. The two-step method frees us from trying to do too many things at once, reducing the temptation to draw Paul into our concerns before we have attended to him in his own terms.

The church and the Bible

We began this study from two concerns, the Christian concern with the church's alienation from the Bible and the scholarly concern with respecting the nature of Paul's texts. The two quickly con-verged, and we have been working within the field of scholarship, focussing on the implications of the scholarly concern. It seems appropriate to ask, by way of epilogue, whether the results offer any small contribution to the massive issues of the church's relationship with the Bible. Some readers may question whether they are not counter-productive. The two-step method has led us to a reading of what Paul was saying in Rom. 1.16–4.25 which might well seem to widen the culture gap and sharpen the sense of alienation. If so, are we being driven harder towards the apparently ahistorical alternatives that are being pioneered?

This work is being done in pursuit of truth, not of immediate relevance. It must be observed, however, that two people have used the method in church study programmes at various levels and found that participants were delighted to come to grips with texts, often for the first time. Working ministers, some very highly qualified academically and some not, found the study of Rom. 1.16–4.25 opening up agendas that were urgent for them. Notable examples were pastoral problems with people who cannot accept forgiveness and the issues of the relationship between the gospel and the various cultures in which it comes to living expression. These outcomes were not simply products of the two-step method, but they show that far from having the alienating effect that might be feared, it can offer new access to Paul's apostolic testimony. This is partly because the unabashed acceptance of the particularity of the texts allows their humanity to shine through. The Bible participates in the particularity of the incarnation.

We noted the importance of the breakdown of the question What does this text mean? In this study, we have been attending to the text as Paul's, from the church's viewpoint, as apostolic testimony. This involves accepting *for this task* the model of meaning as contained in the text and in some sense governed by the author's intention. This enterprise is critical because the gospel is rooted in God's action in a particular time and place, and the story is given to us by the witnesses. Without the historical study, we risk slipping away into solipsism, and creating a revitalized Gnosticism. On the other hand, this is the first step in the church's encounter with the text. Our work does not address the question of whether, and if so how, other models of meaning should also be used. They are in use, and if the scripture is to be appropriated in the church's life, and if the church is to indwell the biblical story, it seems that is a proper pattern, in principle. It is part of the church's continuing task to examine the ways in which other models should be taken up. This involves major hermeneutical and theological questions about the roles of different kinds of readings and the relationships between them, in the church and in the various theological disciplines.

SELECT BIBLIOGRAPHY

Bible

Novum Testamentum Graece, ed. Nestle–Aland et al., 27th edn, Stuttgart: Deutsche Bibelstiftung, 1993.

Septuaginta, ed. A. Rahlfs, Stuttgart: Privilegierte Württembergische Bibelanstalt, 1935.

Other ancient texts

Apocrypha and Pseudepigrapha

Charlesworth, J. H., ed. *The Old Testament Pseudepigrapha*, 2 vols., London: Darton, Longman and Todd, 1983–5.

Athanasius

'Contra Gentes' and 'De Incarnatione', ed. and trans. R. W. Thomson, Oxford: Clarendon Press, 1971.

Augustine

De Spiritu et Littera, in *The Works of Aurelius Augustine, Bishop of Hippo: A New Translation*, trans. and, ed. Marcus Dods, 15 vols., vol. IV, Edinburgh: Clark, 1872, pp. 157–232.

Chrysostom, St John (pseudo-)

'Commentary on the Epistle of St. Paul the Apostle to the Galatians', in P. Schaff et al. (eds.), *A Select Library of the Nicene and Post-Nicene Fathers of the Christian Church*, vol. XIII, New York: Christian Literature Company, 1889, pp. 1–48.

Cicero

De Oratore, trans. E. W. Sutton and H. Rackham, LCL, 2 vols., London: Heinemann, 1967–8.

Letters to Atticus, ed. with trans. by E. O. Winstedt, LCL, 3 vols., London: Heinemann, 1966–70.

Letters to his Friends, ed. with trans. by W. G. Williams, LCL, 3 vols., London: Heinemann, 1965.

Cynic Epistles

See Malherbe, A. J.

Dead Sea Scrolls
The Dead Sea Scrolls in English, ed. and trans. G. Vermes, 3rd edn, Harmondsworth: Penguin, 1987.
Die Texte aus Qumran: Hebräisch und Deutsch, ed. E. Lohse, 2nd edn, Darmstadt: Wissenschaftliche Buchgesellschaft, 1971.

Demetrius
On Style, ed. with trans. by W. R. Roberts in *Aristotle, The Poetics, Longinus, On the Sublime, Demetrius, On Style*, LCL, London: Heinemann, 1965.

Diognetus
The Epistle to Diognetus: The Greek Text with Introduction, Translation and Notes by H. G. Meecham, Manchester: Manchester University Press, 1949.

Epictetus
The Discourses as reported by Arrian, The Manual, and the Fragments, ed. with trans. by W. A. Oldfather, LCL, 2 vols., London: Heinemann, 1926–8.

Eusebius
The Ecclesiastical History and The Martyrs of Palestine, trans. H. J. Lawlor and J. E. L. Oulton, 2 vols., London: SPCK, 1927–8.

Heraclitus
See Malherbe, A. J.: *The Cynic Epistles*.

Justin Martyr
Dialogue with Trypho, in *The Ante-Nicene Fathers: Translations of the Writings of the Fathers down to A.D. 325*, ed. A. Roberts and J. Donaldson, vol. I, Grand Rapids: Eerdmans, reprinted 1987, pp. 154–270.

Midrash Rabbah
Midrash Rabbah: Genesis, trans. J. Neusner, 3 vols., Atlanta: Scholars, 1985.
Midrash Rabbah: Exodus, trans. S. M. Lehrman, London: Soncino, 1939.

Mishnah
The Mishnah, trans. H. Danby, Oxford: Oxford University Press, 1973.

Philo
Philo, with trans. by F. H. Colson, G. H. Whitaker and R. Marcus, LCL, London: Heinemann, 1958–68.

Plutarch
On Listening to Lectures, in *Plutarch's Moralia*, with English trans. by F. C. Babbitt, LCL, vol. I, London: Heinemann, 1927.

Quintilian
Institutes of Oratory, trans. J. S. Watson, 2 vols., London: Bohn, 1856.

Seneca
Letters to Lucilius, ed. and trans. E. Phillips Barker, 2 vols., Oxford: Clarendon Press, 1932.
Suetonius
De Vita Caesarum, in *Suetonius*, trans. J. C. Rolfe, LCL, London: Heinemann, 1965.
Talmud
The Babylonian Talmud, 35 vols., London: Soncino, 1972–84.

Other

Achtemeier, P. J. 'Omne Verbum Sonat: The New Testament and the Oral Environment of Late Western Antiquity', *JBL* 109 (1990), 3–27.
  Romans, Atlanta: John Knox, 1985.
  'Some Things in Them Hard to Understand', *Int* 38 (1984), 254–67.
  'Unsearchable Judgments and Inscrutable Ways: Reflections on the Discussion of Romans', in E. H. Lovering, Jr, ed., *Society of Biblical Literature 1995 Seminar Papers*, Atlanta: Scholars, 1995, pp. 521–34.
Alexander, L. 'The Living Voice: Scepticism towards the Written Word in Early Christian and in Graeco-Roman Texts', in D. A. Clines, S. E. Fowl and S. E. Porter (eds.), *The Bible in Three Dimensions: Essays in Celebration of Forty Years of Biblical Studies in the University of Sheffield*, JSOTSup 87, Sheffield: JSOT, 1990, pp. 221–47.
Aune, D. E. *The New Testament in its Literary Environment*, LEC, Philadelphia: Westminster, 1987.
  'Romans as a Logos Protreptikos in the Context of Ancient Religious and Philosophical Propaganda', in M. Hengel and U. Heckel (eds.), *Paulus und das antike Judentum*, WUNT 58, Tübingen: Mohr (Siebeck), 1991, pp. 91–124.
The Authorized Daily Prayer Book of the United Hebrew Congregations of the British Commonwealth of Nations, new edn, London: Eyre and Spottiswoode, 1962.
Bahr, G. J. 'Paul and Letter Writing in the Fifth Century', *CBQ* 28 (1966), 465–77. (This article refers to the first century and is sometimes cited with 'First' in the title, including by Bahr, *JBL* 87 (1968), 27.)
  'The Subscriptions in the Pauline Letters', *JBL* 87 (1968), 27–41.
Barclay, J. M. G. 'Paul among Diaspora Jews: Anomaly or Apostate?', *JSNT* 60 (1995), 89–120.
Barr, J. *The Semantics of Biblical Language*, Oxford: Oxford University Press, 1961.
Barrett, C. K. *A Commentary on the Epistle to the Romans*, BNTC, London: Black, 1957.
  Freedom and Obligation: A Study of the Epistle to the Galatians, London: SPCK, 1985.
  From First Adam to Last: A Study in Pauline Theology, London: Black, 1962.

'I am not Ashamed of the Gospel', in *Foi et salut selon S. Paul*, AnBib 42, Rome: Pontifical Biblical Institute, 1970, pp. 19–50.

Paul: An Introduction to His Thought, Outstanding Christian Thinkers, London: Chapman, 1994.

Barth, K. *The Epistle to the Romans*, trans. E. C. Hoskyns, 6th edn, Oxford: Oxford University Press, paperback, 1968.

A Shorter Commentary on Romans, trans. D. H. van Daalen, London: SCM, 1959.

Barth, M. *Justification: Pauline Texts Interpreted in the Light of the Old and New Testaments*, Grand Rapids: Eerdmans, 1971.

Barthes, R. *Image – Music – Text. Essays Selected and Translated by Stephen Heath*, London: Fontana/Collins, 1977.

Barton, J. *Reading the Old Testament: Method in Biblical Study*, London: Darton, Longman and Todd, 1984.

Bassler, J. M. *Divine Impartiality: Paul and a Theological Axiom*, SBLDS 59, Chico: Scholars, 1982.

Bauer, W. *A Greek–English Lexicon of the New Testament and Other Early Christian Literature*, trans. and ed. W. A. Arndt, F. W. Gringrich, F. W. Danker, 2nd edn, Chicago, University of Chicago Press, 1979.

Beavis, M. A. 'Literary and Sociological Aspects of the Function of Mark 4.11–12', Ph.D., Cambridge, 1987.

Mark's Audience: The Literary and Social Setting of Mark 4.11–12 JSNTSup 33, Sheffield: JSOT, 1989.

Beker, J. C. 'The Faithfulness of God and the Priority of Israel in Paul's Letter to the Romans', *HTR* 79 (1986), 10–16.

Paul the Apostle: The Triumph of God in Life and Thought, Edinburgh: Clark, 1980.

Benko, S. 'Pagan Criticism of Christianity during the First Two Centuries A.D.', *ANRW* II.23.2 (1980), pp. 1055–1118.

Berger, K. 'Apostelbrief und apostolische Rede. Zum Formular frühchristlicher Rede', *ZNW* 65 (1974), 190–231.

Formgeschichte des Neuen Testaments, Heidelberg: Quelle and Meyer, 1984.

Best, E. *The Letter of Paul to the Romans*, Cambridge: Cambridge University Press, 1967.

Paul and his Converts: The Sprunt Lectures 1985, Edinburgh: Clark, 1988.

Betz, H. D. *Galatians: A Commentary on Paul's Letter to the Churches in Galatia*, Hermeneia, Philadelphia: Fortress, 1979.

Black, M. *Romans*, NCB Commentaries, London: Marshall, Morgan and Scott, 1973.

Blackman, C. 'Romans 3.26b: A Question of Translation', *JBL* 87 (1968), 203–4.

Blass, F. and A. Debrunner *A Greek Grammar of the New Testament and Other Early Christian Literature*, trans. and rev. by R. W. Funk, Chicago: University of Chicago Press, 1961.

Boers, H. 'The Problem of Jews and Gentiles in the Macro-Structure of Romans', *Neot* 15 (1981), 1–11.

Bonner, S. F. *Education in Ancient Rome: From the Elder Cato to the Younger Pliny*, London: Methuen, 1977.

Booth, W. C. *The Rhetoric of Fiction*, Chicago: University of Chicago Press, 1961.

Borgen, P. 'The Early Church and the Hellenistic Synagogue', *ST* 37 (1983), 55–78.

Bornkamm, G. 'Gesetz und Natur (Röm. 2, 14–15)', in *Studien zu Antike und Urchristentum*, 2nd edn, Munich: Kaiser, 1963, pp. 93–118.

'The Letter to the Romans as Paul's Last Will and Testament', in K. P. Donfried (ed.), *The Romans Debate: Revised and Expanded Edition*, Edinburgh: Clark, 1991, pp. 16–28.

Paul, trans. D. M. G. Stalker, London: Hodder and Stoughton, 1971.

'Paulinische Anakoluthe', in *Das Ende des Gesetzes: Paulusstudien*, Munich: Kaiser, 1952, pp. 76–92.

'The Revelation of God's Wrath (Romans 1–3)', in *Early Christian Experience*, trans. P. L. Hammer, London: SCM, 1969, pp. 47–70.

'Theologie als Teufelskunst', in *Geschichte und Glaube II*, Munich: Kaiser, 1971, pp. 140–8.

Botha, P. J. J. 'The Verbal Art of the Pauline Letters: Rhetoric, Performance and Presence', in S. E. Porter and T. H. Olbricht (eds.), *Rhetoric and the New Testament: Essays from the 1992 Heidelberg Conference*, JSNTSup 90, Sheffield: JSOT, 1993, pp. 409–28.

Bowen, J. *A History of Western Education*, vol. I, *The Ancient World: Orient and Mediterranean 2000 B.C.–A.D. 1054*, New York: St Martin's, 1972.

Brinsmead, B. H. *Galatians – Dialogical Response to Opponents*, SBLDS 65, Chico: Scholars, 1982.

Brown, R. E. and J. P. Meier, *Antioch and Rome*, New York: Paulist, 1983.

Bruce, F. F. *The Epistle of Paul to the Romans: An Introduction and Commentary*, NIGTC, 2nd edn, Grand Rapids: Eerdmans, 1985.

'The Romans Debate – Continued', *BJRL* 64 (1981–2), 334–59.

Bultmann, R. 'ΔΙΚΑΙΟΣΥΝΗ ΘΕΟΥ', *JBL* 83 (1964), 12–16.

Der Stil der paulinischen Predigt und die kynisch-stoische Diatribe, Göttingen: Vandenhoeck and Ruprecht, 1910.

Theology of the New Testament, trans. K. Grobel, 2 vols., London: SCM, 1952–5.

Bussmann, C. *Themen der paulinischen Missionspredigt auf dem Hintergrund der spätjüdisch-hellenistischen Missionsliteratur*, Frankfurt: P. Lang/Berne: H. Lang, 1971.

Byrne, B., SJ, *Reckoning with Romans: A Contemporary Reading of Paul's Gospel*, GNS 18, Wilmington: Glazier, 1986.

'Sons of God' – 'Seed of Abraham': A Study of the Idea of the Sonship of God of All Christians in Paul against the Jewish Background', AnBib 83, Rome: Biblical Institute, 1979.

'Universal Need of Salvation and Universal Salvation by Faith in the Letter to the Romans', *Pacifica* 8 (1995), 123–39.

Cambier, J. M. *L'Evangile de Dieu selon l'Epître aux romains*, Exégèse et Théologie biblique, vol. I, Bruges: Desclée de Brouwer, 1967.

Campbell, D. A. *The Rhetoric of Righteousness in Romans 3.21–26*, JSNTSup 65, Sheffield: JSOT, 1992.

'A Rhetorical Suggestion Concerning Romans 2', in E. H. Lovering, Jr (ed.), *Society of Biblical Literature 1995 Seminar Papers*, Atlanta: Scholars, 1995.

Campbell, W. S. 'Did Paul Advocate Separation from the Synagogue? A Reaction to Francis Watson: *Paul, Judaism and the Gentiles: A Sociological Approach*', SJT 42 (1989), 457–67.

'The Freedom and Faithfulness of God in Relation to Israel', *JSNT* 13 (1981), 27–45.

'Historical Context, Exegesis and Preaching with Particular Reference to Paul's Letters', *IBS* 5 (1983), 73–93.

'Romans III as a Key to the Structure and Thought of the Letter', *NovT* 23 (1981), 22–40.

'Why did Paul Write Romans?', *ExpTim* 85 (1973–4), 264–9.

Cerfaux, L. 'Abraham "père en circoncision" des gentils', in *Recueil Lucien Cerfaux*, 3 vols., Gembloux: Editions J. Ducolot, 1954–62, vol. II, pp. 333–8.

Charlesworth, J. H. 'Christian and Jewish Self-Definition in Light of the Christian Additions to the Apocryphal Writings', in E. P. Sanders with A. I. Baumgarten and A. Mendelson (eds.), *Jewish and Christian Self-Definition*, vol. II, *Aspects of Judaism in the Graeco-Roman Period*, Philadelphia: Fortress, 1981, pp. 27–55.

Cioffi, F. 'Intention and Interpretation in Criticism', in D. Newton-de Molina (ed.), *On Literary Intention*, Edinburgh: Edinburgh University Press, 1976, pp. 55–73.

Clark, D. L. *Rhetoric in Graeco-Roman Education*, New York: Columbia University Press, 1957.

Conzelmann, H. *1 Corinthians: A Commentary on the First Epistle to the Corinthians*, trans. J. W. Leitch, Hermeneia, Philadelphia: Fortress, 1975.

Cook, J. G. 'The Logic and Language of Romans 1, 20', *Biblica* 75 (1994), 494–517.

Cranfield, C. E. B. *A Critical and Exegetical Commentary on the Epistle to the Romans*, ICC, 2 vols., Edinburgh: Clark, 1975–9.

Cranford, M. 'Abraham in Romans 4: The Father of All who Believe', *NTS* 41 (1995), 71–88.

Culler, J. *Structuralist Poetics: Structuralism, Linguistics and the Study of Literature*, London: Routledge and Kegan Paul, 1975.

Dahl, N. A. 'Letter', *IDBSup*, pp. 538–40.

'The Missionary Theology in the Epistle to the Romans', in *Studies in Paul: Theology for the Early Christian Mission*, Minneapolis: Augsburg, 1977, pp. 70–94.

'The Particularity of the Pauline Epistles as a Problem in the Ancient Church', in *Neotestamentica et Patristica: Freundesgabe, O. Cullmann zu seinem 60. Geburtstag überreicht*, NovTSup 6, Leiden: Brill, 1962, pp. 261–71.

'Romans 3.9: Text and Meaning', in M. D. Hooker and S. G. Wilson (eds.), *Paul and Paulinism: Essays in honour of C. K. Barrett*, London: SPCK, 1982, pp. 184–204.

Davies, G. N. *Faith and Obedience in Romans: A Study in Romans 1–4*, JSNTSup 39, Sheffield: JSOT, 1990.

Davies, J. G. 'Subjectivity and Objectivity in Biblical Exegesis', *BJRL* 66 (1983–4), 44–53.

Davies, W. D. 'Paul and the People of Israel', in *Jewish and Pauline Studies*, London: SPCK, 1984, pp. 123–52.

Paul and Rabbinic Judaism: Some Rabbinic Elements in Pauline Theology, 4th edn, Philadelphia: Fortress, 1980.

Deissmann, G. A. *Bible Studies: Contributions chiefly from Papyri and Inscriptions to the History of the Language, the Literature, and the Religion of Hellenistic Judaism and Primitive Christianity*, trans. A. Grieve, Edinburgh: Clark, 1901.

Light from the Ancient East: The New Testament Illustrated by Recently Discovered Texts of the Graeco-Roman World, trans. L. R. M. Strachan, London: Hodder and Stoughton, 1910.

Paul: A Study in Social and Religious History, trans. W. E. Wilson, reprint of 2nd edn, New York: Harper, 1957.

Dewey, J. 'Textuality in an Oral Culture: A Survey of the Pauline Traditions', *Semeia* 65 (1994), 37–65.

Dibelius, M. *A Fresh Approach to the New Testament and Early Christian Literature*, London: Ivor, Nicholson and Watson, 1936.

Dodd, B. 'Romans 1:17 – A *Crux Interpretum* for the ΠΙΣΤΙΣ ΧΡΙΣΤΟΥ Debate?', *JBL* 114 (1995), 470–1.

Dodd, C. H. *According to the Scriptures: The Sub-structure of New Testament Theology*, London: Nisbet, 1952.

The Epistle of Paul to the Romans, MNTC, London: Hodder and Stoughton, 1932.

Donfried, K. P. 'False Presuppositions in the Study of Romans', in K. P. Donfried (ed.), *The Romans Debate: Revised and Expanded Edition*, Edinburgh: Clark, 1991, pp. 102–25.

Doty, W. G. 'The Classification of Epistolary Literature', *CBQ* 31 (1969), 183–99.

Letters in Primitive Christianity, Guides to Biblical Scholarship NT Series, Philadelphia: Fortress, 1973.

Drane, J. W. 'Why did Paul Write Romans?', in D. A. Hagner and M. J. Harris (eds.), *Pauline Studies: Essays presented to Professor F. F. Bruce on his 70th Birthday*, Exeter: Paternoster, 1980, pp. 208–27.

Duncan-Jones, R. P. 'Age-rounding, Illiteracy and Social Differentiation in the Roman Empire', *Chiron* 7 (1977), 333–53.

Dunn, J. D. G. 'The Incident at Antioch (Gal 2.11–18)', *JSNT* 18 (1983), 3–57.

'The New Perspective on Paul', *BJRL* 65 (1982–3), 95–122.

'Once More, Pistis Christou', in E. H. Lovering, Jr (ed.), *Society of Biblical Literature 1991 Seminar Papers*, Atlanta: Scholars, 1991, pp. 730–44.

Romans, WBC 38A, B, 2 vols., Dallas, Texas: Word Books, 1988.

Easterling, P. E. 'Books and Readers in the Greek World: 2: Hellenistic and Imperial Periods', in P. E. Easterling and B. M. W. Knox (eds.), *The Cambridge History of Classical Literature*, vol. I, *Greek Literature*, Cambridge: Cambridge University Press, 1985, pp. 16–41.

Elliott, N. *The Rhetoric of Romans: Argumentative Constraint and*

Strategy and Paul's Dialogue with Judaism, JSNTSup 45, Sheffield: JSOT, 1990.

Eschlimann, J.-A. 'La rédaction des épîtres pauliniennes d'après un comparaison avec les lettres profanes de son temps', *RB* 53 (1946), 185–96.

Espy, J. M. 'Paul's "Robust Conscience" Re-examined', *NTS* 31 (1985), 161–88.

Feuillet, A. 'L'antithèse péché-justice dans l'Epître aux romains', *Nova et Vetera* 58 (1983), 57–70.

Fitzmyer, J. A. 'Aramaic Epistolography', *Semeia* 22 (1981), 25–57.

'New Testament Epistles', *JBC*, pp. 223–6.

Romans: A New Translation with Introduction and Commentary, AB, New York: Doubleday, 1993.

Fowler, R. M. *Let the Reader Understand: Reader-response Criticism and the Gospel of Mark*, Minneapolis: Fortress, 1991.

Loaves and Fishes: The Function of the Feeding Stories in the Gospel of Mark, SBLDS 54, Chico: Scholars, 1981.

'Who is "the Reader" in Reader Response Criticism?', *Semeia* 31 (1985), 5–23.

Frege, G. 'On Sense and Reference', in P. Geach and M. Black (eds.), *Translations from the Philosophical Writings of Gottlob Frege*, 2nd edn, Oxford: Blackwell, 1960, pp. 56–78.

Fridrichsen, A. 'Der wahre Jude und sein Lob: Röm 2, 28f.', *SO* 1 (1922), 39–49.

Friedrich, J., W. Pöhlmann and P. Stuhlmacher 'Zur historischen Situation und Intention von Römer 13, 1–7', *ZTK* 73 (1976), 131–66.

Funk, R. W. 'The Apostolic *Parousia:* Form and Significance', in W. R. Farmer, C. F. D. Moule and R. R. Niebuhr (eds.), *Christian History and Interpretation: Studies presented to John Knox*, Cambridge: Cambridge University Press, 1967, pp. 249–68.

Language, Hermeneutic and Word of God: The Problem of Language in the New Testament and Contemporary Theology, New York: Harper and Row, 1966.

Furnish, V. P. *Theology and Ethics in Paul*, Nashville: Abingdon, 1968.

Gadamer, H. G. *Truth and Method*, London: Sheed and Ward, 1975.

Gager, J. G. *The Origins of Anti-Semitism: Attitudes towards Judaism in Pagan and Christian Antiquity*, Oxford: Oxford University Press, 1983.

Gamble, H., Jr *The Textual History of the Letter to the Romans: A Study in Textual and Literary Criticism*, SD 42, Grand Rapids: Eerdmans, 1977.

Gaster, T. H. *Festivals of the Jewish Year*, New York: Sloane, 1955.

Gaston, L. *Paul and the Torah*, Vancouver: University of British Columbia Press, 1987.

Gaugler, E. *Der Römerbrief*, Zurich: Zwingli, 1958.

Godet, F. *Commentary on St. Paul's Epistle to the Romans*, trans. A. Cusin, 2 vols., Edinburgh: Clark, 1880–1.

Guerra, A. J. *Romans and the Apologetic Tradition: The Purpose, Genre and Audience of Paul's Letter*, SNTSMS 81, Cambridge: Cambridge University Press, 1995.

Hadas, M. *Ancilla to Classical Reading*, New York: Columbia University, 1954.

Hafemann, S. J. 'Paul and his Interpreters', in G. F. Hawthorn and R. P. Martin with D. G. Reid (eds.), *A Dictionary of Paul and his Letters*, Leicester: IVP, 1993, pp. 666–79.

Hägg, T. *The Novel in Antiquity*, Oxford: Blackwell, 1983.

Harder, G. 'Der konkrete Anlaß des Römerbriefes', *Theologia Viatorum* 8 (1954–8), 13–24.

Harnack, A. von *Die Briefsammlung des Apostels Paulus und die anderen vorkonstantinischen christlichen Briefsammlungen: Sechs Vorlesungen aus der altkirchlichen Literaturgeschichte*, Leipzig: Hinrichs, 1926.

Harris, W. V. *Ancient Literacy*, Cambridge, Mass.: Harvard University Press, 1989.

Hartman, L. 'On Reading Others' Letters', *HTR* 79 (1986), 137–46.

Havelock, E. A. *Origins of Western Literacy*, Ontario Institute for Studies in Education Monograph Series 14, Toronto: Ontario Institute for Studies in Education, 1976.

Hays, R. B. *The Faith of Jesus Christ: An Investigation of the Narrative Structure of Galatians 3:1–4:11*, SBLDS 56, Chico: Scholars, 1983.

'Have we Found Abraham to be our Forefather according to the Flesh? A Reconsideration of Romans 4.1', *NovT* 27 (1985), 76–98.

'ΠΙΣΤΙΣ and Pauline Christology: What is at Stake?', in E. H. Lovering, Jr (ed.), *Society of Biblical Literature Seminar Papers*, Atlanta: Scholars, 1991, pp. 714–29.

'Psalm 143 and the Logic of Romans 3', *JBL* 99 (1980), 107–15.

Hebert, G. ' "Faithfulness" and "Faith" ', *Theology* 58 (1955), 373–9.

Heil, J. P. *Paul's Letter to the Romans: A Reader-Response Commentary*, New York: Paulist, 1987.

Herbert, G. *The Country Parson, The Temple*, ed. J. R. Wall, Jr, The Classics of Western Spirituality, London: SPCK, 1981.

Hirsch, E. D., Jr *Validity in Interpretation*, Newhaven: Yale University Press, 1967.

Hock, R. F. *The Social Context of Paul's Ministry: Tentmaking and Apostleship*, Philadelphia: Fortress, 1980.

Hooker, M. D. 'Adam in Romans 1', *NTS* 6 (1959–60), 297–306.

Continuity and Discontinuity: Early Christianity in its Jewish Setting, London: Epworth, 1986.

'In his own Image?', in M. Hooker and C. Hickling (eds.), *What about the New Testament? Essays in Honour of Christopher Evans*, London: SCM, 1975, pp. 28–41.

'ΠΙΣΤΙΣ ΧΡΙΣΤΟΥ', *NTS* 35 (1989), 321–42.

Howard, G. 'The "Faith of Christ" ', *ExpTim* 85 (1973–4), 212–15.

'Romans 3:21–31 and the Inclusion of the Gentiles', *HTR* 63 (1970), 223–33.

Hultgren, A. J. *Paul's Gospel and Mission: The Outlook from his Letter to the Romans*, Philadelphia: Fortress, 1985.

'The Pistis Christou Formulation in Paul', *NovT* 22 (1980), 248–63.

Hunter, A. M. *The Epistle to the Romans: Introduction and Commentary*, London: SCM, 1955.

Hyldahl, N. 'A Reminiscence of the Old Testament at Romans 1.23', *NTS* 2 (1955–6), 285–8.

Jeremias, J. 'Chiasmus in den Paulusbriefen', in *Abba: Studien zur neutestamentlichen Theologie und Zeitgeschichte*, Göttingen: Vandenhoeck and Ruprecht, 1966, pp. 276–90.

'Zur Gedankenführung in den paulinischen Briefen', in *Studia Paulina in honorem Johannis de Zwaan septuagenarii*, Harlem: de Erven F. Bohn, 1953, pp. 146–54.

Jervell, J. *Imago Dei: Gen 1, 26f im Spätjudentum, in der Gnosis und in den paulinischen Briefen*, Göttingen: Vandenhoeck and Ruprecht, 1960.

'The Letter to Jerusalem', in K. P. Donfried (ed.), *The Romans Debate: Revised and Expanded Edition*, Edinburgh: Clark, 1991, pp. 53–64.

The Unknown Paul, Minneapolis: Augsburg, 1984.

Jervis, L. A. *The Purpose of Romans: A Comparative Letter Structure Investigation*, JSNTSup 55, Sheffield: JSOT, 1991.

Jewett, R. 'Following the Argument of Romans', *Word and World* 6 (1986), 382–9. An expanded version in K. P. Donfried (ed.), *The Romans Debate: Revised and Expanded Edition*, Edinburgh: Clark, 1991, pp. 265–77.

'Major Impulses in the Theological Interpretation of Romans since Barth', *Int* 34 (1980), 17–31.

Johnson, L. T. 'Romans 3.21–26 and the Faith of Jesus', *CBQ* 44 (1982), 77–90.

Jordan, M. D. 'Ancient Philosophical Protreptic and the Problem of Persuasive Genres', *Rhetorica* 4 (1986), 309–33.

Karris, R. J. 'The Occasion of Romans: A Response to Prof. Donfried', in K. P. Donfried (ed.), *The Romans Debate: Revised and Expanded Edition*, Edinburgh: Clark, 1991, pp. 125–7.

'Romans 14.1–15.13 and the Occasion of Romans', in K. P. Donfried (ed.), *The Romans Debate: Revised and Expanded Edition*, Edinburgh, Clark, 1991, pp. 65–84.

Käsemann, E. *Commentary on Romans*, trans. and ed. G. W. Bromiley, London: SCM, 1980.

' "The Righteousness of God" in Paul', trans. W. J. Montague in *New Testament Questions of Today*, London: SCM, 1969, pp. 168–82.

Kaye, B. N. *The Thought Structure of Romans with Special Reference to Chapter 6*, Fort Worth: Schola, 1979.

' "To the Romans and Others" Revisited', *NovT* 18 (1976–7), 37–77.

Kaylor, R. *Paul's Covenant Community: Jew and Gentile in Romans*, Atlanta: John Knox, 1988.

Keck, L. E. *Paul and his Letters*, Proclamation Commentaries, Philadelphia: Fortress, 1979.

Kelber, W. H. 'Modalities of Communication, Cognition and Physiology of Perception: Orality, Rhetoric, Scribality', *Semeia* 65 (1994), 193–216.

The Oral and the Written Gospel: The Hermeneutics of Speaking and Writing in the Synoptic Tradition, Mark, Paul and Q, Philadelphia: Fortress, 1983.

Kennedy, G. A. *Greek Rhetoric under Christian Emperors*, A History of Rhetoric 3, Princeton, N.J.: Princeton University Press, 1983.

New Testament Interpretation through Rhetorical Criticism, Studies in Religion, Chapel Hill: University of North Carolina Press, 1984.

Kertelge, K. *The Epistle to the Romans*, London: Sheed and Ward, 1972.

Rechtfertigung bei Paulus, Münster: Aschendorff, 1967.

Kingsbury, J. D. *Matthew as Story*, 2nd edn, Philadelphia: Fortress, 1988.

Kinoshita, J. 'Romans – Two Writings Combined: A New Interpretation of the Body of Romans', *NovT* 7 (1964–5), 258–77.

Knox, B. M. W. 'Silent Reading in Antiquity', *GRBS* 9 (1968), 421–35.

Knox, J. 'Introduction and Exegesis for Romans', *IB*, vol. IX, pp. 355–668.

Koester, H. *Introduction to the New Testament*, 2 vols., Philadelphia: Fortress, 1982.

Kuhn, T. S. *The Structure of Scientific Revolutions*, 2nd edn, Chicago: Chicago University Press, 1970.

Kümmel, W. G. 'Paresis und Endeixis: Ein Beitrag zum Verständnis der paulinischen Rechtfertigungslehre', *ZTK* 49 (1952), 154–67.

Kuss, O. *Der Römerbrief Übersetzt und Erklärt*, 2nd edn, vol. I, Regensburg: Pustet, 1963.

Laeuchli, S. *The Language of Faith: An Introduction to the Semantic Dilemma of the Early Church*, London: Epworth, 1965.

Lagrange, M.-J. *Saint Paul: Epître aux romains*, EBib, 4th edn, Paris: Lecoffre, 1931.

Lash, N. 'What Might Martyrdom Mean?', in W. Horbury and B. McNeil (eds.), *Suffering and Martyrdom in the New Testament: Studies presented to G. M. Styler by the Cambridge New Testament Seminar*, Cambridge: Cambridge University Press, 1981, pp. 183–98.

Leenhardt, F. J. *The Epistle to the Romans: A Commentary*, London: Lutterworth, 1961.

Lentz, T. M. *Orality and Literacy in Hellenic Greece*, Carbondale and Edwardsville: Southern Illinois University Press, 1989.

Liddell, H. G. and R. Scott *A Greek–English Lexicon*, rev. H. S. Jones and R. McKenzie, Oxford: Clarendon Press, 1968.

Liddon, H. P. *Explanatory Analysis of Paul's Epistle to the Romans*, 4th edn, London: Longmans, Green and Co., 1899.

Lietzmann, H. *An die Römer*, 4th edn, Tübingen: Mohr (Siebeck), 1933.

Lohse, E. *Märtyrer und Gottesknecht: Untersuchung zur urchristlichen Verkündigung vom Sühnetod Jesu Christi*, Göttingen: Vandenhoeck and Ruprecht, 1955.

Longenecker, B. W. 'ΠΙΣΤΙΣ in Romans 3.25: Neglected Evidence for the "Faithfulness of Christ"?', *NTS* 39 (1993), 478–80.

Louw, J. P. *A Semantic Discourse Analysis of Romans*, 2 vols., Dept of Greek, University of Pretoria, 1979.

Luther, M. *Lectures on Galatians 1535*, ed. J. Pelikan and W. A. Hansen in *Luther's Works*, vols. XXVI, XXVII, St Louis: Concordia, 1963–4.

Lectures on Romans: Glosses and Scholia, ed. H. C. Oswald in *Luther's Works*, vol. XXV, St Louis: Concordia, 1972.

Preface to the Wittenberg Edition of his Latin Writings, ed. L. W. Spitz, in *Luther's Works*, vol. XXXIV, Philadelphia: Muhlenberg, 1960.

Luz, U. 'Zum Aufbau von Röm. 1–8', *TZ* 25 (1969), 161–81.

McGuire, M. R. P. 'Letters and Letter Carriers in Christian Antiquity', *Classical World* 53 (1960), 148–53, 184–5, 199–200.

Mailloux, S. J. 'Reader-Response Criticism?', *Genre* 10 (1977), 413–31.

Malherbe, A. J. *Ancient Epistolary Theorists*, Atlanta: Scholars, 1988.

The Cynic Epistles: A Study Edition, SBLSBS 12, Missoula: Scholars, 1977.

'ΜΗ ΓΕΝΟΙΤΟ in the Diatribe and Paul', *HTR* 73 (1980), 231–40.

Social Aspects of Early Christianity, Baton Rouge: Louisiana State University Press, 1977.

Malina, B. J. *The New Testament World: Insights from Cultural Anthropology*, London: SCM, 1983.

Manson, T. W. 'St. Paul's Letter to the Romans – and Others', in K. P. Donfried (ed.), *The Romans Debate: Revised and Expanded Edition*, Edinburgh: Clark, 1991, pp. 3–15.

Marrou, H. I. *A History of Education in Antiquity*, trans. G. Lamb, New York: Sheed and Ward, 1956.

Martens, J. W. 'Romans 2.14–16: A Stoic Reading', *NTS* 40 (1994), 55–67.

Martin, R. P. *Reconciliation: A Study of Paul's Theology*, Atlanta: John Knox, 1981.

Meeks, W. A. 'The Social Context of Pauline Theology', *Int* 36 (1982), 266–77.

Metzger, B. M. *Manuscripts of the Greek Bible*, New York: Oxford University Press, 1981.

A Textual Commentary on the Greek New Testament, 2nd edn, London: UBS, 1994.

Meyer, B. F. 'The Pre-Pauline Formula in Rom. 3.25–26a', *NTS* 29 (1983), 198–208.

Michel, O. *Der Brief an die Römer*, 14th edn, Göttingen: Vandenhoeck and Ruprecht, 1978.

Minear, P. S. *The Obedience of Faith: The Purposes of Paul in the Epistle to the Romans*, SBT, 2nd series, 19, London: SCM, 1971.

Moffatt, J. *An Introduction to the Literature of the New Testament*, 3rd edn, Edinburgh: Clark, 1918.

Montefiore, H., ed. *The Gospel and Contemporary Culture*, London: Mowbray, 1992.

Moores, J. D. *Wrestling with Rationality in Paul: Romans 1–8 in a New Perspective*, SNTSMS 82, Cambridge: Cambridge University Press, 1995.

Morgan, R. 'The Significance of Paulinism', in M. D. Hooker and S. D. Wilson (eds.), *Paul and Paulinism: Essays in honour of C. K. Barrett*, London: SPCK, 1982, pp. 320–38.

Morris, L. *The Epistle to the Romans*, Leicester: IVP, 1988.

'The Theme of Romans', in W. W. Gasque and R. P. Martin (eds.), *Apostolic History and the Gospel: Biblical and Historical Essays*

Presented to F. F. Bruce on his 60th Birthday, Exeter: Paternoster, 1970, pp. 249–63.

Moule, C. F. D. *The Birth of the New Testament*, San Francisco: Harper and Row, 1962.

An Idiom Book of New Testament Greek, 2nd edn, Cambridge: Cambridge University Press, 1959.

Moxnes, H. *Theology in Conflict: Studies in Paul's Understanding of God in Romans*, NovTSup 53, Leiden: Brill, 1980.

Müller, C. *Gottes Gerechtigkeit und Gottes Volk: Eine Untersuchung zu Römer 9–11*, Göttingen: Vandenhoeck and Ruprecht, 1964.

Müller, U. B. *Prophetie und Predigt im Neuen Testament: Formgeschichtlichen Untersuchungen zur urchristlichen Prophetie*, Gütersloh: Mohn, 1975.

Mullins, T. Y. 'Greetings as a New Testament Form', *JBL* 87 (1968), 418–26.

Munck, J. *Paul and the Salvation of Mankind*, Richmond: John Knox, 1959.

Murphy-O'Connor, J. *St. Paul's Corinth: Texts and Archaeology*, GNS 6, Wilmington: Glazier, 1983.

Murray, J. *The Epistle to the Romans: The English Text with Introduction, Exposition and Notes*, London: Marshall, Morgan and Scott, 1967.

Myers, C. D., Jr 'The Place of Romans 5:1–11 within the Argument of the Epistle', Th. D., Princeton Theological Seminary, 1985.

Newbigin, L. *The Gospel in a Pluralist Society*, London: SPCK, 1989.

Preface to *The Light has Come: An Exposition of the Fourth Gospel*, Grand Rapids: Eerdmans, 1982, pp. vii–xiv.

Nock, A. D. 'The Vocabulary of the New Testament', *JBL* 52 (1933), 131–9.

Nygren, A. *Commentary on Romans*, trans. C. C. Rasmussen, London: SCM, 1952.

Ollenburger, B. C. 'What Krister Stendahl "Meant" – A Normative Critique of "Descriptive Biblical Theology"', *Horizons in Biblical Theology* 8 (1986), 61–98.

Olshausen, H. *Der Brief des Apostels Paulus an die Römer: Erklärt*, Königsberg: August Wilhelm Anzer, 1835.

O'Neill, J. C. *Paul's Letter to the Romans,* Harmondsworth: Penguin, 1975.

Ong, W. J., SJ 'Maranatha: Death and Life in the Text of the Book', in *Interfaces of the Word: Studies in the Evolution of Consciousness and Culture*, Ithaca: Cornell University Press, 1977, pp. 230–71.

Orality and Literacy: The Technologizing of the Word, London: Methuen, 1982.

'The Writer's Audience is always a Fiction', in *Interfaces of the Word: Studies in the Evolution of Consciousness and Culture*, Ithaca: Cornell University Press, 1977, pp. 53–81.

Patte, D. *Paul's Faith and the Power of the Gospel: A Structural Introduction to the Pauline Letters*, Philadelphia: Fortress, 1983.

What is Structural Exegesis?, Guides to Biblical Scholarship NT Series, Philadelphia: Fortress, 1976.

Percy, E. *Die Probleme der Kolosser- und Epheserbriefe*, Lund: Gleerup, 1946.
Perelman, Ch. and L. Olbrechts-Tyteca *The New Rhetoric: A Treatise on Argumentation*, Notre Dame: University of Notre Dame Press, 1971.
Piper, J. 'The Demonstration of the Righteousness of God in Romans 3:25, 26', *JSNT* 7 (1980), 2–32.
Polanyi, M. *Personal Knowledge: Towards a Post-Critical Philosophy*, corrected edn, Chicago: Chicago University Press, 1962.
 The Tacit Dimension, London: Routledge and Kegan Paul, 1967.
Porter, C. L. 'Romans 1.18–32: Its Role in the Developing Argument', *NTS* 40 (1994), 210–28.
Porter, S. E. 'The Theoretical Justification for Application of Rhetorical Categories to Pauline Epistolary Literature', in S. E. Porter and T. H. Olbricht (eds.), *Rhetoric and the New Testament: Essays from the 1992 Heidelberg Conference*, JSNTSup 90, Sheffield: JSOT, 1993, pp. 100–22.
Reumann, J. *Righteousness in the New Testament*, Philadelphia: Fortress, 1982.
Reynolds, L. D. and N. G. Wilson *Scribes and Scholars: A Guide to the Transmission of Greek and Latin Literature*, 2nd edn, Oxford: Clarendon Press, 1974.
Rhyne, C. T. *Faith Establishes the Law*, SBLDS 55, Chico: Scholars, 1981.
Richardson, P. *Israel in the Apostolic Church*, Cambridge: Cambridge University Press, 1969.
Ricoeur, P. *Interpretation Theory: Discourse and the Surplus of Meaning*, Fort Worth: Texas Christian University Press, 1976.
 'What is a Text? Explanation and Understanding', in J. B. Thompson (ed.), *Paul Ricoeur: Hermeneutics and the Human Sciences. Essays on Language, Action and Interpretation*, Cambridge: Cambridge University Press, 1981, pp. 145–64.
Roetzel, C. *The Letters of Paul: Conversations in Context*, 2nd edn, Atlanta: John Knox, 1982.
Roller, O. *Das Formular der paulinischen Briefe: Ein Beitrag zur Lehre vom antiken Briefe*, Stuttgart: Kohlhammer, 1933.
Rowland, C. 'Reading the New Testament Sociologically: An Introduction', *Theology* 88 (1985), 358–64.
Rowland, C. and M. Corner *Liberating Exegesis: The Challenge of Liberation Theology to Biblical Studies*, Louisville: John Knox, 1989.
Russell, D. S. *The Method and Message of Jewish Apocalyptic 200 B.C.–A.D. 100*, Philadelphia: Westminster, 1964.
Sanday, W. and A. C. Headlam *A Critical and Exegetical Commentary on the Epistle to the Romans*, ICC, 5th edn, Edinburgh: Clark, 1902.
Sanders, E. P. *Paul and Palestinian Judaism: A Comparison of Patterns of Religion*, London: SCM, 1977.
 Paul, the Law, and the Jewish People, Philadelphia: Fortress, 1983.
Sanders, E. P. with A. I. Baumgarten and A. Mendelson (eds.), *Jewish and Christian Self-Definition*, 3 vols., Philadelphia: Fortress, 1980–2.
Sandmel, S. *The Genius of Paul: A Study in History*, Philadelphia: Fortress, 1979.

Schenk, W. 'Die Gerechtigkeit Gottes und der Glaube Christi: Versuch einer Verhältnisbestimmung paulinischer Strukturen', *TLZ* 97 (1972), 161–74.

'ἱερός κτλ', *TDNT*, vol. III, Grand Rapids: Eerdmans, 1965, pp. 221–83.

Schlatter, A. *Gottes Gerechtigkeit: Ein Kommentar zum Römerbrief*, 4th edn, Stuttgart: Calwer, 1965.

Schleiermacher, F. D. E. *Hermeneutics: The Handwritten Manuscripts*, Missoula: Scholars, 1977.

Schlier, H. *Der Römerbrief*, HTKNT VI, Freiburg: Herder, 1977.

Schmidt, H. W. *Der Brief des Paulus an die Römer*, Berlin: Evangelische, 1963.

Schmithals, W. *Der Römerbrief als historisches Problem*, Gütersloh: Gütersloher, 1975.

Scroggs, R. *The Last Adam: A Study in Pauline Anthropology*, Oxford: Blackwell, 1966.

'Paul as Rhetorician: Two Homilies in Romans 1–11', in R. Hamerton-Kelly and R. Scroggs (eds.), *Jews, Greeks and Christians: Religious Cultures in Late Antiquity. Essays in Honor of William David Davies*, SJLA 21, Leiden: Brill, 1976, pp. 271–98.

Segal, A. F. *Rebecca's Children: Judaism and Christianity in the Roman World*, Cambridge, Mass.: Harvard University Press, 1986.

Siegert, F., ed. *Drei hellenistisch-jüdische Predigten*, Tübingen: Mohr (Siebeck), 1980.

Smith, J. Z. 'The Social Description of Early Christianity', *Religious Studies Review* 1 (1975), 19–21.

Snodgrass, K. R. 'Justification by Grace – To the Doers: An Analysis of the Place of Romans 2 in the Theology of Paul', *NTS* 32 (1986), 72–93.

Stendahl, K. 'The Apostle Paul and the Introspective Conscience of the West', *HTR* 56 (1963), 199–215.

'The Bible as Classic and the Bible as Holy Scripture', *JBL* 103 (1984), 3–10.

'Biblical Theology, Contemporary', *IDB*, vol. I, pp. 418–32.

Final Account: Paul's Letter to the Romans, Minneapolis: Fortress, 1995.

'Paul among Jews and Gentiles', in *Paul among Jews and Gentiles and Other Essays*, Philadelphia: Fortress, 1976, pp. 1–77.

Stirewalt, M. L., Jr 'The Form and Function of the Greek Letter-Essay', in K. P. Donfried (ed.), *The Romans Debate: Revised and Expanded Edition*, Edinburgh: Clark, 1991, pp. 147–91.

'Paul's Evaluation of Letter-Writing', in J. M. Myers, O. Reimherr, H. N. Bream (eds.), *Search the Scriptures: New Testament Studies in Honor of Raymond T. Stamm*, Leiden: Brill, 1969, pp. 179–96.

Stowers, S. K. *The Diatribe and Paul's Letter to the Romans*, SBLDS 57, Chico: Scholars, 1981.

Letter Writing in Graeco-Roman Antiquity, LEC 5, Philadelphia: Westminster, 1986.

'Paul's Dialogue with a Fellow Jew in Romans 3:1–9', *CBQ* 46 (1984), 707–22.

A Rereading of Romans: Justice, Jews and Gentiles, New Haven: Yale University Press, 1994.

'Social Status, Public Speaking and Private Teaching: The Circumstances of Paul's Preaching Activity', NovT 26 (1984), 59–82.

Stuhlmacher, P. 'The Apostle Paul's View of Righteousness', in Reconciliation, Law, and Righteousness: Essays in Biblical Theology, trans. E. R. Kalin, Philadelphia: Fortress, 1986, pp. 68–93.

Der Brief an die Römer: Übersetzt und erklärt, NTD 6, Göttingen: Vandenhoeck and Ruprecht, 1989.

Gerechtigkeit Gottes bei Paulus, Göttingen: Vandenhoeck and Ruprecht, 1965.

Suggs, J. M. ' "The Word is Near You" ': Romans 10.6–10 within the Purpose of the Letter', in W. R. Farmer, C. F. D. Moule and R. R. Niebuhr (eds.), Christian History and Interpretation: Studies presented to John Knox, Cambridge: Cambridge University Press, 1967, pp. 289–312.

Suleiman, S. R. 'Introduction: Varieties of Audience-Oriented Criticism', in S. R. Suleiman and I. Crosman (eds.), The Reader in the Text: Essays on Audience and Interpretation, Princeton: Princeton University Press, 1980, pp. 3–45.

Sumney, J. L. Identifying Paul's Opponents: The Question of Method in 2 Corinthians, JSNTSup 40, Sheffield: JSOT, 1990.

Talbert, C. H. 'A Non-Pauline Fragment at Romans 3.24–26?', JBL 85 (1966), 287–96.

Taylor, G. M. 'The Function of ΠΙΣΤΙΣ ΧΡΙΣΤΟΥ in Galatians', JBL 85 (1966), 58–76.

Tey, J. The Daughter of Time, Harmondsworth: Penguin, 1954.

Theissen, G. 'The Strong and the Weak in Corinth: A Sociological Analysis of a Religious Quarrel', in The Social Setting of Pauline Christianity: Essays on Corinth, SNTW, Edinburgh: Clark, 1982, pp. 121–43.

Thomas, R. Literacy and Orality in Ancient Greece, Key Themes in Ancient History, Cambridge: Cambridge University Press, 1992.

Thyen, H. Der Stil der jüdisch-hellenistischen Homilie, FRLANT 47, Göttingen: Vandenhoeck and Ruprecht, 1955.

Uniting Church in Australia Basis of Union, Melbourne: Uniting Church, 1982.

Vaughan, C. J. Η ΠΡΟΣ ΡΩΜΑΙΟΥΣ ΕΠΙΣΤΟΛΗ: St. Paul's Epistle to the Romans with Notes, London: Macmillan, 1870.

Via, D. O., Jr 'A Structuralist Approach to Paul's Old Testament Hermeneutic', Int 28 (1974), 201–20.

Vorster, W. S. 'The Historical Paradigm – Its Possibilities and Limitations', Neot 18 (1984), 104–23.

Wallis, I. G. The Faith of Jesus Christ in Early Christian Traditions, SNTSMS 84, Cambridge: Cambridge University Press, 1995.

Walters, J. C. Ethnic Issues in Paul's Letter to the Romans: Changing Self-Definitions in Earliest Roman Christianity, Valley Forge, Pa: TPI, 1993.

Watson, F. Paul, Judaism and the Gentiles: A Sociological Approach, SNTSMS 56, Cambridge: Cambridge University Press, 1986.

Wedderburn, A. J. M. 'The Purpose and Occasion of Romans Again', *ExpTim* 90 (1978–9), 137–41.

The Reasons for Romans, SNTW, Edinburgh: Clark, 1988.

Weiss, J. *The History of Primitive Christianity*, London: Macmillan, 1937.

Wengst, K. *Christologische Formeln und Lieder des Urchristentums*, Gütersloh: Gütersloher, 1972.

Westerholm, S. *Israel's Law and the Church's Faith: Paul and his Recent Interpreters*, Grand Rapids: Eerdmans, 1988.

White, J. L. *The Form and Function of the Body of the Greek Letter: A Study of the Letter-body in the Non-literary Papyri and in Paul the Apostle*, SBLDS 2, 2nd edn, Missoula: University of Montana Press, 1972.

Light from Ancient Letters, FFNT, Philadelphia: Fortress, 1986.

'Saint Paul and the Apostolic Letter Tradition', *CBQ* 45 (1983), 433–44.

Wiefel, W. 'The Jewish Community in Ancient Rome and the Origins of Roman Christianity', in K. P. Donfried (ed.), *The Romans Debate: Revised and Expanded Edition*, Edinburgh: Clark, 1991, pp. 85–101.

Wilckens, U. *Der Brief an die Römer*, EKKNT VI/1–3, 3 vols., Cologne: Benziger, 1978–82.

Wilder, A. *Early Christian Rhetoric: The Language of the Gospel*, 2nd edn, Cambridge, Mass.: Harvard University Press, 1971.

Williams, S. K. 'Again Pistis Christou', *CBQ* 49 (1987), 431–47.

'The Hearing of Faith: ΑΚΟΗ ΠΙΣΤΕΩΣ in Galatians 3', *NTS* 35 (1989), 82–93.

'The "Righteousness of God" in Romans', *JBL* 99 (1980), 241–90.

Wills, L. 'The Form of the Sermon in Hellenistic Judaism and Earliest Christianity', *HTR* 77 (1984), 277–99.

Wimsatt, W. K. 'Genesis: A Fallacy Revisited', in D. Newton-de Molina (ed.), *On Literary Intention*, Edinburgh: Edinburgh University Press, 1976, pp. 116–38.

Wimsatt, W. K. and M. C. Beardsley 'The Intentional Fallacy', in D. Newton-de Molina (ed.), *On Literary Intention*, Edinburgh: Edinburgh University Press, 1976, pp. 1–13.

Winter, B. W. *Seek the Welfare of the City: Christians as Benefactors and Citizens*, First Century Christians in the Graeco-Roman World, Grand Rapids: Eerdmans, 1994.

Wire, A. C. 'Pauline Theology as an Understanding of God: The Explicit and the Implicit', Ph.D., University of Michigan, 1974.

Wright, N. T. 'The Messiah and the People of God: A Study in Pauline Theology with Particular Reference to the Argument of the Epistle to the Romans', D.Phil., Oxford, 1980.

'Romans and the Theology of Paul', in E. H. Lovering, Jr (ed.), *Society of Biblical Literature 1992 Seminar Papers*, Atlanta: Scholars, 1992, pp. 184–213.

Wuellner, W. 'Paul's Rhetoric of Argumentation in Romans: An Alternative to the Donfried–Karris Debate over Romans', in K. P. Donfried (ed.), *The Romans Debate: Revised and Expanded Edition*, Edinburgh: Clark, 1991, pp. 128–46.

Yates, F. A. *The Art of Memory*, Chicago: University of Chicago Press, 1966.

Young, F. and D. F. Ford *Meaning and Truth in 2 Corinthians*, Biblical Foundations in Theology, London: SPCK, 1987.

Zahn, T. *Der Brief des Paulus an die Römer*, Leipzig: Böhme, 1910.

Zeller, D. *Der Brief an die Römer: Übersetzt und erklärt*, RNT, Regensburg: Pustet, 1985.

Ziesler, J. *The Meaning of Righteousness in Paul: A Linguistic and Theological Enquiry*, SNTSMS 20, Cambridge: Cambridge University Press, 1972.

Paul's Letter to the Romans, Trinity Press International NT Commentaries, London: SCM, 1989.

'Salvation Proclaimed: IX. Romans 3.21–26', *ExpTim* 93 (1981–2), 356–9.

INDEX OF BIBLICAL AND OTHER ANCIENT
SOURCES

Biblical

250   Index of biblical and other ancient sources

GENERAL INDEX

Accounting for all of the text, 36, 38, 42–3, 45, 47, 63, 107–8, 171
All, *see* Πᾶς
Apostle, The, *see* personae in the text
Audience, 21, 28–30, 55–6, 58, 60, 69–72, 78, 96–107, 110, 114, 120–2, 122–4, 212–14
Authorial intention, 4–5, 35–42, 44, 63, 79–80, 210–11, 227–8, 229–30; *see also* meaning in texts

Basic conception, the, 6–7, 10, 15–18, 20, 109–10, 208–9, 229–30

Causal exposition, causal explanation, 22, 24–7, 29–30, 34, 42–3, 44, 182–4, 185, 206–7, 211–12, 222
Coherence, criteria of, 42–3, 211–12, 214
Congregation, The, *see* personae in the text
Conservative, The, *see* personae in the text
Creator–creature relationship, 26, 192–5, 196–8, 202–3, 205–6, 222–3

Faith, 23–5, 30, 49–50, 73, 116–17, 118–19, 121–2, 124, 144–6, 148–9, 153, 154, 155–61, 163, 186, 189, 191, 196–8, 198–9, 217–21

God's righteousness, 10, 13–15, 17–18, 22–4, 57, 62, 73, 74, 94–5, 101–2, 111–12, 113, 116–18, 119–22, 124–6, 127, 136, 137–8, 141, 144–8, 149–50, 152–3, 172, 178–9, 186–7, 189, 191, 196–8, 199–200, 208, 223–4
Grammatical problems of Rom. 3.21–6, 14–15, 49, 56–7, 112, 147–8, 172

Historical-critical exegesis, scholarship, 3–4, 5, 27–9, 34–5, 79–80, 91, 179, 182, 185, 207, 209–23, 223

Intelligibility, criterion of, 95–6, 114, 215–22

Justification account, justification framework, 6–7, 16–18, 20, 22, 24, 29, 44–5, 183–4, 185, 208–9
Justification theology, Paul's, 18–19, 26, 33, 38, 182, 183–4, 185–91, 196–8, 200–3, 205, 206, 208–9; *see also* basic conception, causal exposition

Law, 7, 8–9, 10, 12, 61, 66, 68–9, 110, 124–5, 130–3, 135–6, 140–1, 144, 153–5, 156–9, 162, 173–5, 186, 196, 203–5, 206
Letter, *see under* nature of the text

Meaning in texts, 28, 30–1, 34–40, 45, 46, 107–8, 109, 114, 115, 171, 184–5, 210–11; *see also* authorial intention

Nature of the text, the
    exegetical question, the, 20, 33, 44–5, 63–4, 76, 107–8, 210–12
    letter, 1, 3, 4, 5, 21, 32–3, 34, 40, 41, 64, 76–9, 215
    oral-aural, 78, 81–90, 95–6, 114, 136–7, 215
    pastoral, 1, 3, 4, 5, 22–4, 27, 29, 30, 64–5, 71–2, 74, 139, 161, 177–81, 183, 211, 224–5; *see also* nature of the text: preaching
    preaching, 22–4, 30, 67, 73–4, 90–6, 102–3, 110–11, 121–2, 133, 139, 172–7, 179–81, 182–3, 208, 213–14

DATE DUE